NOV 2 1 2003

3000 800055 34378
St. Louis Community College

D0204034

Forest Park Library
St. Louis Community College
5600 Oakland
St. Louis, MO 63110-1393
314-644-9210

Images That Injure

IMAGES THAT INJURE

Pictorial Stereotypes in the Media

Second Edition

Edited by Paul Martin Lester and
Susan Dente Ross

Foreword by Everette E. Dennis

Westport, Connecticut
London

Library of Congress Cataloging-in-Publication Data

Images that injure : pictorial stereotypes in the media.—2nd ed. / edited by Paul Martin
   Lester and Susan Dente Ross ; foreword by Everette E. Dennis.
      p. cm.
   Includes bibliographical references and index.
   ISBN 0-275-97846-X (alk. paper)—ISBN 0-275-97845-1 (pbk. : alk. paper)
   1. Stereotype (Psychology) in mass media.   I. Lester, Paul Martin.   II. Ross,
Susan Dente.
P96.S74I45   2003
303.3'85—dc21   2003042941

British Library Cataloguing in Publication Data is available.

Copyright © 2003 by Paul Martin Lester and Susan Dente Ross

All rights reserved. No portion of this book may be
reproduced, by any process or technique, without the
express written consent of the publisher.

Library of Congress Catalog Card Number: 2003042941
ISBN: 0-275-97846-X
      0-275-97845-1 (pbk.)

First published in 2003

Praeger Publishers, 88 Post Road West, Westport, CT 06881
An imprint of Greenwood Publishing Group, Inc.
www.praeger.com

Printed in the United States of America

The paper used in this book complies with the
Permanent Paper Standard issued by the National
Information Standards Organization (Z39.48–1984).

10   9   8   7   6   5   4   3   2   1

This edition is dedicated to Travis Linn,
friend and mentor who is surely missed.

CONTENTS

FOREWORD

When Walter Lippmann transformed a common printing term—stereotype—into a concept now better known in its social and psychological form, he understood that those "pictures in our head" can simplify, distort, and even do injury to meaning.[1]

On the one hand, stereotypes are rather negatively defined as "a conventional, formulaic and oversimplified conception, opinion, or image,"[2] whereas on the other they communicate dramatically and well without much subtlety or nuance. For visual communicators, whether they are photographers, videographers, filmmakers, graphic artists, informational graphics designers, or cartoonists, stereotypes are useful devices because they are easily understood and make a clear, if unfair, and, at times, even hurtful point. For cartoonists such depiction is central to their job description, but for communicators charged with an accurate representation of news and information, entertainment, or advertising, they can be damaging and dangerous.

Visual messages play a profound role in the construction of social memory, as video capturing the collapse of the World Trade Center towers, film of the anguished mourner at Kent State, and the flag raising at Iwo Jima all attest. Some visual messages that were once fresh and imaginative can become, when overused, hackneyed material that is eventually parodied because it is so predictable. Of far greater consequence, however, are what Paul Martin Lester, Susan Dente Ross, and the contributors to this volume call images that injure in the form of pictorial and verbal stereotypes in the communication media. They grapple with various forms of prejudice or images that prejudge without reference to facts and reality.

Along the way, this gathering of gifted scholars, commentators, and analysts examines racial and ethnic stereotypes, as well as those involving gender, age, physical disabilities, sexual preference, and other characteristics. They assess head-on the most overt and blatant representations as well as those that are subtler and, in some cases, even unintended. Always there is concern for the impact of an image on its collective audience in a social sense and on individuals, as well. As it takes a serious look at the impact and consequences of these hurtful images, the book cuts new ground both in a theoretical sense and in offering a variety of measures— both quantitative and qualitative.

More than most books that critically examine the media, this one is open to different modes of analysis and thus different ways of knowing. This variety has value for the scholarly literature as well as for individual readers of varying backgrounds and especially for students of media and media institutions. There is also much of value here for the professional communicator. At a time of sometimes reflective and politically correct assessment, most of these studies are anything but predictable and push readers toward their own analysis and opinion. Always there is the question of what to do with such intelligence—whether to act on it and thus constrain ultimate freedom or to use it to engender understanding and tolerance. All that is a matter of judgment and taste, and the editors of this volume leave much of that to individual cogitation.

In a nation that preens itself on tolerance and equality, claiming both, these studies are a sobering account of how far we are from that illusive goal. Still, to the extent that the ideas offered here are followed by thoughtful action, we might just see a diminution of images that injure and thus give this work lasting and important impact.

—Everette E. Dennis

IMAGES THAT INJURE:
AN INTRODUCTION

Paul Martin Lester and Susan Dente Ross

Each one of us is a medium for communication.
Each one of us is a river that flows to the sea.
Each one of us is an individual—
Independent, unique, and linked—
To all who have been and all who will be.

The scope and range of this book is broad. This book is about pictures and words, images and symbols, the array of raw materials with which we form our communication, fix our memories, and shape our realities. The authors in this collection specifically examine newspapers, books, films, advertisements, cartoons, commercials, television, magazines, and the World Wide Web. Their discussions illuminate how each of these media and each of us individually and collectively participate in a sea of meaning that is simultaneously personal and social, unique and shared, linked and independent.

Some authors in this volume examine a single droplet of the constant flow of communication to give new insight into the contribution of one discrete element to our construction of reality. Others look at many media, and through their scrutiny of the vast and varied forms of communication—both interpersonal and mediated—they offer a new understanding of the complex, intricate, and multifaceted process through which we give symbols meaning and transform hieroglyphs into representations of our world.

Both a detailed study of contemporary messages and an abstract discussion of the effects of symbolic representation, this book can, and should, be read on many levels. The specific examples presented in these pages provide a wealth of material for students and professionals in journalism, advertising, public relations, ethics, gender studies, and more. The theoretical foundation and elaboration offer an opportunity for readers to critically examine the ways in which they affect and are affected by the swirling waters of archetype, stereotype, and symbol.

Readers should not assume from the title of this book that the authors intend to bash the media. Many of the authors have been media professionals; others teach in an array of media programs around the country. We study media stereotypes here not because media stereotypes are somehow unique or different but precisely because the media stereotype just as individuals stereotype. We all stereotype. As human beings, our brains naturally classify what we see; we cannot help but notice the differences in physical attributes between one person and another. We attribute meaning to these differences, and we respond to the meaning we have created.

But it is neither natural nor necessary to move beyond observation and classification to stereotyping. As with the printing term from which the word comes, the word *stereotype* is a shorthand way to describe a person with collective, rather than unique, characteristics. To stereotype is, in both a real and a metaphorical sense, to lose sight of the individual. History has shown that stereotyping can lead to scapegoating, which can lead to discrimination, which can lead to segregation, which can lead to physical abuse, which can lead to state-sponsored genocide.

Although media stereotypes are not inevitable, media experts suggest several reasons why the media stereotype:

- Advertisers demand quickly interpreted shortcut pictures.
- Lazy or highly pressured reporters do not take or have the time to see things in a new way or to explore issues within their multifaceted and complex contexts.
- Too few members of diverse cultural groups work as photographers, reporters, editors, or publishers in media organizations.
- Media professionals assume that readers and viewers are conditioned to accept only certain images of diverse members—images that place these individuals within a limited range of content categories, professions, and castes.
- Finally, culturalism may explain why mainstream media are slow to cover human catastrophes in remote sections of the world such as Rwanda,

Somalia, or even south-central Los Angeles. Culturalism is a term used to describe the belief that one cultural group—whether based on ethnicity, economics, education, and so on—is somehow better or worse than some other cultural group. This value judgment may inform news decisions about who and what is worthy of coverage.

Sometimes media stereotypes are flagrant. More often they are subtle. The news media stereotype because typically they portray members of diverse cultural groups within specific content categories—usually crime, entertainment, and sports—and almost never within the categories of general interest, business, education, health, and religion. Entertainment media similarly typecast actors by their gender, ethnicity, age, dress, and race.

Such media stereotypes reinforce and magnify our personal stereotypes. As a consequence, media stereotypes play a significant role in the social disintegration that produces hatred, violence, and misunderstanding. News and entertainment images are especially powerful because visual messages are products of our sense of sight, not our cognition. Pictures are highly emotional objects that have long-lasting staying power within the deepest regions of our brain. But both textual and visual media messages that stereotype individuals by their concentrations, frequencies, and omissions become a part of our long-term memory. And when certain individuals or ethnicities appear only as criminals, entertainers, and sports heroes, we forget that the vast majority of people—regardless of their particular cultural heritage—have the same hopes and fears as the rest of us.

Essays in this work concern the cultural images of African, Irish, Mexican, and Native Americans; Pacific Islanders; Jewish persons; men, women, and children; older adults; the physically disabled and the vision impaired; gay and lesbian persons; politicians; computer users; and media personnel. Chances are, the mental image you have of a member of one of these groups is a mediated image—it comes from print, television, motion pictures, or computers.

New to this edition is a section on stereotypes related to the coverage of the 9/11 aerial attacks. Stereotypical images of patriotic symbolism, terrorists, and Arabs are featured in the chapters that highlight the significant and important effects of media stereotypes on our national psyche.

But each of us, whether media producer or consumer, bears responsibility for these images that injure. We should recall that we see stereotypes in the media because we stereotype in our own heads, among our friends, within our families, and across society. We know this is true. There are signals, warning signs, and obvious examples everywhere we turn:

- Next time you're in a public restroom, notice the disabled persons' stall. Have you ever seen someone in a wheelchair using that toilet? Something is wrong.
- Next time you're sitting in your seat on an airplane, notice that almost always the flight attendants are women whereas the voice welcoming you to 35,000 feet is a man's. Something is wrong.
- Next time you're watching a video movie that features a child at home alone successfully defending himself against two, large burglars, notice how easy it all is for the boy. Something is wrong.
- The next time you're watching a basketball game, notice how often all the players on the court are African American whereas all the fans in the stands are screaming Anglos. Something is wrong.

It is our responsibility, individually and collectively, as critical producers and consumers of the messages that convey our world, to change what we know to be wrong in society. There is little chance of change in media images without a change in us because the media are not a mirror of our society, they are its fabric. The media are not *them;* the media are all of us.

The simplest key to avoiding stereotypes is to perceive richness. When we truly see the unique abundance of an individual, we no longer willingly submerge those individual quirks and qualities into generalized, inchoate stereotypes. To avoid stereotyping, it may be helpful to do the following:

- Expand our vision. Become involved with diverse cultural groups in everyday life situations.
- Explore social issues. Have the courage to use words and pictures to examine the underlying social problems at the heart of violence.
- Encourage others. Establish national competitions that foster positive portrayals of members from diverse cultural groups.
- Increase attention. Advocate more space and time in print, broadcast, and computer media to publish long-term photojournalism projects and in-depth essays that more fully explain the context of the images we usually see.
- Educate yourself. Learn all you can about visual literacy so you can really look at the images in newspapers, magazines, films, and on television.
- Be a critical observer. Take the time to study the snapshots of your family and friends and the images printed, broadcast, and downloaded and question yourself and all who will listen about the meaning and ethics of the images we make and see.

We produce and perpetuate stereotypes, but through conscious effort we instead can communicate the wealth of difference that enriches the sea of our lives.

Part I

A GENERAL OVERVIEW

Chapter 1

MORAL RESPONSIBILITIES AND THE POWER OF PICTURES

Deni Elliott

Pictures are powerful. Publishing strong images makes economic sense, whether or not the images injure subjects or audience members. But economics is not ethics.

Pictures are almost always legal to publish even if they stereotype the subjects or cause harm. But the fact that some action is legal does not make it ethical.

Pictures that stereotype are often aesthetically appealing. They make some of us laugh or feel compassion or feel anger. But aesthetics is not ethics.

This essay is about ethics. Specifically, I describe the ethical[1] responsibilities that follow from one (or one's news organization or advertising agency or public relations firm) having the power to disseminate images to a general audience. Publishing images that injure is a morally questionable act. Sometimes morally questionable acts can be justified. Other times the actions turn out to be wrong. Publishing images that injure requires good moral (not economic, legal, or aesthetic) reasons to justify the harm caused. Sometimes that justification can be accomplished; sometimes it cannot. Here I differentiate between the cases in which harm can be justified and when it cannot.

THE MEANING OF HARM

Economics, aesthetics, and freedom of the press aside, it is wrong, in a prima facie sense, to do things that cause harm to other human beings.

This tenet echoes throughout 2000 years of Western moral philosophy. Whether one studies the basic three historical theories of utilitarianism, deontology, and virtue theory or contemporary mixed formalism and feminist critiques, the minimal level of morality remains the same: Don't cause harm unless you have what an impartial audience would judge to be a very good reason.

For the purposes of this chapter, I am considering the term *injure* (as in *Images That Injure*) to be synonymous with *harm*. Harm, as the word is used in a philosophically technical sense, includes direct harm (being killed, being caused pain, being disabled, or being deprived of pleasure or opportunity) and harm that is sometimes direct and sometimes indirect, such as when someone breaks a promise to you, cheats or deceives you, disobeys the law resulting in injury to you, or deprives you of duty.[2] Harm is indirect when the person harmed is not aware of having been harmed or the harm caused is more dilute, as is the case with deception. If someone successfully deceives me, I do not know that I have been deceived, yet I have been caused harm by being deprived of accurate information. If someone unsuccessfully attempts to deceive me, I have been directly harmed by the knowledge that I have been lied to. In addition, the whole community has been harmed by a decrease in trust by at least two people (the deceiver and me) in what others say to us.

Images that injure can cause harm in both direct and indirect ways. As a woman of average height and weight, I am directly harmed by the images of women that advertising puts forth. The subtle computer manipulation that elongates legs and narrows hips to idealized proportions causes me pain and deprives me of pleasure. I am harmed because I know that empirical evidence shows that young women develop eating disorders and low self-esteem because they compare themselves with such images. I am harmed because the presentations make me angry. The presentations also cause indirect harm in that the idealized presentations suggest to the full society that real women fall short in some way. Creating physical expectations that women cannot reasonably fulfill causes harm to relationships throughout society.

Some philosophers have argued that causing offense is different from causing harm. Indeed, eighteenth-century philosopher John Stuart Mill would argue that it is important that we expose ourselves to ideas that we find offensive so that we can better know the truth. However, he also counsels that if a message needs to be presented that some will find offensive, the message giver has a moral (but not legal) responsibility to present that message in as civil and inoffensive way as possible.[3] The key element is in deciding what messages *need* to be presented. The answer to the question of need can be found by appeal to the particular social functions that different media fulfill.

THE SOCIAL FUNCTIONS OF MASS MEDIA AND MORAL CONSIDERATIONS

This dictate—do not cause unjustified harm—is coupled with another maxim that echoes throughout Western moral philosophy: Do your job. Do your job means that one should work to fulfill one's role-related responsibilities. Role-related responsibilities are those associated with being in relation to others, such as parent, student, life partner, and professor. We have a moral responsibility to fulfill those duties to others. In a similar way, media institutions, like other social institutions, exist because they fulfill some legitimate role. News media exist to tell citizens what they need to know for self-governance. Persuasive media exist to provide their clients' messages to the audience. Entertainment media exist to provide amusement and to disseminate culture.

It is not surprising that these minimal ethical requirements to do one's job and not cause unjustified harm reflect basic human intuition. If someone causes harm to you or to someone you care about, you quite rightly demand an explanation. We all want others to do their jobs in regard to us because, when they don't, we are likely to be caused direct or indirect harm. What is irrational to want for oneself (being caused harm without reason) is immoral to cause others.

Most writing in historical and contemporary ethics takes the reader well beyond this minimal maxim to an examination of the responsibility that we all have to promote good. However, most urgently, moral analysis starts with a question of blameworthiness. Did someone do something that caused harm? Does that person have moral culpability for that harm? Is there anything that mitigates, explains, or justifies the harm caused? The questions of agency, culpability, and justification are questions that must be answered; and they must be answered by analysis of criteria within the scope of moral consideration.

Considering injury within the scope of moral consideration is different from examining that injury from the perception of economic, legal, or aesthetic concerns. Economics is important to the running of a media business, whether the focus of that business is entertainment, persuasion, or news. Mass communication industries, like other endeavors, require an economically stable base from which to operate. However, the need for economic stability does not excuse immoral behavior. Physicians in private practice, for example, are financially dependent upon their patients, but we would not excuse a doctor's unethical activity by her need to make money. Doctors who take kickbacks from labs and specialists in exchange for patient referrals are quite rightly accused of having a conflict of interest.

In this example, it is easy to see that a doctor's role-related responsibility is to her patient. Her recommendations are correctly made based on the clinical needs of the patient rather than on the opportunity for her to make additional income. In a similar way, corporations, including media organizations, have a role-related responsibility to provide the service they have promised to provide, but it doesn't follow that any means to that end is acceptable. The responsibility of all mass media image creators and managers is to recognize their power in creating viewer perception and to use that power judiciously by (1) presenting images accurately or clearly labeled as fiction, parody, or photo illustration, and (2) being responsible for the symbolic as well as the literal meaning of the image.

Fulfilling that responsibility plays a fundamental role in explaining or justifying the publication of particular images. An image is more easily justifiable when its presentation relates directly to the media's role-related responsibility. It is more difficult to justify an injurious image when this direct connection does not exist. For example, news photos that cause audience members and the families of subjects harm, but that relate directly to what citizens need to know for self-governance, such as pictures of dead and wounded soldiers in a war fought on our behalf, are strongly justified. Feature photos that show people in public in accidentally compromising positions are less easily justified. Whether a picture works in a marketing sense is morally irrelevant.

A harmful image cannot be justified by appeal to law. The law allows the publication of almost all text and pictures. However, the fact that almost any image *can* be published does not imply that all such images *should* be published. For example, whereas it was legal to publish the pictures of people who were killed in the attacks of 9/11, most news organizations refrained from showing identifiable corpses. They found insufficient justification to offset the harm caused to those viewing the pictures and the families of the deceased.

Aesthetics is often at the core of an argument to publish a picture that is morally questionable. If a photo lacks aesthetic appeal, no one will argue for its publication. In almost all cases, images likely to be published are compelling in an inviting or in a disturbing way. However, the fact that an image is a "helluva picture" doesn't provide justification for publishing a picture that will cause someone to suffer harm.

MORAL CAUSALITY AND THE
SUFFERING OF HARM

Sometimes people suffer harm and it is no one's fault. If I go to my favorite restaurant, which does not take reservations, and find that all of the tables are filled and other prospective diners are lined up in front of me, no one there is to blame for my continuing hunger or for my disappointment at an hour's wait outside the restaurant door. I have suffered harm (hunger/disappointment), but no person caused my harm, unless you want to include my choice to go to this particular restaurant for dinner. If, while I wait outside the restaurant for a table to be free, I fall victim to a drive-by shooting, the diners who got there first are not to blame for my untimely demise. It is not their fault, even though it is because of them that I am standing outside. The other diners create what Aristotle would call the proximate cause of my harm. But they are not morally blameworthy.

Moral blameworthiness requires either an intention to cause harm or the neglect of one's responsibility. Images that injure are rarely produced with malice or with the intent to cause harm to individuals or to the community. Because the media have power, however, they have two role-related responsibilities: to fulfill their social function and to use their power judiciously. Media have the power to influence how viewers perceive events or individuals. Media practitioners have a responsibility to provide presentations that are accurate or, in the case of entertainment or persuasion, are either accurate or are clearly presented as fiction or parody. The power and influence of mass media create special responsibilities for image providers to be aware of the harm they do or could cause and to publish images that injure only with knowledge of that harm and willingness to justify the harm.

Power creates special moral obligations. Any time there is a relationship with inequality in power, the more powerful party incurs special responsibilities in regard to the more vulnerable party. We are most familiar with this in the parent–child or teacher–student relationship. I have particular responsibilities toward my stepdaughter, Allison, and toward my students that I don't have toward those who are not vulnerable to my power.

For example, if I wear my gay and lesbian pride button as I walk through the local town, I am likely to pass some stranger who is offended by the pink triangle and its symbolic reference. I don't have a special relationship in regard to that homophobic individual. Conventions, as well as the primacy of liberty and free expression, allow individuals to hold and express beliefs that may offend others. I am no more morally blameworthy for the harm (offense) I cause the stranger than I would be blameworthy for the harm (disappointment) caused by my buying the last ticket to a showing of a new movie.

However, if I wear the same button to Allison's summer camp performance, I am morally accountable because of my relationship to my stepdaughter. I can reasonably predict that some of the more conservative parents and campers will react to that button in a way that has negative consequences for Allison. Unlike the situation in which I offended the stranger on the street, I now need to justify causing my stepdaughter to suffer harm. Wearing the pride button in a situation in which I can predict it is likely to have negative consequences for her is, prima facie, morally questionable. I may justify my choice by deciding that it is important to increase the level of tolerance toward gay and lesbian people. I might believe that my wearing the button and provoking rude remarks to my stepdaughter will teach her how to take responsibility for her family's unpopular beliefs. My justification may be weak or strong, but justification of some sort is necessary because, unlike the stranger on the street, my stepdaughter is vulnerable to my power.

MEDIA AND POWER

Media institutions are powerful. The connection between expressive media and receptive audience embodies an amazing description of the mediated reality that all citizen–consumers live. Children between the ages of 2 and 17 watch an average of 25 hours of television each week; adults are estimated to spend half their leisure time watching television or consuming other media; 60 million copies of the 1,500 daily newspapers and the 7,600 weekly or semi-weekly newspapers are sold each day; more than 60,000 different periodicals are in publication, with 40,000 books rolling off the presses each year. Considering the amount that we think we know about the world, only a small percentage of that knowledge is based on first-person sense experience. The media provide the vicarious experience and then shape our perceptions of it. How evil an influence this mediated reality might be is a point of contention among scholars. However, it is a given that media of all types sell more than the literal product of information, persuasion, or entertainment. From the choice of who or what counts as newsworthy to deciding which body images promote sales and building the contexts for situation comedies, media managers promote some lifestyles and make it difficult for members of the audience to value others.

Media practitioners are responsible for the impact of their work, even if there is no intention on the part of the practitioner or on the part of the industry to cause harm. Individuals in the audience are necessarily vulnerable to the impact of the media in all of its social functions.

JUSTIFICATION FOR PUBLISHING IMAGES THAT INJURE

Justification is the process by which a morally questionable act is made morally permissible. Sometimes the justification is weak, sometimes it is strong, and sometimes it is nonexistent. For example, publishing the police sketch of an African American rape suspect in the local newspaper causes harm to African American men by contributing to the stereotype of African American men as criminals. Publishing the picture certainly causes harm to the suspect. However, publishing the picture is strongly justified by the need for the suspect to be apprehended. Imagine now the same news staff putting together a multipage photo-essay as part of a year-end wrap up. The overwhelming number of pictures of African American men that appear in that photo-essay are those of suspects in crime, those convicted of crimes, or those playing basketball. The staff cannot justify the harm caused the audience and African American men by contributing to the stereotype by appealing to the newsworthiness of the pictures. Realizing that the vast majority of editorial pictures of African American men fit the stereotype may indicate to someone the desperate need for diversity training, but that is not adequate justification for publishing photos that cause harm. Publishing news photos or illustrations in which race is important or evident is justified by the connection of the artwork to the news organization's responsibility to tell citizens information that is important for self-governance. The more direct that connection, the stronger the justification.

However, the fact that there is a strong connection between the communicator's social function and the injurious image does not necessarily justify the act. If there are ways of fulfilling one's social function without including images that injure, that choice is always the better one. To return to the presentation of photos from the attacks on 9/11, the horror of that story could be told without close-up, identifiable photos of those who jumped to their deaths from the upper floors of the World Trade Center buildings.

SYSTEMATIC MORAL ANALYSIS FOR IMAGES THAT INJURE

The following is a series of steps that can be used to determine whether or not specific instances of images that injure are justified:

1. Identify the injury. This is the level of conceptualization. Describe who is being hurt by the image and how one knows that.

2. Ask if it is reasonable to hold the image maker/distributor morally blameworthy for the injury. Is it reasonable to predict that the audience, subjects, or other vulnerable people will be directly or indirectly harmed by the image? What is the evidence for this prediction?

3. Describe the social function of the media and how this particular image connects to the imagemakers doing their jobs. The more tenuous the connection between the role-related responsibilities and the image, the less justified the image. If the role-related responsibility can be met without the use of an injurious image, the image also is less justified.

Chapter 2

STEREOTYPING, PREJUDICE, AND DISCRIMINATION

Willard F. Enteman

Media are essentially businesses, and, as economists teach us, business is an amoral enterprise committed to the singular purpose of maximizing profits. If ethical issues are raised in such a context, they will be resolved by actions that promise to maximize profits. Motives are unimportant; results count. The title of this book suggests we should be concerned with images that injure. However, in the media business, as long as images do not threaten to injure the corporate bottom line, they will receive little more than perfunctory attention.

Within media in general, journalism is a shrinking domain that by tradition has held to professional standards beyond merely economic ones. Because many journalists resist being designated professionals, we should be careful with our terminology. However, the history of journalism is replete with people such as *Wall Street Journal* correspondent Daniel Pearl, who was kidnapped and executed covering a story in Pakistan, who put themselves in harm's way to get the story right. Pearl was a writer, but similar stories can be told about pictorial journalists, and it is their craft that will be the focus of this chapter. The way to change the behavior of corporate managers is to convince them that changed behavior will help maximize profits. I do not have the data to do that, and I suspect in many cases the data would not support the conclusion. The way to deal with business professionals is to show them what kinds of motives and actions are consistent with a standing as professionals, which means as morally motivated people. We can hope to do that here.

UNDERSTANDING TERMS

Though the origin of the word *stereotype* has been almost entirely lost in the dim recesses of linguistic history, it is most closely associated with journalism as a trade. The older print people among us will remember that the original stereotype was a printing plate, sometimes called a *fong,* that facilitated reproduction of the same material. The typesetter could avoid recasting type by using the stereotype. Thus, a stereotype imposes a rigid mold on the subject and encourages repeated mechanical usage. It offers mechanistic efficiency. We have taken the word *stereotype* beyond its original intent to a metaphorical one that retains overtones of the original. Those who promulgate metaphorical stereotypes use them as substitutes for careful analysis.

The term *prejudice* has a more direct history. It was meant to convey what it does: prejudge. It is ironic, however, that as journalists we should be concerned about our own prejudgments. Our craft is dedicated to helping people make judgments based on facts and evidence in order to liberate them from prejudice. Nevertheless, we dare not evade the truth here. There is prejudice and stereotyping in journalism in general and, sadly, in pictorial journalism in particular. As professionals, journalists should want to be aware of unintentional stereotyping and prejudice and should move to eliminate them.

In this context, we may give brief attention to *discrimination.* As it is used here, discrimination builds upon and moves beyond prejudice and stereotyping. With discrimination, we can no longer speak of unintentional prejudgment; it is intentional. Like the drug addict, the discriminatory person presents a public face of self-righteous denial. However, even what is claimed to be thoughtless discrimination arises out of a studied desire to evade conflicting evidence.

SOME PRELIMINARIES

The combination of stereotypes with prejudice and discrimination is lethal. A productive manner in which to understand what has happened is to borrow a term from the legal community—the *artificial person.* In law, an artificial person is an unreal and constructed person such as a corporation. Stereotyping converts real persons into artificial persons. In our stereotypical acts, we treat people as proxies for a group we have decided they should represent. In short, we deny them their humanity. Prejudice and discrimination magnify the dangers of stereotyping because the natural laziness that is a historical part of stereotyping is extended by another natural laziness: tenuous generalization.

The combination of stereotyping and prejudice becomes even more virulent in the context of pictorial imagery. The hackneyed phrase holds that a picture is worth a thousand words. We might suggest a new one to the effect that even a million words may not be able to undo the negative impact of a single bad picture.

If we are to challenge pictorial stereotyping ethically, we should pay attention to some prerequisites for the consideration of ethical issues. There are three such conditions that I call the three Cs of ethics: confusion, choice, and commitment.

The person who acknowledges no confusion about the world or some aspect of it is a dangerous person. She will see no reason to change either her attitudes or her behavior. The primary hope for her is a good liberal education. Even more than most other professions, journalists need a solid, rigorous, and challenging liberal education that will undermine their prejudices. The person who does not acknowledge confusion will not have enough self-awareness to think about her stereotypes.

In regard to choice, fortunately, we do not have to enter the complex debates among philosophers on the subject of free will. What we can say, I think, is that ethics demand choice. Where there is no choice, there is no room for sensible ethical judgment. The opening comments about business managers are based on the economists' deterministic view that they have no effective choice but to maximize profits. If, eventually, scientists conclude human free will is a mere superstition, we shall be forced to revise radically our thinking about ethics. In the meantime, we should note that scientific determinism is a presumption rather than a conclusion.

The final precondition of ethics is one of a commitment to do what is right.[1] As a philosopher, I have no special insight that enables me to persuade immoral people to abandon their way of life. I may, however, be able to help the committed person determine what is right in a particular situation. This chapter and, perhaps, the book at large assume we are dealing with people who will permit themselves to be confused, who have choices, and who are committed to doing what is right.

ETHICAL THEORIES AND APPLICATIONS

We may proceed initially by outlining the general perspectives of two broadly different ethical philosophies. The first, which for our purposes I will call *personalism,* is most closely associated with Immanuel Kant. The second, typically identified as *utilitarianism,* is most closely associated with Jeremy Bentham and John Stuart Mill. In considering practical topics such as ours, the former is typically dismissed as too abstract and too rigid. However, I am going to suggest that Kant's approach is the better one for responding to stereotypes, prejudice, and discrimination.

Kant argued for making a distinction between persons and things. Things have a price and can be exchanged, one for the other, as prices change. In the marketplace, this is accomplished most efficiently with money. Here we have the origin of the expression "Every*thing* has its price."

By way of contrast, Kant said persons are beyond all price. Marx would pick this point up later in his complaint that capitalism turns everything, including people, into a commodity. People have what Kant called a dignity, and the invasion of that dignity cannot be justified, no matter what price someone is willing to pay. Thus, the expression "Every*body* has his or her price" is a cynical one and should be rejected morally for the reason Kant suggests: people are not things. Because we all view ourselves as persons, not things, the only consistent view to take is that everyone should be treated as a person with dignity and not as an object to be manipulated.

The very nature of stereotyping, prejudice, and discrimination is that they convert real persons into artificial persons and, as a consequence, treat human beings as objects. Thus, a common tactic of those who would strip others of their dignity is to deny that they are humans. Such rationalizations underlie the history of prejudice and discrimination.

Utilitarianism is the ethical perspective that suggests we should make our ethical decisions by selecting that course of action that is most likely to lead to the greatest happiness for the greatest number of people. In many cases, that seems to have a double advantage: it is harmless and it allows for a broader range of practical application. However, utilitarianism may also provide support for stereotyping in that, whereas it may hurt some people, it may, nevertheless, promote the greatest happiness for the community at large. When I have heard editors justify stereotyping, the defense has usually been a utilitarian one, but I think it should be challenged along Kantian lines. Listed below are some examples.

Harmlessness. There are those who argue that some cases of exploitation are harmless or nearly so. For example, some think it is acceptable to stereotype white Anglo males. They sometimes suggest first that such stereotyping is an appropriate corrective for prejudices of the past, and, second, such people retain so many levers of power that stereotyping is harmless. But if the underlying principle is that treating people as objects is wrong, there is no justification for compensatory prejudice. Stereotyping those with power may be less morally obnoxious than stereotyping those without power, but it remains morally obnoxious. The cure for centuries of stereotyping and prejudice is not more refined and sophisticated stereotyping and prejudice; it is cessation.

Communication. I have heard some journalists argue that stereotyping and prejudice can be justified in the interest of communicating to a broader audience. Since the basic job of journalism is to communicate, they say whatever aids in the process of communication is justified. In short, as the utilitarian would have it, undermining the rights of a few may be defended if it is to the advantage of many. However, as our advertising colleagues could tell us, usually more than the surface message is communicated to an audience. The use of stereotypes, especially in pictorial form, ends up communicating much more than may have been intended; it positively reinforces a history of exploitation.

Professional Obligations to Readers, Listeners, or Viewers. This is, perhaps, the most frequent justification I have heard from journalists for stereotyping activities. In the context of this rationalization, we can find all sorts of pictorial examples, as when we show pictures of grieving parents or severely injured persons, or picture after picture of arrests that consistently show people from diverse cultures being arrested when, as a matter of fact, Anglos are arrested in greater numbers than any other ethnic group. Journalists do have obligations to readers, viewers, and listeners, but they have obligations to others, also. Journalists do not withdraw from the human race when they pick up their notepad or their camera. The issue should always be whether there are ways of getting the story told without stereotyping someone else and reinforcing prejudice. A journalist always has choices in reporting a story. They should be made in light of respect for persons.

History. Utilitarian journalists sometimes justify their stereotyping activities by suggesting that they are preparing the first draft of history. Thus, even though living people may be exploited, they think it is justified if future generations can learn valuable lessons. The historical argument is strengthened from a utilitarian perspective because reference to future generations increases the number of people affected and, thus, expands the greatest number to find the greatest happiness. Such justifications may be challenged because, if the purpose is to leave a record of stereotyping and prejudice, it is enough to say that it exists without engaging in it. In addition, there is plenty of independent corroborating evidence of stereotyping without adding to or duplicating the exploitation.

Entertainment. Another justification I hear regularly for stereotyping and prejudice is that it is entertaining. As often as not, the entertainment sought is a humorous one that makes it even more difficult to object. I believe the news media have set themselves on a dangerous course in accepting the role of entertainer as part of their effort. Certainly, we want readers, viewers, and listeners to pay attention to what we do, and I most assuredly do not suggest academic lectures or publications as models. Nevertheless, too much questionable activity is admissible under the guise of entertainment for us to be entirely comfortable with that role. In the pictorial area, the temptation is even greater because of the potential impact of pictures. There is no doubt that people make fools of themselves visually, but we need to be careful that in our effort to entertain others we do not perpetuate stereotypes and exploit subjects.

There is another approach to ethical issues that has been receiving attention recently. It is usually called *virtue ethics* for it recommends we follow the example of admirable and virtuous people. If we follow Kant in establishing what is virtuous, I think this approach might be both helpful and practical. To put the matter simplistically, we need roles more than rules. The ethical problems in journalism spring more often from people avoiding their professional responsibilities than from people pursuing them too aggressively. What we need are examples of journalists who have solved the problems that have been articulated even within this area of journalistic ethics. We need to hear from or about journalists who have faced some of the issues identified and overcome them successfully. Committed journalists want to communicate; they want to get the real story across; they want to have pictures and tapes that tell the real story. They do not want to deal in stereotypes or prejudice. Committed journalists want to aid readers, listeners, and viewers as persons, just as committed teachers want to help students as persons, committed physicians want to help patients as persons, and committed clergy want to help parishioners as persons.

We might apply the reasoning we have developed to other issues that seem so intractable in journalism. A newsroom with narrowly selected reporters and editors may not be confused about what it is doing and may not recognize it has choices because there is no palpable articulation of them. From the perspective of the reliable presentation of the news, it is critically important that newsrooms be diversified. Talk of a pluralistic society is often little more than political cant, but it is also revelatory of an observable fact of our society. As much as some would like to deny it, the fact is that we have a remarkably diverse and diversified society. It is not enough to imagine how others with different experiences, different backgrounds, and different aspirations might react. It is important for people with that diversity to be living witnesses in order to expand both confusion and choice. My argument here is not for preferential hiring. It is not the condescending view that some groups of people need "a hand-up rather than a hand-out." Both sides of that equation reinforce stereotypes and prejudice. My argument is directly related to improving the quality of the news and serving the readers, viewers, and listeners. The pictorial media folks should be at the forefront. They know better than anyone about different perspectives. Diversity of background in the newsroom is essential.

At the same time, pictorial imagery is, perhaps, more susceptible to the use of stereotypes and the reinforcement of prejudice. When it comes time to prepare written material, reporters and editors still have at their command the whole range of choices given by the language in terms of vocabulary and syntax. When it comes time to prepare pictures, video, or digital images back in the newsroom, all are constrained to choose from among the alternatives that appear before them. Thus, it is important that the choice be as wide as possible. The bedeviling problems that occur when editors and others are presented with choosing the lesser of evils will not all be solved by the development of choice, but they may be moderated.

Pictorial imagery should be looking for what is remarkable, what is noteworthy, what is singular about the subjects, not what makes them representative of some preconceived image. The pictorial image should extend the vision of the viewer; it should not confine or constrain that vision. People already have prejudices and stereotypes. Reinforcing them is not part of the news beat. Extending the perspective of the viewer is. The issues we face in our society are too complex and too important to be reduced to thinking by stereotypes. That does not contribute to the national dialogue; it detracts from it.

If we ensure we have a diversified newsroom of committed journalists who have been liberally educated and who are presented with a wide array of genuine choices, we can have some faith the conclusions of that newsroom will ensure we do not stretch bounds thoughtlessly. Obviously, even the most diversified, conscientious, and well-educated newsroom can make mistakes. The notion that we might reach perfection comes from unjustified human arrogance. However, we can do better. We can create the conditions under which prejudicial, discriminatory, and stereotypical behavior is minimized. The choice is ours to determine whether we are committed.

Chapter 3

MEDIA METHODS THAT LEAD TO STEREOTYPES

Travis Linn

"Hi, honey, I'm home!"

For most situation comedy (sitcom) programs on television, a man's role begins and ends with that exclamation (it also identifies the role of the woman as the patient homemaker). The image of a man is shallow, usually depicting him as a bumbling idiot, having to rely on his wife for almost everything around the house, and inept at raising the children.[1]

Such a stereotype arouses the righteous anger of many men and women. Stereotypes used in humor are particularly hurtful when they are based on many of the categories found in this edition that are both inevitable and irrelevant to personal worth.

And yet, stereotypical views of others are part of our shared culture. We participate in these views even when we consciously reject them. It is this reality upon which the writers of sitcoms rely.

The job of a sitcom is to make people laugh, and that is done through prejudices and stereotypes that are common to the culture. The Polish joke, the Jewish joke, the Catholic joke, the New Englander joke—all these play upon images that may or may not have any basis in fact. Certainly, they are prejudicial in that they characterize classes of people. Yet they are considered funny because either we share those prejudices, or we are aware of them and sufficiently accepting of them that we can laugh while telling ourselves that we do not share their perspective. In fact, the humor depends partly on the recognition that the stereotypes are stereotypes, that they are not universal truths. The jokes about Jews' obsession with wealth would not be jokes if we believed that all Jews were so obsessed. Instead of laughing, we would nod knowingly. At the same time, the jokes wouldn't be understandable if we didn't share at least the knowledge of the stereotype. Our reaction would be, "What's that about?"

The use of stereotypes is equally common, however, in dramatic programs that purport to represent life as it really is (at least to the point of credibility). Gang members on television are almost always Latino or African American. Southern women are blonde, tough, and wise underneath a layer of practiced charm, and so on. Stereotypes are used as a way of gaining credibility. A stereotype is, after all, an artifact of common belief. Most people believe that most gang members are Latino or African American because law enforcement officers tell us that is the case, and the evening news confirms it. The truth is that there are many Anglo gangs. Thus, the use of this stereotype in a dramatic program is one that appears to fit reality, and, because it appears to fit reality, the program gains the confidence of the viewer in that regard.

The use of an ethnic stereotype tends to reinforce the common belief that it relies upon, thus hardening attitudes about multicultural groups. Stereotypes lead viewers to believe that only Latino and African Americans are gang members. The writer of the dramatic program is thus faced with a paradox: casting Latinos as gang members reinforces an ethnic stereotype and is injurious and prejudicial, but taking another course—perhaps having an interracial gang—is at odds with common belief to the extent that the dramatic presentation is robbed of some of its credibility and thus its power.

THE JOURNALIST FACES A SIMILAR DILEMMA

In news, one could argue, stereotypes have no legitimate role. Humor is not the objective of the newscast (at least one would not think so!). It would seem an appropriate goal of the journalist to portray people as they are, not as we think them to be. Indeed, journalism is most compelling when it shows us that reality is different from what we have assumed it to be. Yet, the journalist inevitably leans on the same stereotypes as the writer of comedy or drama but for somewhat different reasons. The journalist also faces a different dilemma, but one no less central to the craft.

WHY JOURNALISM STEREOTYPES

One of the most obvious ways journalists preserve stereotypes is in the selection of examples, or cases, to illustrate stories. A sales tax increase is proposed. The assignments editor calls for a story that shows how the increase might affect a so-called typical family. What is a typical family in our society? The answer used to be that it is an Anglo family with a working male, a stay-at-home wife, and two children, aged about three and about six. Now, chances are the wife will have a job, but the rest will be the same. On the other hand, the reporter may be keenly aware of societal changes that are going on, and so she may seek out an unmarried Latina mother of three children. This family may actually be less typical than the traditional one.

The problem in this scenario, as far as a discussion of stereotyping goes, is not the selection of one family or another. It is the concept of picking a typical family. In American society, diversity is so widespread and variety so pronounced that it is too great a stretch to designate any family as typical. Focusing on one kind of family—any family—as being illustrative is a practice that ignores the majority of society.

What, then, is the solution? Should the journalist use 3, 5, or 10 different examples? This technique would provide some context and perspective, but it would take up a prohibitive amount of time or space. Should the journalist avoid examples altogether, presenting only statistics that can describe the whole population? This procedure would avoid stereotyping, but it would make the story dull and, to many, incomprehensible. Certainly it would take the humanity out of the story, leaving it cold and bloodless.

Thus, the journalist's dilemma comes from the role as a storyteller. If a story is to be meaningful and interesting, it has to be about people, specific people. But when that is done, imbalance is introduced. It is similar to the dilemma of a researcher. When the researcher uses anecdotal evidence, the research has life and meaning, but it loses significance because anecdotes can and do distort; they leap out from their contexts and assume unwarranted importance. Statistics, fairly presented, maintain the balance and are significant (or at least they can be), but they are also dull and possibly incomprehensible. The compromise that is often adopted is to present the statistical tables accompanied by anecdotes or quotations that illustrate the major findings. This improves the report and makes it more understandable, but it is a compromise. The anecdotes and quotations that are used tend to be remembered more vividly than the dry statistics that provide the context.

For the journalist, it is the same. Some of us who were conscious at the time have vivid memories of the 1968 Democratic Convention in Chicago. We remember the riots, the pictures we saw on television of protesters throwing rocks, bottles, and excrement at the police, the pictures we saw on television of the police teargassing and clubbing the protesters. Most people would say the television coverage focused on the rioting, diverting attention from the convention itself. Yet only a small fraction of the television coverage was of the rioting. The vast majority of television time was taken up by the activities in the convention hall and the related meetings. The coverage was not balanced in favor of the rioting, but our attention was, and our memory is. Furthermore, if the journalists at the time had told the television audience, "They're rioting outside, and police are hauling away hundreds of people, but we're not going to show you that activity because it's minor compared to the selection of a presidential candidate," the home viewer might have rioted.

This selective perception is a phenomenon so familiar that it is standard to textbooks on communications. It affects those who send messages as well as those who receive them, and it is based upon and reinforces stereotypical thinking. All of us evaluate new information by comparing it with the perceptions that we already have—perceptions that we accept as true, as having stood the tests of previous comparisons. Occasionally, we allow the new information to change our perceptions, but more frequently we accept, reject, or reshape the new information in such a way as to preserve our existing perceptions, perceptions that could be called *worldview* or *prejudice*.

Here is another paradox. If we see all new information in the light of beliefs already held, we are bound to preserve prejudices and to ignore new insights. If, on the other hand, we set aside previously held beliefs— as if that were possible—we would have no basis on which to judge new information, and for us every day would be our first day in the world.

How, then, are journalists to resolve these paradoxes? There can be no true resolution, of course. Otherwise, these examples would not be paradoxes. However, there can be honest grappling with the issues. What follows are a few suggestions or thoughts on ways journalists can avoid the unconscious use of stereotypes.

ENERGETIC, THOROUGH REPORTING

In journalism, laziness and stereotypical thinking go together. The reporter asks two or three questions, gets a good quote or sound bite, and moves on. The first line of defense against prejudice in journalism is thorough reporting. The more questions asked, the more observations made, the more concrete and particular the reporter's notes, the more the journalist is focused on a person, a family, or an incident, rather than taking a face and a name and plugging those into a set of assumptions.

SUSPENSION OF BELIEF

Writers of fiction hope for *suspension of disbelief*. They want their readers to set aside rationality for the moment and accept the sometimes unlikely premises of their creations. In journalism, we should seek suspension of belief. We should consciously recognize the assumptions that lace common knowledge and suspend our belief in those assumptions as we consider the facts of a given situation. We cannot erase long-held perceptions from our minds, but we can suspend their application until we get the facts of the situation at hand. As reporters, too often we (literally or in principle) write the first draft of the story in the car en route to the scene, subject only to minor adjustments to accommodate obvious contradictions.

AVOIDANCE OF GENERALITIES AND QUALITATIVE ADJECTIVES

Journalists unconsciously add opinion and prejudice to stories through the use of generalities and qualitative adjectives.

Generalities such as "when it gets hot, we get lazy" or "kids need action; just listening to someone talk isn't fun" assign behaviors to groups or classes. They are per se stereotypical. Such generalities are often used as soft leads to stories so that we can contrast an individual case. The rest of the sentence is "but John Smith gets busier as the temperature goes up" or "but these kids turn off their video games to hear their teacher explain something."

Qualitative adjectives are those that apply judgment to the subject rather than describing something that can be observed. *Angry* is a qualitative adjective in that it is the application of the writer's judgment rather than the observation of behavior. *Slamming the telephone down* is a modifying phrase that describes behavior. It is also a more powerful image than angry. Description of attributes and action is simultaneously less judgmental and more powerful than the attribution of qualities. Words like *normal, ordinary, unusual,* and *rare* apply the journalist's (often unfounded) opinion to people and events.

The inevitable conclusion is that stereotypical thinking and writing are linked with lazy journalism. A reporter who fails to do enough background research and fails to ask all the questions falls into the trap of using generalities to fill the gaps. The writer who fails to find the precise words allows stereotypical phrases to creep into the copy. The photographer who relies on visual clichés perpetuates harmful stereotyping. Simply put, an energetic, thorough journalist has no room in a story or photograph for vague generalities and convenient stereotypes.

Chapter 4

UNCONSCIOUS, UBIQUITOUS FRAMES

Susan Dente Ross

When a sympathetic protagonist declares sincerely, "I've been framed," in a popular television show or motion picture, we all know malevolent forces have conspired to misrepresent facts and falsify evidence to set the poor slob up as the fall guy. Evil forces acted maliciously and intentionally. The protagonist's dilemma is neither accidental nor inevitable.

Often, our poor hero—and the evil forces fighting against her—is immediately recognizable to us. The good character, and the bad, is identifiable by her ethnicity, her clothing, her language, and her behavior. The hero represents a group of like individuals, all of whom we assume share similar traits and behaviors. Thus, the swarthy Arab striding across a screen is likely to be the villain (see Chapter 8), and the blonde bombshell is sure to be the virtuous maiden in distress.

These stereotypes are not accidental. They are the product of an individual's decision "not to work harder than necessary to achieve a superficially acceptable result" (Enteman, 1996, p. 9). We know some of the information transmitted through these stereotypes is inaccurate and unfair, but we rely on stereotypes anyway because they are easy and efficient. Stereotypes reduce our effort; they allow us to transmit huge amounts of information without engaging in careful, individual analysis. And, we argue, we can always make exceptions to our own sweeping, cruel, or exaggerated remarks, as when we say, "Well, she's not really *black* black," or "He's not like *most* athletes."

Thus, knowing the costs, we still *choose* to represent people not "as they are, [but] as we think them to be" (Linn, 1996, p. 16). We engage willingly in a calculated shorthand that enables us both to sweep the individual into the general and to generalize from the single case. We decode the data, "black, male, 23," within a context where "driving while black" or even being black and male in America is evidence of crime.[1] Or we allow one fraudulent welfare recipient to represent everyone who ever has relied on government assistance. If we are thoughtful and self-critical, we may rationalize such stereotyping in the name of simplicity, or we may develop strategies to minimize our use of stereotypes. Either way, we assume stereotypes are neither accidental nor inevitable. They are produced and altered by intentional action. Studies suggest that such attention can eliminate or at least minimize the harm of stereotypes. Yet subtler and less intentional factors also skew our vision of reality.

Whereas media professionals like to perceive themselves as cataloguers of reality, neutral observers of the world around them, this is not entirely true. Reporters, news directors, journalism professors, and students construct the ideal of objectivity and argue that the media not only can but also must serve as an unbiased crucible of public opinion formation. Yet, despite their training and desire for objectivity, journalists are simultaneously constructing and being shaped by the culture in which they work. The truth is, we cannot tell stories we do not hear. We cannot convey pictures we do not see. The images photojournalists see and capture and the stories journalists hear and tell are at once a response to professional imperatives and a reflection of personal experiences and acculturation. The images and stories journalists see and share are dictated not only by where reporters go to find stories and with whom they talk, but by what journalists understand to be important in what is seen and heard. The views and values of journalists shape the content of their messages, and these views and values are shaped as much by personal and social history as by professional environments and norms.

This is normal. Human perception is selective and partial. As framing theory suggests, human beings do not perceive the universe neutrally, uniformly, or completely. We filter; we ignore; we exaggerate. What we perceive, and what we are able to communicate to others, is affected by our identity, our culture, our experience, our worldview: in a word—our *frame*. In a now-famous analogy, Gaye Tuchman (1978) described our mental frames as problematic windows on the world:

> The view through a window depends upon whether the window is large or small, has many panes or few, whether the glass is opaque or clear, whether the window faces a street or backyard. The unfolding scene also depends

upon where one stands, far or near, craning one's neck to the side, or gazing straight ahead, eyes parallel to the wall in which the window is encased. (p. 1)

Our personal, professional, and cultural frames delimit how we make sense of, and how we portray, the world. Some scholars believe the structure and organization of media bias journalists toward certain frames (Ghanem, 1996; Gitlin, 1980; Hofstetter, 1976; Perkins & Starosta, 2001; Shoemaker & Reese, 1996; van Dijk, 1991; Weston, 1996). Print deadlines (Hofstetter, 1976), story form, journalistic routines (Shoemaker & Reese, 1996), and editing (Liebes, 2000) create structural and procedural constraints that lend themselves to certain frames of reality (Ghanem 1996; van Dijk, 1991). News values dictate that conflict and violence warrant attention; happy coexistence does not. Journalists' training tells them the legislature generates news and the garden club does not. Our education and personal experiences incline us to believe the comments of a university professor are noteworthy; the words of an illegal immigrant are not.

But framing involves much more than story and source selection. Content frames emerge through word choice and decisions about how the story is told and who gets quoted, about what, and where in the story. Frames include "keywords, stock phrases, stereotyped images, sources of information, and sentences that provide thematically reinforcing clusters of facts or judgments" (Entman, 1993, p. 52). Unlike Tuchman's window frame, content frames are only partly visible. Much of framing lies deeply embedded in text and is decoded by audience members who recognize the cultural meanings of certain words, images, narratives, or juxtapositions. Thus, frames consist of more than just the text and images on the page; frames encompass the meanings those things convey (van Dijk, 1991). The systematic semantics of news discourse ties each story to others and to a wealth of cultural myth and legend, to cultural beliefs of how the world works, and of how stories end. Framing connects today's news with our personal and social histories and with the myriad of images and stereotypes we use to represent reality.

In these ways, framing encourages certain definitions of problems, identification of causes, and possibilities of solutions. Framing narrows the range of likely interpretations of events. Its association with predecessors circumscribes each story. Framing builds upon cultural associations and reinforces the human tendency to generalize and to transform individuals into representatives of a group or class. Framing encourages us to view the details of a story, not in their own particulars, but in their tendency either to exemplify or to contradict a social or cultural norm. Stories that ask us to develop a new understanding are jarring and, often, unconvincing. Instead, framing encourages us to look through the specifics of the event to *recognize* a story as an exemplar. Media framing is both the product and the producer of ubiquitous cultural frames. It is both the reflection and the construction of our worldview. It is inevitable and largely unconscious.

Through selection, emphasis, and omission, journalists direct the attention of their audience toward the aspects of daily life that consistently warrant—and do not warrant—consideration. This selective emphasis is not random or transient. Rather, the frames employed by journalists are durable reflections of internalized professional values and social norms. Indeed, some might suggest that selective attention is one of the primary values of responsible media. The selective attention of the media helps set the agenda for public discussion of social issues. By framing some ideas as credible, others as laughable, media simplify the task of harried citizens with little time to devote to complicated issues. By disseminating government depictions and analyses of issues and events, media oversee government and inform the public. By omitting the assertions of small, powerless, or unpopular groups, media endorse social values, disassociate themselves from radicals, and reflect the role of power in society.

Of course, good journalists try to tell both sides—or even many sides—of a story. But journalists' understanding of the sides of any story is somewhat predetermined. Journalists expect a balanced news story to include both the pro and the con. For example, the city's proposed road project will improve traffic flow through the business district; it also will require increased local taxes. But a balanced and professional report on the road project does not need to include an explanation of the complex history of the issue, the role of increased roads in ozone depletion, or thousands of other potentially important pieces of information. Who will build the road isn't newsworthy, generally, *unless* the contractor is the nephew of the mayor. The precise composition of the paving material isn't worth reporting *until* the road collapses because the pavement failed to meet federal requirements. The list could go on and on. What journalists include—and what they exclude—in stories reflects their frame of what is newsworthy.

Research suggests that media framing affects the mental constructs each of us carries around about the world. Media frames are particularly powerful when they relate to people, places, or issues about which we have no direct information. Media frames tend to be most influential when they provide a means for us to interpret and understand the unknown. The frames we encounter in media provide a template for our vision of the foreign, the marginal, the other. And these images are durable, though not permanent. Education and direct personal experience can enlarge or reshape our mental windows, or redirect our gaze. Even a glass house, though, does not permit us to look simultaneously and with equal intensity out the front and the back, and professional norms and cultural standards lead us to look in one direction rather than another. No amount of good will or effort can eliminate the fact that what we see depends on who we are and where we look.

Critics of media sensationalism, pack journalism, media consolidation, and "if it bleeds, it leads" news values express concern that recurrent news media frames fail to portray either the diversity or the complexity of events. They assert that what the media say and how they say it is formulaic and misrepresentative. When dozens of media outlets focus their resources on the same events and the same sources like a marauding pack of wolves or a complacent herd of sheep, nominally independent news outlets produce little plurality of content. When this occurs, the critics say, it should surprise no one that the images and texts produced by multinational media conglomerates tend to reflect the dominant ideas and ideals of society's elite and powerful. These media images create and perpetuate stereotypes.

Some argue that media support of the status quo is the product of conspiracy or coercion, but framing theory suggests that reporters and editors simply are more likely to accept the ideas that dominate their own culture than the ideas of outsiders. Certainly the media are subject to the pressures of the profit motive, but personal and professional training also shutters journalists' insights. Journalists have less exposure to individuals and groups outside their beats (which conform to the powerful inner circles of society). If journalists alternately ignore or caricature and render as buffoons or demons those at the margins of society, this treatment is less the result of intentional choice than the logical outcome of circumscribed personal and professional lives.

Whereas individual journalists and media organizations sometimes break loose from cultural blinders, much media content—both visual and textual—tends to create, perpetuate, and reinforce images that resonate with deeply held cultural biases and myths. It may be said that news is really a continuation of the old. Stories and images of society's weak, poor, and radical appear when they conform to familiar narratives. The realities of personal challenges are rendered as fables of redemption and self-realization. The details included, or omitted, from such stories conform to simplistic tales of good and evil, self-sufficiency, and the value of hard work that permeate our society. The narratives and the images endure: the criminal, the rich, the homeless, and the intellectual. We know what they look like, and we have expectations about how they will behave. More important, perhaps, are the others whose images we never see in the media. Their stories are not told, and their portraits are not ingrained in our social tableau. It is difficult to say whether these people are absent from news pages because they have been dismissed from society or they are powerless because the media render them invisible. But it is exceedingly difficult for the poor, the weak, or the undereducated to reshape effectively our image of reality.

This is not the fault of the media. This is a human problem. What we call *the media* is no more, and no less, than an assemblage of individuals doing their jobs, sometimes well, sometimes poorly. Journalists employ incomplete and unfair frames and stereotypes because they are people, and people often find it easier and more comfortable *not* to confront their ingrained stereotypes and prejudices.

It is probably most accurate to say that journalists both mirror and frame reality. The media are both the product and the producers of the cultures in which they exist. As producers and consumers of media, it is our job to understand the concept of framing and to study its implications. If we wish to consume media messages critically and work as responsible journalists and educators, we must recognize and challenge our own frames. That is our only hope for a broader, deeper, and more nuanced image of reality.

Chapter 5

IMAGES THAT HEAL

J. B. Colson

If all the makers and all the consumers of all the media were to read, understand, and reflect on the contents of this book, there would be a whole lot of healing going on. But we are all guilty, at least some of the time, of fast, easy, and false generalizations about *the other,* people who are not like us.

These generalizations injure not only the apparent victims of stereotypes, who, of course, are likely to be hurt the most, but all of us who participate in the production and consumption of images that shortchange the unique and positive characteristics of individuals and groups.

As Everette Dennis notes in the introduction, stereotypes function well in terms of easy, clear messages for visual communicators and their viewers. Thus, despite their potential damage, stereotypes seem inevitable in an era of slick, facile media and its time-pressed readers.

It is not images themselves that injure, but the messages they are part of and the way they are received, so the subtitle of this book, *Pictorial Stereotypes in the Media,* is necessary for the assumption of the book's title. Words and layout design are also key parts of almost all pictorial presentations, with words at least implicitly directing our interpretations of images. To think about images that heal requires thinking about all aspects of a message, including its presentation context. For all those images that seem a priori injurious, I believe a presentation context can be imagined where they would serve healing functions. However, the bulk of this book is about media presentations of images that are in varying degrees inaccurate and unjust, images that in a variety of ways hurt the people depicted and there-fore all of the society involved. Can we imagine, then, images with positive psychological and social effects that would improve the well being of those involved, or better, images presented in such a way that would so serve?

What would media images that heal, that serve the opposite function to pictorial stereotypes that injure, look like? This is a natural, potentially useful question for a text that discusses media stereotypes so thoroughly, from so many points of view, but a difficult question with less-certain answers than the business of deciding what imagery injures.

It is easy enough, perhaps, to read this text carefully and avoid the obvi-ous sins of pictorial injury that it details. Beyond that, the question of images that heal becomes a greater challenge. In a large part this book is a catalogue, thoughtful and analytical as it is, of definable existing problems. This, and the fact that stereotypes are an easy, unthoughtful approach to representation, suggests a void for the definition of thoughtful, positive rep-resentations.

It would be surprising if anyone who reads through this book carefully does not at some point think, "I never thought of that," and elsewhere, "I don't agree with that." (This certainly happened for me.) With a lack of awareness and a lack of agreement at stake, we are often less than clear about what constitutes injury and what serves to heal.

THE DIFFICULTY OF INTERPRETATION

Vicki Goldberg puts it well in her book, *The Power of Photography:* "Photographs are mute artifacts. They do not speak but can only be inter-preted, and interpretation is a notoriously tricky game." She explains that one reason we are so easily fooled into believing we understand photogra-phy is that we carry over the ease with which we can read its denotation into the much less certain business of connotation. Does a photograph of a disabled person performing an everyday task with effort honor that person or victimize him? Details of photographic treatment seen in the image, such as camera angle, lighting, and facial expression, can certainly influ-ence our interpretations, but usually not as much as our attitudes and expectations.

EFFECTS OF PRESENTATION

This point, already made above as a caution against assuming too much inherent communication in an image, is worth additional emphasis. Titles, cutlines, headlines, and text regularly accompany photography. Because the connotation of photographs is so uncertain, those words exert a great deal of force on interpretation. Change the words and you change the apparent meaning of the image and thereby also help determine its social effect.

Other important aspects of presentation include the expectations for the specific medium used (the *New York Times* versus supermarket tabloids) and image size and placement.

OUR OWN PROJECTIONS

In his thoughtful book about the nature of photography, *Camera Lucida,* the philosopher Roland Barthes muses on a photograph of his mother, about which he says in a point of irony, as well as honesty: "I cannot reproduce the Winter Garden Photograph. It exists only for me. For you, it would be nothing but an indifferent picture, one of the thousand manifestations of the 'ordinary'" (p. 73). A matter of indifference to us is a keystone to the nature of photography for Barthes. (He suggests an important facet of the medium of photography is the viewer's reaction to the picture.) The difference is what he brings to the image.

The uncertainty of connotation inherent in photography, to the extent that it is not directed by presentation context, is open to influence by our personal knowledge and attitudes. Regarding reaction to stereotyping, it is assumed that members of a stereotyped group will have a common negative reaction, based on their common experience as members of that group. If the corollary of that were true, only members of that group would effectively appreciate imagery showing them well, or images that heal. This is probably true at least some of the time, but it need not deny a larger appreciation for showing human diversity realistically.

As Paul Martin Lester discusses in his book *Visual Communication Images with Messages,* the more we know, the more we see. This is a difficult concept to accept and to work with. In the case of stereotypes, we are working with what we assume we know. The challenging task for those producing messages is to see openly what, in many cases, we do not yet know. For viewers the task is to see and accept openly the unexpected and unfamiliar in media representations.

Just run down the list of titles in the table of contents for this book; with how many of these groups do you not identify? If it is difficult for us to consider stereotyping from the point of view of so many groups, it is even less likely that we can imagine the diverse personal psychology involved in responses to images.

SEPARATION OF PHOTOGRAPHERS
FROM VIEWERS

Writers in this book have noted the need for more diversity among media practitioners. The low percentages of African Americans, Latinos, and women in key media positions do not contribute to an understanding of their attitudes and needs. As this book demonstrates, we have many other identifiable and significant subcultures to know about and honor. In addition to fundamental differences between producers and consumers of media, the nature of mass media is to limit the chance for them to interact.

To produce messages for media is to be distanced from the viewers of those messages. In closer social contexts, discussion with skill and good motivation can convert injury into healing, a process not available to most people involved with mass media. Though we can expect the increasing diversity of media staffs occurring now to continue, we cannot expect media to closely represent the increasing diversity of our society. What we hope for is well-trained and sensitive media producers who will do justice to the people they report on, to their viewers, and to the ethics of their profession.

To produce media is also to be part of media subgroups, each with its own values, attitudes, and operating sociology. Newspaper photojournalists, for example, have quite different values and working methods than news writers, but both groups tend to respect deadlines, bylines, and peer group approval. So do writers and photographers for magazines, who, as a group, are defined by some important working differences from newspaper people. The issue of struggle for success in peer group terms often results in media professionals working to standards quite different from those the public uses to judge their images. The dramatic angles and stunning moments of prize-winning photographs or articles may be difficult to read or offensive to an everyday viewing public.

GETTING TO IMAGES THAT HEAL

The damages of images that injure are well described in various ways by other writers in this text. Though the injuries in many cases are bad feelings, they can extend to extremes far beyond temporary psychological states. Alienation for individuals to the point of suicide and for groups to the point of physical conflict are some of the extremes that have actually happened.

The goals for images that heal, broadly stated, are improved conditions for individuals and better social relations for everyone involved. Working to understand how all this can be defined, understood, and made to happen is one obvious task, a project for both media professionals and academics. Professional societies, most of which have ethical charters, can play a major role in this effort.

Compassion. The personal attitude at stake in working for images that heal is compassion. With true compassion, our motivation to heal is natural; our awareness of others, their nature, and their situation is heightened.

The Other. We construct our identities with a set of personal definitions that typically separates us from others. When we reduce our separation and include others in our definition of our own well being, we will work with concern for them as well as ourselves. With a truly open mind, we will see that there is no *other* absolutely separated from us.

Education. Reading this book is one example of educating ourselves, a lifelong responsibility we have in a rapidly changing world. Whereas all levels of education are at stake in the issue of stereotyping, and we can hope for a lot more from our public school systems, most authors of this book work in university programs related to media production. Inspiring the students in these programs to avoid stereotyping and to produce images that heal is one of the most effective ways we have of achieving our goals. To the extent that we can help our universities show leadership in media ethics and practice, rather than function so decidedly to provide workers for an industry, we will be effective.

The Special Role of Documentary Photography. The subject of *documentary photography* referred to here is one of social situations, examining them carefully and reporting them in interesting and useful ways. Although journalism often produces and presents documentary projects, the nature of documentary photography is separated from everyday journalism by scope and depth. The time, effort, resources, and skills required for documentary photography are substantial. They can be developed especially well in university programs where documentary practice is understood and supported. In addition, documentary attitudes and skills can be brought to journalism and all reportorial practice.

The Problem of Resources. This text is an example of the problem of resources. Limited resources prevent the inclusion of images in this edition, so we have no examples to illustrate our discussions. Media, universities, governments, and individuals all seem to have decreasing resources and increased responsibilities and challenges. These pressures do not facilitate avoiding stereotypes and putting time and effort into the difficult task of producing accurate, insightful representations. Most of the control of resources and most of the executive power over image production is not in the hands of those who directly make the images for media. The values and actions of these executives are therefore a most important factor in eliminating stereotypes from media.

RIGHTS AND RESPONSIBILITIES OF MEDIA PARTICIPANTS

In its innocent form, imagery that injures is the result of ignorance. As malicious enterprise, it is about the abuse of power. If not ignorance and not malice, it is the result of placing values such as visual impact or the public's right to know over the feelings of people as individuals and members of groups. These value judgments may or may not be ethically appropriate, but in all cases of social injury due to the depiction of people, ethics are at stake.

A traditional approach to finding clarity in ethical dilemmas is to consider the rights and responsibilities of all the parties involved. Informed communicators with positive ethical motivations are needed if we are to replace stereotypes in significant numbers with images that heal. Educators have the responsibility of training a public well able to read and critique images intelligently. All of us have the responsibility to provide feedback to the media we consume, not only complaining about stereotypes but also expressing gratitude and encouraging positive efforts. University educators have a responsibility to train media producers who will avoid making injurious image messages. The victims of stereotypes need to do what they can in their part of the process by calling stereotypes to task and supporting efforts on behalf of their interests. However, because most of the power is in the hands of the imagemakers and those who finance them, these individuals have the most responsibility for producing media that recognize the diversity and complexity of human experience. We all have the right to accurate, insightful images in our media.

Part II

STEREOTYPES FROM SEPTEMBER 11, 2001

Chapter 6

VISUAL SYMBOLISM AND STEREOTYPES IN THE WAKE OF 9/11

Paul Martin Lester

When Ernest Hemingway first moved to Key West, Florida, he hung out at the original Sloppy Joes bar, now called Capt. Tony's Saloon. It's quite different from the touristy Sloppy Joes on Duval Street. Capt. Tony's is a much smaller, seedier, and more comfortable bar around the corner on Greene Street. It is also the oldest drinking establishment in town.[1]

Three months after the aerial attacks of September 11, 2001, I found myself sitting at the bar at Capt. Tony's sipping a Bushmill's Irish whiskey on the rocks and listening to a young, heartfelt woman with a guitar, a microphone, and an amplifier belt out classic saloon hits such as "Brown Eyed Girl," "Hotel California," and "House of the Rising Sun."

For the most part her performance was lost on the drinkers left alone with their private thoughts that afternoon, until she announced the last song of her set. And incredibly, when she started singing, almost everyone in the bar put down their drinks and sang along with her.

Since that afternoon, I've seen the title of that melody displayed with black, sans serif typefaces on storefront displays in my hometown and throughout the country when I travel. I've heard it sung by flag-waving fans at half time and seventh-inning stretches countless times. I've seen and heard it so often that I wondered if there would be a serious movement to make the song the new national anthem because it is much easier to sing and contains lyrics that are much easier to remember. Through a little research, I found out that in the 1930s, when "Papa" was drinking in Capt. Tony's, many in this country felt the same way.

The song, of course, is Irving Berlin's "God Bless America."

On one of several Web sites devoted to Irving Berlin and "God Bless America" it is noted, "America's 'unofficial national anthem' was written during the summer of 1918 at Camp Upton, located in Yaphank, Long Island, for his Ziegfeld-style revue, *Yip, Yip, Yaphank.*" Another famous tune written for the musical was "Oh How I Hate to Get Up in the Morning," but "God Bless America" was left out. Berlin thought the tone seemed too serious for a comedy.[2]

Interestingly, "God Bless America" started out as a peace song. When war was ravaging Europe again 20 years later, Berlin wanted to write a song that would calm his anxious fellow citizens. He recalled his abandoned tune, changed some of the lyrics, and had singer Kate Smith introduce it through a radio broadcast on Armistice Day, 1938. As today, the song was such a success that many wanted to replace the national anthem with it. "Berlin soon established the God Bless America Fund, dedicating the royalties from sheet music sales to the Boy and Girl Scouts of America."[3]

"God Bless America" is a song that was written during World War I, first became popular just before World War II, was little heard during the Korean, Vietnam, and Gulf wars, and now has regained its popularity during our current War on... Terrorism, Al Qaida, Taliban, Osama bin Laden, the "Axis of Evil"—Iraq, Iran, and North Korea—Filipino insurgents, or drug smugglers and rebels in Columbia.

As the woman and the bar crowd sang the song, I looked around Capt. Tony's and for the first time noticed all the patriotic graphic symbols around me—the God Bless America sticker with its red, white, and blue typography stuck to the singer's guitar case, the small American flags placed inside empty beer steins on the bar, and the jacket of the woman sitting across from me with a flag lapel pin on it.

Within 48 hours of the 9/11 aerial attacks, Kmart sold 200,000 American flags nationwide. You could see flags everywhere—cut out of newspapers and stuck to house windows, displayed large on the side of shopping malls, painted on the side of buildings, and flapping until dirty and frayed while tenuously attached to car antennae. Without doubt, the use of the American flag is fair game to communicate American ideals and products.

However, it wasn't always that way. American flags on shirts, pants, and even diapers got people arrested in previous eras. Abbie Hoffman of Chicago Seven fame was arrested in 1968 for wearing a shirt that resembled an American flag. He was released when it couldn't be determined if the shirt was made from an actual flag.[4] A man in Ohio was arrested and convicted in 1972 for wearing a flag sewn on a back pocket. An Ohio appeals court upheld the conviction because it was determined that the flag was placed "over the anus" and thus was subject to the state's desecration law. However, the Ohio Supreme Court overturned the decision noting that the anus is not under a person's pocket area (Hill, 1997). *Hustler* publisher Larry Flynt wore a flag diaper "to deliver a court fine in 1983 and spent five months in federal prison for desecration of the flag" (Zeller, 2002).

The clearest indication of how times have changed for the flag is to note a product from Atlanta-based Paragon Trade Brands, the country's largest manufacturer of disposable diapers. It recently introduced its Little Patriots line of red-white-and-blue–starred diapers that were sold in Wal-Mart stores. The colorful package shows a baby in front of a stars-and-stripes backdrop, waving a flag while sitting on what appears to be a toilet, with text that includes the obligatory message, "A portion of the proceeds (10 percent) benefits the American Red Cross" (Zeller, 2002).

Of course, the original meaning of the American flag and the meaning for many today is not one based on a protest or eye-catching ability in an advertisement. Through the years, the red color of the flag has come to symbolize valor and zeal. White has a sociological meaning in the flag as hope and purity. The color blue is for reverence to God, loyalty, sincerity, justice, and truth. A star, an ancient Egyptian symbol for sovereignty, represents each state in the Union, whereas the 13 stripes stand for the 13 original colonies. George Washington described the symbolism of the flag: "We take the stars from Heaven, the red from our mother country [England], separating it by white stripes, thus showing that we have separated from her, and the white stripes shall go down to posterity representing Liberty."[5]

Berlin once said that "a patriotic song is an emotion and you must not embarrass an audience with it, or they will hate your guts." For this book, an appropriate paraphrase might be that the use of a flag is an emotional choice that must not embarrass its audience. But far too often, many in this country have been embarrassed and disturbed by the flagrant display of visual patriotism in the mass media, advertising, and by ordinary, well-meaning citizens.

PATRIOTIC SYMBOLISM IN THE MASS MEDIA

Jennifer Lambe and Ralph Begleiter of the Department of Communication at the University of Delaware examined the use of patriotic symbolism in local news shows through a survey of news directors of television stations across the United States.

The two researchers noted the difference between visual symbolism used with television news reports during the Gulf War of 1991 and the current war.

> While many broadcasts adopted the names of the U.S. missions in the Gulf, such as "Operation Desert Shield" and "Desert Storm," color schemes used in newscasts generally did not involve red-white-and-blue and American flags were not prominently in evidence on TV news screens. All that changed dramatically after the horrific attacks of September 11, 2001. As the American people wrapped themselves in their flag for comfort, TV stations followed suit. As Americans hung flags from their windows and flew them from their cars, television news programs used patriotic symbols to express solidarity with their American viewers. (Lambe & Begleiter, 2002)

With red, white, and blue graphic elements and typography, news stations—both local and national—were quick to produce slogans and designs that undeniably presented a pro-government, pro-war theme. Slogans such as "Assault on America," "America Fights Back," and "Americans United" conveyed solidarity, if not necessarily journalistic objectivity, to the American public, with words and graphic symbols (Lambe & Begleiter, 2002).

Newspaper front pages and magazine covers are also important areas for research into the word, picture, and design choices made by journalists and editors regarding events of 9/11 and beyond. The Web site of the Poynter Institute, a media-training and resource center based in St. Petersburg, Florida, reproduced many newspaper front pages from around the world that were published on September 12.[6] As expected, every paper printed a large, colorful photograph of the destruction. Some of the best designs used images that expressed the human element—people running in fear, crying, and holding each other, or erecting an American flag. One striking difference between U.S. and foreign front pages is the use of red, white, and blue–colored text, backgrounds, and graphic rules. The effect of the use of the patriotic colors was to link symbolically the coverage with the country's tragedy.

The covers of the major U.S. news magazines, *U.S. News & World Report, Newsweek,* and *Time,* were no exception. *U.S. News* used the headline "UNDER SIEGE" and a picture of a firefighter attaching an American flag to a streetlight stand. *Newsweek* used the headline "God Bless America" with an image of three firefighters erecting a flag. *Time* showed an image of President Bush waving a small American flag with the headline "One Nation, Indivisible." *Time* also displayed patriotic colors in the most blatant way with the T in red, the I in white, and the M in blue.

Perhaps symbolic of America's struggle, the E was printed in black. Although not a news magazine per se, *The New Yorker* cover was quite different. It showed a dark illustration by Art Spiegelman of the twin towers titled "Ground Zero" that contributed to the serious tone of the stories that reflected the solemn mood of the country.[7]

The World Wide Web is, of course, a medium that has a wealth of media messages related to 9/11 and patriotic themes with few qualms about not being objective. For example, on About.com there is a collection of "cartoons, funny pictures, doctored photos, and patriotic art targeting Osama bin Laden and boosting America's war on terrorism." On the site is a long list of collected works that mostly provide stereotypical humor related to the events covered in the media. Jihad for Dummies, Absolut Dead Man, The Turbanator, and Afghanistan Terrorist School are pictures you can click on. In a piece called New World Trade Center Design, there is a picture of five World Trade Center buildings—the middle one is higher than the other four.[8]

PATRIOTIC SYMBOLISM IN ADVERTISING

Many would probably conclude that using the flag to sell diapers is over the top, but all kinds of products are being sold with 9/11 visual symbolism tie-ins—most with an American flag motif.

For $795 you can buy a pair of red, white, and blue Manolo Blahnik heels from Neiman Marcus. Two new Beanie Babies, a bear named America and a dog named Courage, come from Ty Inc. For $16 an American flag embroidered on a baby's burp cloth can be had from babyobaby.com. Sturbridge Yankee Workshop of Portland, Maine, sells liberty pillows that a spokesperson says, "speak our love and belief in country and freedom." Flag-themed prom dresses and wedding gowns allow you, through photographs, to remember "the year that American freedom was under challenge." You can get a barbell for your pierced tongue that has a small American flag on the end and buy toilet paper with each sheet printed with Osama bin Laden's picture with a bull's-eye on his forehead and "Wipe Out Terrorism" printed below (De Lisser, 2002).

Television commercials have also used 9/11 patriotic symbolism. General Motors used a "Keep America Rolling" theme while AT&T had a "Let Freedom Ring" telephone pitch. Most notably, during Super Bowl XXXVI, Anheuser-Busch showed a commercial of their famous Clydesdale horses digitally kneeling at the site of Ground Zero in New York City.

The Topps Company, most known for their baseball trading cards and Bazooka Joe bubble gum, is also quick to produce cards on topics of significant interest to the general public. For example, Topps published a set of cards about the Korean War called "Freedom's War," a set titled "Man On The Moon," three series having to do with the Gulf War, and, most recently, a 90-card set titled "Enduring Freedom." In an appeal to parents to purchase the cards for their children, the Topps Web site proclaims that the company "presents the New War on Terrorism in a format that children understand. Not included are the disturbing images shown repeatedly on national newscasts." The advertising pitch uses the language of President George W. Bush: "Kids need to understand that the President (and his team) will keep them safe and that evildoers will be punished. Our cards deliver the details in a medium with which they are familiar and comfortable."[9]

Each pack contains seven cards plus a sticker with patriotic symbolism. The cards are divided into seven sections: "September 11, 2001," "To the Rescue," "The World Supports America," "The Investigation," "America Unites," "The Nation's Leaders," and "Defending Freedom." On the front of each pack is a close-up photograph of an American flag with a red, white, and blue illustration that shows a stern-looking soldier in battle gear, another stylized American flag, and the words "ENDURING FREEDOM" (De Lisser, 2002).

Within a pack recently purchased is a sticker of an American flag with the words, "THESE COLORS DON'T RUN" under it and seven cards: "Secretary of State Powell Meets the Press," "Sailors Aboard the *USS Theodore Roosevelt*," "Army Paratroopers Boarding an Aircraft," "FEMA Director Allbaugh Meets with Bush," "Prepping Aircraft Aboard *USS Theodore Roosevelt*," "Condoleeza Rice, National Security Advisor," and "Air Force's SOS MH-53J Pave Low IIIE." On the back of each card is a brief description about the subject of the card with a photograph, two American flag illustrations, a white star, and red, white, and blue typography. "The last thing we wanted to do was tug heartstrings," says Arthur Shorin, Topps' chairman and CEO. He adds that there is a market for "an encyclopedic" collection of cards explaining events and effects of 9/11 in a manner to which children can relate (De Lisser, 2002). Nevertheless, consumers of these cards, who are mostly children, receive a highly colorful and one-sided, governmental, pro-war message within an advertising context.

PERSONAL PATRIOTIC SYMBOLISM

Personal statements of patriotism by journalists through the wearing of flag lapel pins sparked controversy at some television news stations. In response to the Lambe and Begleiter survey, one news director wrote, "I assume you are aware of the situation at the NBC affiliate in Columbia, Missouri, owned by the University of Missouri School of Journalism. The news director there banned anchors from wearing patriotic displays" (Lambe & Begleiter, 2002).

But another news director wrote,

> Any journalist who believes that by displaying the symbol of our nation that he/she cannot be an objective, responsible journalist is either: (1) a lousy journalist, (2) a lousy American. Our flag is not Democratic or Republican; it is not George Bush's flag or Ted Kennedy's flag. It belongs to EVERY American, bought and paid for by the bloodshed and sacrifices of millions of American soldiers and citizens. If I can't be an excellent journalist and a proud American, then I don't deserve to be either. This is the saddest controversy I've ever seen the media embroiled in. (Lambe & Begleiter, 2002)

Like the country, members of the journalism profession are divided as to the appropriateness of displaying patriotic symbolism.

Entertainers and sports figures have contributed to personal patriotic displays. Through public testimonials, concerts, and commercial endorsements, celebrities show their colors in a symbolic way. Many players—for all the major sports—wear embroidered flag ribbons on their jerseys or uniforms. Chad Kreuter, catcher for the Los Angeles Dodgers baseball team wears a highly stylized American flag graphic enameled to the back of his mask.

PATRIOTIC SYMBOLISM AND STEREOTYPES

Ira Glass, the thoughtful host of Public Radio International's *This American Life,* has misgivings about too outward a display of patriotism. Glass relayed that on the "first day [after the attacks], it felt like waving a flag was an act of mourning. But now that we're going to war, waving a flag feels like giving carte blanche to Congress and the President to do whatever. And I don't believe that."[10]

Glass and others believe that a danger in all the flag waving and other patriotic displays is that they can stir up resentments against specific cultural groups—namely, those individuals of Arab descent (see Chapter 9).

Soon after the attacks of 9/11,

> …mosques were firebombed, Arab Americans were vocally abused and physically attacked, and at least six persons of Arab descent were murdered. Five months after the attacks, Arab Americans filed 260 claims of work-

place discrimination with the federal government, an increase of 168 percent over the same time period the previous year. Equally alarming was a CNN/Gallup poll that asked Americans if they would support a policy requiring all individuals of Middle Eastern heritage to wear some form of identification indicating they had been checked by security. Half of those polled would support such a policy. (Lester, 2003, pp. 105–106)

Consequently, Glass warned his girlfriend, who is Arab American, "that she ought to put up a flag, since the other houses on her block are displaying them."[11]

When mass media, advertising, and personal messages employ patriotic symbolism in too strident and prevalent ways, the result can turn American against American.

Back at Capt. Tony's Saloon, almost everyone in the dark and smoky bar, along with the guitar-strumming singer, finished "God Bless America" with the familiar last line, "My home sweet home." The patriotic saloon singers immediately exploded into applause.

However, when the performer didn't miss a beat and went right into the chorus of another famous song by John Lennon and Paul McCartney, the clapping stopped. Some say it, too, is a call for peace and just as patriotic as "God Bless America": the verse says, "All we are saying is give peace a chance."

Chapter 7

TERRORISTS WE LIKE AND TERRORISTS WE DON'T LIKE

Deni Elliott

Smoke billowed from the World Trade Center buildings on 9/11 as photo-journalists made that day's attacks the most documented in the world's history. Associated Press (AP) photographer Mark D. Phillips caught in a picture's frame smoke that evoked an eerie combination of eyes, nose, mouth, and horns that some viewers saw as the face of Satan and others saw as an image of Osama bin Laden.[1]

Jack Stokes, AP Media Relations manager, said the photo had not been manipulated. "The smoke in this photo, combined with light and shadow, has created an image which readers have seen in different ways," he said.

Smoke and light and shadow may influence the meaning viewers bring to some photographs, but U.S. photojournalists provided images of terrorism both before and after 9/11 that included cues to tell viewers how they should feel. In providing negative cues regarding some non–U.S. terrorists, news media have reported nationalistically, in line with whom the U.S. government has termed *evil*. However, in situations in which the U.S. government's view is ambiguous regarding the appropriateness of terrorist activity, news media are similarly nonjudgmental.

U.S. citizens need something from news media that is different from that which they get from government. To make educated decisions for self-governance, citizens need a media perspective that is broader than the governmental rhetoric, and citizens need images that do more than serve the government's agenda.

This chapter explores alternative views of those labeled terrorists, with a special focus on images related to the attacks of September 11, 2001, and those related to the Israeli/Palestinian conflict.

TURBANS AND GENERIC IMAGERY

Type in keywords *terrorism* and *images* in any Web-based search engine and what comes up first and continually are image galleries from 9/11. Few would need to explore those galleries to be reminded of the images we carry in our memories: jet airliners crashing into the Twin Towers, both buildings collapsing, shocked and sweat-covered survivors, jumpers frozen in their eerily elegant falls to deaths, and pictures of grief made public.

The primary images of terrorism from 9/11 are of the consequences of the acts. The actors are less specific. Published images of the suicide bombers who carried out the attacks blur into a generic mug shot of a man of Middle Eastern ancestry. The pictures of Palestinians purportedly celebrating in response to the attacks include women in veils and men in turbans. Osama bin Laden is portrayed as the face of evil on "Wanted, Dead or Alive" posters, but his turban and other-than-Anglo features identify him most easily.

Just as the juxtaposition of airliners slamming into the world's most impressive office buildings creates an inescapable subtext of American power crumbled by American technology, the religious and cultural symbols of regional dress became icons for evil. When terrorists look different from the Anglo American dominant society, it is easy to label that look as evil. It is easy to extend that label to stereotypically include other people who happen to share a religion, culture, or physical look, or even to encompass an entire geographical region as the home of terrorists.

Americans used the turban as a symbol of terrorism long before 9/11, said Eli Sanders, *Seattle Times* staff reporter. Sanders suggested this tendency "may stem from the Iran hostage crisis" of the late 1970s. The symbolic connection between turbans and evil is blamed for hundreds of unprovoked post 9/11 attacks on Sikh men, although there is no connection between Sikhs and the 19 men who carried out the hijackings (Sanders, 2001).

The entertainment industry "has been at war with Islam for the last two decades," said Akbar Ahmed (2002), who teaches Islamic Studies at American University. Films that show Muslims in negative ways have "conditioned the American public to expect the worst from a civilization depicted as 'terrorist,' 'fundamentalist,' and 'fanatic.' So powerful has this image been that popular culture makes the equation without thinking about it" (Ahmed, 2002). Long before September 2001, Americans were becoming acclimated to equate Middle Eastern look and dress with threat. People unfamiliar with those traditions may be made uneasy by differences in dress or religious traditions, but what permeated the American subconscious was not Muslim difference but Muslim threat. The image of this threat became an icon for terrorism.

PALESTINIAN SUICIDE BOMBERS

A photograph released by the Israeli army in June 2002 showed a Palestinian toddler dressed as a suicide bomber with explosives strapped to its body. The child wore a headband proclaiming allegiance to Hamas. (Hamas is a militant group that has claimed responsibility for the majority of the 71 suicide bombings in Israel in less than two years.)

Publication of the photograph reinforced and perpetuated the concept of the Middle Eastern terrorist, according to both Israeli and Palestinian sources. "The photograph of the baby suicide bomber symbolizes the incitement and hatred which the Palestinian leadership have been using to brainwash an entire generation of Palestinian children who have, unfortunately, taken in this message like mother's milk," said Dore Gold, a senior adviser to Israeli Prime Minister Ariel Sharon. Palestinian Labor Minister Ghassan Khatib accused the Israeli media of using the photo to "further distort" the Palestinian position.[2] Dressing the child as a suicide bomber was explained as a joke.

DEFINING TERRORISM

Terrorism is defined by Title 22 of the United States Code, Section 2656 f (d), to include premeditated, politically motivated violence perpetrated against noncombatant targets by non–state-sanctioned agents.[3] One of the primary things that distinguishes terrorism from military engagement is that while some civilians may be slain in military engagements, these unintended and unfortunate victims are *collateral damage*. In terrorism, civilians are the intended targets. In addition, terrorists differ from state-sanctioned military combatants because the latter fight on behalf of a recognized nation-state. Terrorists instead are funded and supported generally through less-formal means, including individual support, coalitions, and the informal support of some governments.

The actions and tactics that define terrorists often have little to do with how we distinguish terrorists we like—or that are portrayed in a positive way by mainstream U.S. media—and those we don't. Distinguishing good terrorists from bad terrorists is difficult when their tactics and complexions are the same, as with the Catholics and Protestants in Belfast. The distinction of good and bad terrorists is also made difficult when the U.S. government fails to recognize either side as threatening U.S. national interests. But when the U.S. government labels terrorists "freedom fighters," or "rebels," or the "opposition army," they are not likely to be condemned or presented in a negative light by media. The distinction between terrorist and freedom fighter, however, often turns on little more than the appearance of the non–state-sanctioned combatants, what our governmental leaders call them, and whether the current U.S. government supports their political agenda.

This permits terrorists to be transformed overnight. For instance, in 1985 then-President Ronald Reagan received a group of Afghan mujahideen and called them "freedom fighters" (Ahmad, 2001). Eqbal Ahmad, professor of international relations, examined 20 official U.S. documents on terrorism and found that "not one offers a definition" (Ahmad, 2001). In this way, "the terrorist of yesterday is the hero of today, and the hero of yesterday becomes the terrorist of today" (pp. 12–13).

Osama bin Laden, himself, was an ally of the United States in the mid-1980s. Ahmad writes:

> When the Soviet Union intervened in Afghanistan…Zia ul-Haq saw an opportunity and launched a jihad (a struggle) there against godless communism. The U.S. saw a God-sent opportunity to mobilize one billion Muslims against what Reagan called the Evil Empire. Money started pouring in. CIA agents started going all over the Muslim world recruiting people to fight in the great jihad. Bin Laden was one of the early prize recruits. (p. 22)

According to Ahmad, bin Laden remained loyal to the United States until the end of the Gulf War.

After Saddam was defeated, the American foreign troops stayed on in the land of the kaba (the sacred site of Islam in Mecca). Bin Laden wrote letter after letter saying, "Why are you here? Get out! You came to help, but you have stayed on." Finally he started a jihad against the occupiers. His mission is to get American troops out of Saudi Arabia. His earlier mission was to get Russian troops out of Afghanistan (p. 23).

THE COSTS OF POLITICALLY MOTIVATED LABELS

Portraying some terrorists as evil and some as not interferes with citizens' ability to understand the world in which they live. Understanding requires that one know the perspective that purported terrorists bring to their cause. Without that understanding, it is not likely terrorist activity can be prevented.

Chapter 8

UNEQUAL COMBATANTS ON AN UNEVEN MEDIA BATTLEFIELD: PALESTINE AND ISRAEL

Susan Dente Ross

What was true before September 11, 2001 is equally true afterward: the media rarely present both sides of a conflict neutrally and evenhandedly.

To create a clear, simple image of the complex and competing issues involved in a conflict, the media tend to endorse the credibility of the favored side and to excise the disfavored side from news coverage (Liebes, 1992). Media invest one side of the story with credibility and allow it to dominate the news (Gamson, 1992).

Like the Roman coliseum in which lions were loosed upon unarmed captives, today's media arena bestow privileges upon those individuals who have political support over their challengers (Steuter, 1990; Tilly, 1978; Wolfsfeld, 1997). When a conflict involves *us* versus *them, they* are clearly the bad guys (Liebes, 1992; Wolfsfeld, 1997). American media tend to endorse the position of the U.S. government (Schlesinger, Elliot, & Murdock, 1984). When a conflict does not so directly involve U.S. interests, such as in the Israeli/Palestinian conflict, *our* side may not be obvious.

Yet the media enemy is not chosen at random. A symbiotic relationship exists between government initiatives toward terrorists and media. It is no accident, for example, that "terrorism news bears a remarkable resemblance to many sentiments common in U.S. foreign policy, and, indeed, conservative North American political culture" (Steuter, 1990, p. 274). By emphasizing difference and schism, polarization and conflict, U.S. media portray individuals "who oppose established order [as] terrorists, while state terrorism is a category that is virtually never used unless it refers to the Communist bloc" (Steuter, 1990, p. 262).

Media also are drawn to crisis and violence (Shinar, 2000), which serves the interests of terrorists. Terrorists seek out media coverage "to make an ideological point through dramatic impact...[and] to amplify this impact...by reaching the broadest possible audience" (Stossel, 2001, p. 35). In this way, Stossel argues, it may be that "the television viewers of America were more important than the initial targets" of the 9/11 attacks in serving the goals of the terrorists (Stossel, 2001, p. 35). The media affinity for the spectacle of violence skews media coverage toward conflict and away from peace negotiations (Wolfsfeld, 1997).

Media emphasis on ideology and spectacle also contributes to the creation of an enemy *other*. Media demonize an enemy through stereotypes that exaggerate preexisting fears and perceptions of difference. This is not new. American media participated in the shameful transformation of Japanese Americans from citizens to enemies during World War II that justified their internment in camps on the West Coast. The media also served both as the medium and the target of the red scare of McCarthyism that dominated the Cold War years with recurrent anti-Communist messages. In the years since the Cold War, fears and images of hate have coalesced around deeply held stereotypes of the Middle East that harm others and distort public decision making. These media stereotypes strongly influence what Americans believe about important international issues and contribute to the intractability of intercultural conflicts (Cappella & Jamieson, 1996; Shinar, 2002).

STEREOTYPES OF MUSLIMS, ARABS, AND PALESTINIANS

For decades, scholars like Edward Said have identified a persistent tendency for Western media to perpetuate derogatory and racist stereotypes of Islam (Said, 1981). This does not mean that Arabs and Muslims are portrayed only and entirely as evil. Rather, it means that the "negative images of Islam are very much more prevalent than others, and...such images correspond not with what Islam 'is'...but to what prominent sectors of a particular society take it to be" (Said, p. 136).

John Esposito, one of America's leading authorities on Islam, agrees. In his 1995 book, *The Islamic Threat, Myth or Reality?*, Esposito wrote:

> Islam's relationship to the West [remains] marked by mutual ignorance, stereotyping, contempt, and conflict....Western fears and antipathies are

fed...by media reports and headline events....Old stereotypes of "the Arab" and Islam in terms of Bedouin, desert, camel, polygamy, harem, and rich oil sheiks have been replaced by those of gun-toting mullahs or bearded, anti-Western fundamentalists. (pp. 25, 230)

This unfair caricature in part reflects the human difficulty or reluctance to portray difference equitably. Each of us is more able (and more willing?) to uncover and describe traits and behaviors we recognize and find familiar. The difficulty in finding objective terms of description increases when we feel contempt, dislike, or hostility toward someone.

Selective, crisis-oriented media coverage of the Middle East also contributes to a biased and unfair view of Arabs and Islam that emphasizes difference and violence. Headlines repeatedly proclaim the threat of a radical, Islamic holy war by an undifferentiated mass of Arabs and Muslims intent upon eradicating the Western way of life.[1] One example is the lead article in *Atlantic Monthly*'s September 1990 issue, "The Roots of Muslim Rage" (Lewis, 1990). A bearded, turbaned, glowering, dark-skinned Muslim with American flags reflected in his piercing eyes fills the cover of the magazine. Two illustrations accompany the article: in one, a snake marked with stars and stripes slithers across a desert; in the other, the snake rears for attack behind a praying Muslim. Clearly the theme is one of mutual antagonism, confrontation, and threat.

Movies for the big and small screen do little to moderate this image. The tendency of American films to define Arabs as the evil, uncivilized, terrorist *other* began well before 9/11 and is so pervasive that it has been dubbed the *Hollywood Arab*. In examples from the 1977 release of *Network* through the controversial 1998 opening of *The Siege*, American films have presented Arabs as violent, religious fanatics (National Conference for Community and Justice, 1998). The overwhelming message of the 20th Century Fox film *The Siege* is that every Muslim is a fundamentalist and a potential terrorist. The enemies of America in *Wrong Is Right* (1982), *Iron Eagle* (1986), and *True Lies* (1994) are nuclear-bomb wielding, fundamentalist Arab terrorists. And, according to the American Arab Anti-Discrimination Committee (ADC), every Muslim or Arab in HBO's drama, "Path to Paradise: The Untold Story of the World Trade Center Bombing" (1997), is portrayed as an "ugly stereotype." The ADC called "Path to Paradise" "one of TV's most racist movies" ever. The stereotyping was so extreme and the American Arab outcry was so severe that the film aired with a disclaimer indicating the movie did not reflect the beliefs of most Muslims and Arabs, but the movie remained unchanged.

The American Arab community again mobilized in 2000 to call for an international boycott of the Paramount Pictures release of *Rules of Engagement* (2000). The film prominently features the military slaughter of more than 80 unarmed civilian Yemeni men, woman, and children as potential threats to the American ambassador. The Arab American Anti-Discrimination Committee said the film embodied the clearly racist message that all Arabs deserve to be killed because of their inherent hatred of America and Americans (Okwu, 2000).

Since 9/11, the small screen has continued this steady portrayal of the Arab as villain. The clichés begin with the title of the CBS TV movie *The President's Man: A Line in the Sand* (2002). Featuring Chuck Norris, the movie about swarthy Arabs attempting to detonate a nuclear bomb in Texas outrageously vilifies Arab Muslims, Arab Americans, and Islam and inflames American anti-Arab sentiments. CBS series, including *JAG, The District, The Agency,* and *Family Law,* have represented Arabs as deceitful, brutish, lunatic terrorists and murderers, and recent episodes of NBC's *The West Wing* and ABC's *Alias* portrayed Arabs as hateful (Shaheen, 2002).

ONE NEWSPAPER'S VIEW

But how does one of the nation's most prestigious and credible sources of news, the *New York Times,* represent Arabs and Israelis on its editorial page? In the 13 months surrounding the aerial attacks of 9/11, the official voice of the *New York Times* discussed the Palestinian/Israeli conflict 34 times, for an average of slightly more than one editorial every two weeks (Ross, 2002). The first impressions given by the titles of these editorials suggest an emphasis on U.S. strategic interests and stability in the region.

Several editorials represent the United States as a powerful, active player in the regional conflict in which Arabs, and particularly Yassir Arafat, are relatively powerless. Arafat is portrayed as a lame duck whose fate will be decided by other world players, including the United States. The editorials stereotypically tend to equate or conflate Arabs and Palestinians, as if Palestinians have no unique traits, interests, or challenges. Though the editorials sometimes present a strong negative image of Arabs as belligerent arms smugglers or suicide bombers, they also sometimes portray Arabs as legitimate brokers of peace. In contrast, relatively few editorials explicitly name Israel. These Israeli-identified editorials are almost exclusively negative in tone and tend to describe concrete Israeli military atrocities.

Editorial emphasis on violence and detailed descriptions of specific acts of bloodshed create an image of senseless brutality in which the two sides alternately serve as aggressor. Palestine and Israel are feuding neighbors engaged in a senseless cycle of violence. But the two sides are not presented as equally culpable. Ariel Sharon is a largely unwilling participant in the carnage; Yassir Arafat is an impotent, unreliable, Janus-faced sponsor of terrorism. Arafat is condemned for a "strategy of talking peace while waging war [that] is spreading death across Israel" (Ross, 2003). Sharon is neither even-tempered nor consistent, but he is a strong, well-informed, rational leader who is in charge of his own destiny. He shares a podium with the White House and U.S. and foreign diplomats.

The editorials portray Palestinians as members of an antiquated, murderous caste consumed by old hatreds, constantly stoking tensions with peace-loving Israelis, and intent upon eliminating the state of Israel. Palestinians are stereotyped as racist, anti-Semitic, terrorist suicide bombers. Palestinians are never presented as the moral victims. The need for Palestinian sovereignty and security is routinely presented as secondary to the same interests of the Israelis. What Israel deserves, Palestine is only begrudgingly and conditionally granted. And it is Arabs, not Palestinians, who are linked to editorial discussions of cease-fires, diplomatic efforts, and the peace process.

The recurrent graphic descriptions of suicide bombings in the *New York Times* editorials about Israeli/Palestinian conflict convey an impression of Palestinian terrorism and Israeli victimization. The image presented by the editorials is that the entire Palestinian population consists of suicide bombers. The typical Palestinian is a conflagration of hate, a plague of death, a suicide cult, and a puppet spouting venomous anti-American and anti-Israeli vitriol. Palestinians engage in random killing of "Israelis on an almost daily basis." They murder "a 10-month-old Jewish baby" and pack bombs "with nails and bullets that [tear] through a crowd of innocent teenagers" and leave "Israeli families in mourning" (Ross, 2003). Palestinians are faceless, unprovoked, and unreasonably bitter.

Recognition of Palestinian humanity is rare and often backhanded. For example, an editorial denouncing Israeli occupation of Ramallah acknowledges the "victimhood" of the Palestinians but also calls them "Israel haters" and says, "They have not taught their young the virtues of peaceful coexistence." The number of Palestinian dead goes unreported. Or when 20,000 Israeli troops "in full battle dress, riding in tanks and backed by fire from Apache attack helicopters ripped their way through large refugee camps," the harm is summarized simply as "more than 160 Palestinians" dead. The human losses from the "destruction of hundreds of houses, the innumerable roadblocks and daily Palestinian humiliation" go unmentioned (Ross, 2003).

The Israelis, in the eyes of the editorial writers, are human beings and family members who have been terrorized and traumatized. They are weeping widows, orphans, and childless parents. Funerals fill the land of Israel, and the individuals and families that make up the nation suffer unjustly. Israel and its leaders are long-suffering, law-abiding individuals who have been provoked into violence. It is the Israeli troops—the legitimate defense of a nation under attack—not the people of Israel that have retaliated against an uncounted number of nameless Palestinians. Israelis are not terrorists or murderers; instead, their military sometimes overzealously protects the nation's legitimate interests. The excesses of Israeli military incursions are justified as a necessary means to advance the safety of Israeli citizens or as reasonable retaliation for brutal terrorist Palestinian assaults. Israel's recurrent efforts at peace and negotiation have been ignored or rebuffed. Palestinian intransigence and failure to staunch violence are the baseline.

In rare editorials that look at the historical context of the current conflict, Israelis sometimes are said to share in responsibility for the continuous carnage and endless cycle of bloodthirsty revenge. These editorials blame both sides for senseless bloodletting, and they acknowledge that both Israelis and Palestinians share the plight of their destiny together on a tiny, arid plot of land. But most editorials present the history of the conflict as short term. History means last week or last year. Regional history begins in 1967 or, at the earliest, 1948. Historical enmity, distrust, and violence between Arabs and Israel are not explained. Readers instead are left with images of violence and stereotypical images of Palestinian terrorists and Israeli victims. The state-sponsored violence of the Israel military is accepted as part of an undesirable but nonetheless necessary governmental order.

CONCLUSION

Television, movie, and news images of Arabs as villains and terrorists continue in abundance. These stereotypes appear in documentaries, made-for-TV fiction, news coverage, and editorials. They reach our children through animated films and melodies, shape our adolescents through news magazines and commentary, and inform our beliefs about who is to blame for international violence and how it can be eliminated.

These images are not real. They are not accurate. They are not productive. They injure their messengers, their recipients, and their subjects. They promise a future of continued misunderstanding, mutual contempt, and hatred.

Hope for peace cannot be found in continued images that injure and rhetoric that distorts. Hope for understanding cannot be found in stereotypes that obscure who we are and what we believe. Hope for an end to violence cannot be found in media messages that excise individuals, demonize cultures, and value some lives more than others.

Hope for justice begins with a level playing field on which all parties feel fairly treated. Hope for peace begins with an individual commitment to recognize the unique value of others. Hope for an end to violence begins with a personal desire to eradicate images that injure and to replace them with images of inclusion, compassion, and tolerance.

Chapter 9

POST-9/11 DISCRIMINATION AGAINST ARABS AND MUSLIMS

James W. Brown[1]

Prediction

FBI Director William Sessions and other law enforcement officials were also at the Capitol today to testify about the bombing of the World Trade Center in New York, which killed at least five people and injured 1,000. Lawmakers are writing anti-terrorist legislation, and they wanted to know if the February 26 attack could be the beginning of a new cycle of terrorism in the United States. NPR's Anthony Brooks reports.

Linda Wertheimer, All Things Considered, March 9, 1993

Prejudice

Offended? I, too, am offended. I get offended when I can't show my patriotism because it might offend someone from around the world that landed here to go to school. It offends me when I have to give up prayer in school. Once again because it might upset Hadji Hindu or Buddy Buddha. I don't believe the founding fathers were either of these.

Truth is, they were Christian and believed in the one true God of the universe. Talk about majority. When I look around I see no Mosque, or fat, bald guys with bowls in their laps. I see churches. I'm offended when I turn on a television show and without fail a queer is in the plot just like it's a natural thing. America put God in the closet and let the queers out. When the planes struck the twin towers I never heard anyone utter, "Oh, Ellen." I heard a lot of, "Oh, my God." Now we want to pull God off the shelf, rub His head and expect a miracle.

Dennis Nail, assistant police chief, Martinsville, Indiana in a 2001
letter to the editor, Martinsville Daily Reporter

Prophecy

Dear Friends in Peace-

Hi! I know you had nothing to do with it. So I ask if you want to be my peace partner. I don't want to make fun of you and I don't want anyone else to do so either. I think it doesen't [*sic*] matter what anyone else says it just matters whats in your heart. I want you to know that were praying for you and we hope you won't be treated terrible any more. Becuse [*sic*] we know you didn't do anything to deserve this. *Your Peace Friend: Sarabeth Marshall.*

From a letter sent by grade school student Sarabeth Marshall
to the Islamic Society of North America, Plainfield, Indiana,
September 20, 2001 (language not corrected)

9-1-1

Prior to September 11, 2001, we thought of nine-one-one as numbers to dial for emergency response from police, fire, or emergency medical services. Now we think of those numbers as a date.

We will forever remember that date as one in which nearly 3,000 people died as a result of four simultaneous airplane hijackings. Nineteen Islamic men using mere industrial box cutters as weapons commandeered four aircraft. Most of the men were from Saudi Arabia. The stock market would shut down for a few days, the airline industry came perilously close to bankruptcy, and the feeling of security within our borders disappeared.

The September 12 edition of the *New York Times* used 300 reporters, 30 staff photographers, and several dozen freelancers. U.S. ATTACKED in 96-point type was the point of entry for 74 bylines on 67 stories. Only Neil Armstrong's walk on the moon and President Richard Nixon's resignation had ever warranted a 96-point headline (Auletta, 2002).

When we remember that date, we remember raw emotions—anger, fear, depression, sympathy for the victims and their families, and hate, especially hate. Immediately after the attack, we didn't know who to hate, but we were sure to find a suitable target.

Our cowboy president, George W. Bush, tentative in the first days of his presidency, began to act like a president. Even those of us who didn't vote for him rallied behind him and his tough talk. He was going to hunt them down and make them pay. Even though he didn't initially know who *them* was—in our panic, we believed in him.

On September 14, investigations pointed to the Middle East after five Arab men were identified among the suicide teams. Also on September 14, the U.S. Catholic Bishops and Muslim Leaders issued a joint statement that said, "We believe that the one God calls us to be peoples of peace. Nothing in our Holy Scriptures, nothing in our understanding of God's revelation, nothing that is Christian or Islamic justifies terrorist acts and disruption of millions of lives which we have witnessed this week." The statement implored Americans to refrain from "sinking to the mentality and immorality of the perpetrators of Tuesday's [September 11, 2001] crimes" (U.S. Catholic Bishops & Muslim Leaders, 2001). By September 21, President Bush put other world leaders on notice that they were either with him or with the terrorists. By September 23, the United States had placed a $50 million price on Osama bin Laden, who, at that time, was being shielded by Taliban leader Mullah Mohammed Omar in Afghanistan. On October 8, the United States began war with the Taliban by launching air strikes against terrorist training camps in Afghanistan ("Timeline: Countdown to US Air Strikes," 2001).

It was then we knew whom to hate.

What enemy state had committed this cowardly act? None. Who was the enemy? They were radical fundamentalists who profess the Islamic religion but who are geographically dispersed throughout the world. The war against terrorism will require different strategies and tactics, and it will go on for a long time, perhaps for centuries.

HARASSMENT AND VIOLENCE AND PROFILING

As a nation, before 9/11 we had begun critically examining racial profiling, recognizing that DWB (driving while black) should not be a traffic offense. New Jersey state police policies were being rewritten. After 9/11, African Americans could take a little breather. A new class of usual suspects had emerged—Arabs. Anyone who fit the misguided perception of what an Arab was supposed to look like was suspect. Sikhs, Indians [Eastern], Greeks, or anyone who had darker skin was a potential target.

Within six days after September 11, there already had been hundreds of acts of violence and harassment directed against Muslims and others perceived as being Muslim.[2] An Indian was shot to death at his gas station in Arizona. Arsalan Tariz Iftikhar, Midwest communications director of the Council of American Islamic Relations, wrote:

In the two weeks after the tragic events, Muslim store owners have been murdered, women wearing scarves have been assaulted by bat-wielding gangs, and a mosque has had a Ford Mustang driven through it. On certain

Northwest and Delta flights, pilots have refused to fly with passengers they
thought looked like Arabs or Muslims. (Iftikhar, 2001)

Ziad Asali, president of the American Arab Anti-Discrimination Committee
(ADC), said, "These incidents range from simple assault and battery to arson,
aggravated assault, and at least six murders. These acts have been random,
spontaneous, and without geographical concentration. These hate crimes
were concentrated mostly in the seven weeks following September 11."

President Bush visited a mosque two miles from the White House to
pointedly condemn violence and harassment against American Muslims.
He hoped to forestall negative world opinion that our military response
would be directed against the Muslim religion ("Another Kind of War,"
2001).

"The [Arab American] community also continues to face a serious problem with racial profiling and a new form of security-related discrimination, the illegal denial of services on airplanes after boarding," ADC
President Asali said. "ADC has confirmed over 70 cases involving more
than 250 people in which persons perceived to be Arabs have been
expelled from aircraft after or during boarding on the grounds that passengers or crew do not like the way they look. Someone was told to disembark
because his name was Mohammed" ("Crossroads: Race, Rights and
National Security," 2002).

Racial profiling is back in full force—and the target profile is young,
Arab American men.

ENEMY BY ASSOCIATION

Historically, our behavior toward Americans whose former homelands
became enemies has not been kind. Japanese Americans were summarily
rounded up and imprisoned during World War II. Mari Matsuda, a Japanese American professor of law at Georgetown University Law Center,
thinks conservative members of the Japanese American community are
supporting the Arab American community because they have a greater
understanding than others of the effects of such racial profiling. It is really
guilt by association, says Matsuda,

> ... that because of this threat, this grave danger to our country, we don't
> have time to discern the dangerous from the not dangerous, the loyal from
> the disloyal, the terrorist from the immigrant who is just here to earn a liv-
> ing. So we are going to have to make sweeps and we are going to have to

use race and religion to determine who we sweep, who we search, who we detain, who we question, what organizations we are going to shut down. ("Crossroads: Race, Rights and National Security," 2002)

TRAITOR

Not all Muslim response from within the country was patriotic. Mohammed Junaid, 26, bought a one-way ticket to Pakistan to join the Taliban. His mother had actually been rescued at the World Trade Center. Damon Johnston, reporting for *The Daily Telegraph* (Sydney), quoted Junaid,

> I'm willing to kill the Americans. I will kill every American that I see in Afghanistan. And I'll kill every American soldier that I see in Pakistan. My mother was in the north tower of the World Trade Center, but I still feel absolutely no remorse about what happened on September 11. I saw the towers collapse but felt nothing for the Americans inside. I may hold an American passport but I am not an American—I am a Muslim. (Johnston, 2001)

Junaid left a $140,000-a-year job as a computer programmer to kill his American brothers.

FREEDOMS ARE ABRIDGED

Now, under President Bush's war on terrorism tactics, American citizenship is not a guarantee of a speedy trial or access to an attorney.

Two Americans are being held in military brigs without access to lawyers while two foreigners accused of terrorist activities are being tried in federal court with the protections usually accorded citizens (Seelye, 2002). Louisiana-born Yasser Hamdi was captured in Afghanistan and was sent to the detention camp in Guantánamo Bay in Cuba. He was moved to the mainland after the government discovered he was a citizen, but the government now argues his citizenship does not matter and keeps him from speaking with his attorney. The argument is that Hamdi is being detained for protection of the country, not for prosecution. Jose Padilla, born in Brooklyn, is being kept in a military brig based on the implication that he was involved in a plot to detonate a radioactive dirty bomb in Washington, D.C. He has not been charged and does not have access to an attorney. John Walker Lindh, the so-called American Taliban, does have access to an attorney and will go on trial for providing support to terrorists. He was captured in Afghanistan. Foreigners Zacarias Moussaoui, accused of being the twentieth hijacker in the 9/11 attacks, and Richard Reid, who attempted to detonate a shoe bomb on an airplane, have both had access to lawyers.

Matsuda, of Georgetown University, is particularly troubled by the administration's willingness to abandon legal protections in the new environment of terrorism on American soil. Matsuda said:

> And what we stand for, at rock bottom, is a government constrained by law. And you don't take people and lock them up with no eyes on it. The press is not there; the judges are not there; we don't know these people's names; they haven't been charged with anything. We don't know how long they are going to be locked up for. And our government is not telling us anything about the reasons why they are being detained. Because they are telling us the reasons have to remain classified. Now tell me, anyone, where is the check, where is the balance? ("Crossroads: Race, Rights and National Security," 2002)

New York Times reporter Katharine Seelye quoted a top Bush administration official as saying, "We're not in the criminal justice business, we're in the national defense business. First things first" (Seelye, 2002).

MEDIA BIAS

There is no doubt that the media have fed the bias against Arabs and Arab Americans and other people of Middle Eastern origin. Immediately after the 1995 bombing of the Alfred P. Murrah Federal Building in Oklahoma City, the media speculated that we should look to the Middle East for the person or persons responsible. The perpetrator turned out to be Timothy McVeigh—a white man, a veteran, and a zealot.

There was a regional conference of the Islamic Society of North America in Tulsa, Oklahoma that weekend. Dr. Sayyid Sayeed, secretary general of the Islamic Society of America of Plainfield, Indiana, was very disappointed by early reporting on the bombing. Sayeed said:

> I turned on the television. The news of that great tragedy was being reported, and right from the beginning the media was directly jumping to the conclusion saying this was the job of Islamic fundamentalists. And to my disappointment, within a few minutes they got the local congressman from Oklahoma, and he said, with full confidence, he said it is the job of Islamic terrorists, and we have many of them in Oklahoma, and they have a headquarters of their organization in Plainfield, Indiana. And they had come

here this weekend to provide a cover to this tragedy. You can imagine that once this was said and once the media was abetting this kind of understanding—hell was let loose—to all the country. In Oklahoma itself, a frenzied mob attacked a Muslim house; they broke the door open and went in and there was one woman there who ran to her bathroom, locked herself in. They broke the bathroom door as well. By this time she had had a miscarriage. (Personal communication, May 6, 2002)

Mona Charen, in her October 28 column, wrote that we must expel Arabs on student and travel visas. "[T]here is no constitutional right to visit the United States," Charen wrote. "There is no constitutional right for foreign students to study here.... As for those missing hazardous materials drivers, the only answer is ethnic profiling. Every Middle Eastern–looking truck driver should be pulled over and questioned wherever he may be" (Charen, 2001). Leonard Pitts, Jr., another columnist, commented on Charen's propositions, "It's an idea so absurd in its xenophobia you can hardly take it seriously. Then you realize it's so absurd you can't afford not to" (Pitts, 2001). Pitts argued that you couldn't save freedom by killing it.

MUSLIM VICTIMS

Muslims were also victims of 9/11.[3] Some were workers in the World Trade Center.

Meher Tariq was married to Tariq Amanullah, an assistant vice president at Fiduciary Trust located on the 90th floor of the south tower. They had been living in the United States for 13 years. Meher Tariq, quoted in the *Sunday Times* (London), said:

Tariq was not an extremist person, but he tried to follow Islam in every aspect of his life. I haven't been watching the news. I can't take it. I'm very uneasy about the war on both sides. I wasn't afraid of being a Muslim in America, but I'm afraid now. It's hard enough wondering how to take care of my children by myself, but now people are turning against Muslims. ("The Muslim Wife," 2001)

The 2000 U.S. Census shows that New York state is second only to California in numbers of people of Arab descent (0.6 percent). Many of New York City's 300 private Islamic schools closed for fear of misplaced reprisals. Arab American and Muslim children are fearful and have trouble understanding why their people committed these acts (Burgard, 2001).

In a November 12 article in the *Daily News* (New York), Mike Claffey reported that leaders of New York's Pakistani community had complained to federal officials that the war on terrorism "has made it open season on Muslim immigrants from their homeland" (Claffey, 2001). Nearly 100 Pakistani Americans complained to FBI and Immigration and Naturalization Service representatives. They said about 50 people had been detained, some without bail and unable to contact relatives.

Touri Bolourchi, a retired nurse, was one of the 65 passengers on board United Airlines Flight 175. She was an Iranian-born Muslim who had lived in the United States since 1979. She was returning to her home in Los Angeles when her flight was hijacked to crash into the World Trade Center south tower. Stephanie Chavez, *Los Angeles Times,* quoted Bobby Turan, Bolourchi's 15-year-old grandson, at the funeral, "Grandma, I will never forget the way you knew about everything, the way you could do almost anything. I will never forget your smile; it was as reliable as your Honda. Your kisses will always be like a renewal of energy for me" (Chavez, 2001).

CONCLUSION

The tragedy of September 11, 2001, will live in infamy. Thousands of lives were lost. Post-attack government policies have restricted rights and freedoms that are the foundation of our nation. Many people have fought and died protecting these rights. Ultimately, the consequences to our society of our loss of freedoms may far exceed the consequences of the catastrophic loss of life. Peace-loving Arabs and Muslims have suffered harassment and violence because of stereotyping.

Babies are not born with hate. Hate is an entirely learned emotion. Society's task is to break the chain of hate. Amnesty International's crisis response guide for junior high and high school students is the kind of material that every child should read (Amnesty International, 2001).

Media coverage of the 9/11 tragedy and response was a little more cautious than the coverage following the Oklahoma City bombing in 1995. Instead of immediately assuming bomb equals Muslim fundamentalist, as was done in Oklahoma, press coverage after 9/11 was clearly aiming for better accuracy. However, some Americans, through ignorance or prejudice, are still attacking other Americans.

Already, our freedoms are significantly and measurably restricted. We are subjected to long lines at airports and screening at music performances, sporting events, etc. Such restrictions are a price we pay for the perception of safety.

Just because we are at war does not mean we can jettison human rights. Patriotism does not mean unquestioning support of our president or the government. Citizens in a democratic society should constantly be a check on the government. The United States cannot hold people indefinitely, without specific charges, without access to attorneys or due process. We are fighting for democracy, and we cannot, at the same time, conveniently forget freedoms that we have won. And we cannot selectively apply human rights to only certain categories of our citizens. Ultimately, people should be judged by their actions, not by the color of their skin, not by their religious beliefs, and not by how they dress.

In a free society, good speech should be used to drive out bad speech. While we may be offended by Dennis Nail's opinions (chapter opening quote), we must defend his right, in this country, to have any opinion that he wishes to hold—even when we believe his opinion to be idiotic.

The diverse groups and individuals who create it make our society richer. America, in its diversity, creates an amalgam that is brighter and stronger than its individual elements.

Chapter 10

ARABS AND ARAB AMERICANS: ANCIENT MIDDLE EAST CONFLICTS HIT HOME

Nancy Beth Jackson

Long before *Middle Eastern descent* became a description for ethnic profiling, Arabs and Arab Americans were stereotyped negatively in the West. Although often equated with Muslim, *Arab* is a broad term that goes beyond religion, skin color, nationality, or politics. A Semitic people like the Jews, Arabs originated in the Arabian Desert in biblical times. According to the Old Testament, the Arabs are the descendants of Ishmael, the son of Abraham and Hagar, an Egyptian slave. Abraham banished Hagar and her son to the desert with bread and an animal skin filled with water after his long-barren wife Sarah gave birth to Isaac. The biblical tale of illegitimacy and outcasts helped establish early stereotypes of Arabs. Until the last century, the Bible was the main source of information about Arabs and the Middle East for most Americans.

Arabs have always been robed in mystery, intrigue, and danger in the West and portrayed as the enemy since the Crusades. Modern media magnified and circulated that image more widely in covering decades of oil embargoes and terrorist attacks. Ronald Stockton, a political science professor at the University of Michigan-Dearborn, suggested a decade ago, however, that anyone examining the Arab image needed to go beyond the headlines and into the early history of humans. "The images of Arabs cannot be seen in isolation but are primarily derivative, rooted in a core of hostile archetypes that our culture applies to those with whom it clashes. The roots of these archetypes are in ancient conflict or cultural teachings that go back centuries or even millennia" (McCarus, 1994, p. 120).

Muhammad, the founder of Islam, united desert tribes in the seventh century. Today 22 diverse Arab nations stretch 5,000 miles from the Atlantic coast of North Africa to the Arabian Sea. The League of Arab Nations, founded in 1945, joins them politically, but language and culture provide the common bond. Arabs created algebra, pioneered optics, mapped the world, advanced medicine, preserved Greek knowledge during the Middle Ages, and introduced Europeans to everything from artichokes to the zero, but their contributions have remained only a footnote in the history of Western civilization. Arabs are more often remembered for their incursions into Europe and their battles against Christian knights during the Crusades.

The stereotypes of Arabs as evil aggressors determined to destroy the West did not begin with the attacks on the World Trade Center in 1993 and 2001. The image originated nearly 1,400 years ago as fierce warriors on horseback advanced out of the Arabian Desert and threatened to absorb Europe in the name of Islam. One of the seminal dates in Western history is 732, when Charles Martel vanquished the Saracens at the Battle of Poitiers in southwestern France, but conflict between the cultures continued to shape geography and history in the centuries that followed. Arabs and the West developed in what amounted to parallel universes, jihads and crusades defining their relationship instead of diplomacy. Subjugated by the Turks in the eleventh century, Arabs were part of the Ottoman Empire until its demise after World War I. Whether the region was labeled Arab, Ottoman, or Muslim, it was as *other* as other could be, feared and misunderstood then and now. The designation of *Middle East* did not become popular until the twentieth century.

Arab traders served as intermediaries between Europe and the Orient, but over the centuries the Middle East remained a veiled land associated with mystery, intrigue, and danger. *Ali Baba and the Forty Thieves, Scheherazade,* exotic spices, water pipes, belly dancers, and desert sheiks in flowing robes inspired Western composers, writers, and artists, but romanticized images did not increase understanding.

CONTEMPORARY STEREOTYPES

"To a large extent the Arabs are misjudged in the West—and caricatured in a manner once reserved for blacks and Hispanics—for the simple reason that they *are* different. Their language, dress, prayers, behavior, and thoughts don't fit into any neat pattern easily grasped by Westerners," the journalist David Lamb wrote in 1987. "Being Arab is a liability everywhere but in the Arab homelands, for virtually everywhere else the Arab is stereotyped in negative terms."

Arabs existed in a faraway land even into the twentieth century when oil embargoes, the Israeli/Palestinian conflict, and international terrorism created new and far less romantic, stereotypes of Arabs as enemies of the West, images that appeared regularly in the morning headlines and the nightly news. Arabs were reduced to crude caricatures: hawk-nosed camel jockeys, playboy sheiks, and movie villains. Arab women were either exotic belly dancers or faceless creatures enveloped in veils and robes.

"It is only a slight overstatement to say that Muslims and Arabs are essentially covered, discussed, apprehended, either as oil suppliers or as potential terrorists. Very little of the detail, the human density, the passion of Arab Muslim life has entered the awareness of even those people whose profession it is to report the Islamic world," Edward W. Said, the Palestinian-born Columbia University scholar, charged in 1981 when he addressed media stereotypes (Said, 1981, p. 16).

In the oil crisis of the 1970s, the media found its inspiration for photo ops and editorial cartoons in traditional male clothing such as the long shirtdresses worn instead of trousers and the distinctive and practical headdresses, which protect against heat and sandstorms in the Arabian Peninsula and Palestine. By the 1990s, Muslim Arab women fully veiled or in headscarves became the threatening image in the Western media after Islam was designated to fill the enemy void created by the collapse of the Soviet Union and the end of the cold war. But until that February Friday in 1993, such exotic images remained a foreign menace.

With the bombing of the World Trade Center, Middle East terrorism became a local story in the United States. The villains were not members of an elite hit squad out of a Le Carré novel, but Arab immigrants who drove taxis, wore baseball caps backward, and plotted in American cities.

On July 5, 1993, *Time* magazine pictured Arab immigrants as "The Terror Within," identifying them as "a deadly new threat to America's public safety" (Church, 1993, p. 22). An 11-page spread in the October 4, 1993 issue described "a new breed of militant zealot" and provided details of "how an immigrant cabdriver from Egypt became an alleged ringleader of the gang that planted the powerful bomb at the World Trade Center." The red-haired Egyptian, shown playing with his small children in the park, was "the epitome of the modern terrorist, a self-made commando pursuing a homemade agenda to disrupt Western civilization." Leaving few tracks as he moved his family around predominately Arab neighborhoods in New York City and New Jersey, he was labeled the "Teflon terrorist" (Behar, 1993, pp. 55–56). More disquieting was evidence that he had not acted alone. In an eerie foreshadowing of the photos of the 19 Arab hijackers in the 9/11 attack, almost a full page was given over to headshots of the bearded immigrants who were among the 22 alleged conspirators.

The images on television and in the press played up the Arab involvement in the intrigue as a blind Egyptian religious leader, taxi drivers, hospital technicians, a chemical engineer, and grocery store clerks were linked to the attack and plans to blow up tunnels and other New York landmarks. Two years later when another bomb in a rental van destroyed the Oklahoma City's Alfred P. Murrah Federal Building, media too quickly reported that the FBI had issued an alert for several males described as "Middle Eastern with dark hair and beards." Anglo American males were arrested for the crime, but the initial report encouraged an anti-Arab backlash. More anti-Arab sentiment was fueled when a suspected millennium terrorist attack on the Los Angeles Airport was foiled when an Algerian was arrested in December 1999 trying to enter the United States from Canada with explosives in his car trunk. Bombings of U.S. embassies in Africa and the attack on the USS *Cole* in Yemen cemented the image of the Arab as terrorist in many American minds.

Newscasters on September 11, 2001 announced almost immediately that the world had changed forever with the terrorists' attacks on U.S. soil, but no one's world changed more radically than that of Arab Americans. President Bush was quick to condemn hate crime reprisals and call for greater understanding, but profiling increased even as concern grew about infringements on civil liberties. Over a thousand Arabs and Arab Americans were detained without being charged with a crime; the Justice Department sought interviews with 5,000 Middle Eastern men on temporary visas. Being or appearing to be Arab led to extensive questioning and searches at airports. Some passengers were told they could not fly simply because the pilots did not feel comfortable with the way they looked. In October 2001, Republican Congressman Darrell Issa, a Lebanese American from San Diego, was turned away at Dulles International Airport when he checked in for a flight to Saudi Arabia, traveling as a representative of President Bush. An Arab American Secret Service agent, assigned to protect the president, was barred from a flight to Dallas on Christmas Day that year. A CNN/*USA Today*/Gallup poll found that more than half of those interviewed supported more intensive security checks for travelers of Arab heritage in the interest of safety, and almost half favored special identity cards for Arabs, including American citizens.[1]

U.S. IMMIGRATION

In the United States, few peoples have been portrayed in such negative light as the Arabs, forever associated with conflict in the Middle East, ancient and contemporary. Once the most invisible of minorities, Arabs were late in coming to America, arriving in separate and vastly different waves, mere ripples in U.S. immigration history. Arab Americans in the United States are estimated to number about 3 million, but no one knows for sure because the U.S. Census Bureau classifies Arab Americans as white rather than a separate group. Over the years they have been labeled as turk, turko, African, Asian, and European. The ethnic identification as Arabs did not gain popular usage until the 1930s and then was associated more with politics than demography.

The first immigrants, mostly Orthodox and Eastern Rite Christians from what is now Lebanon and Syria, entered the United States between the 1870s and 1920, seeking jobs and eager to assimilate after fleeing the Ottoman Empire. Few Muslims came during this period because they feared they would lose their religion in America. Like Catholic immigrants at the time, the Christian Arab immigrants encountered discrimination and prejudice because of their religious practices, but they soon blended into the mainstream. Arab Americans remain predominately Christian, with less than a quarter adhering to Islam.

After World War I, when isolationism and xenophobia grew in the United States, Congress narrowed the gate by barring illiterate immigrants. The Origins Quota Act of 1921 clearly reflected a growing fear—contrary to the experience of the early Arab immigrants—that non–Northern Europeans would be more difficult to assimilate. Quotas favored immigrants from northern Europe, with few Arabs arriving until after World War II.

Arab immigration resumed after 1952 when immigration quotas expanded to welcome political refugees and newcomers with desirable job skills and continued to grow following immigration reform in 1965. But the world and the Arab immigrant had changed dramatically. The first wave had been mostly poorly educated and from agrarian backgrounds. Many, like Jewish immigrants of the period, began their life in America as peddlers but over time became leaders in the business community. Part of the postwar brain drain, the new immigrants entered as students and scholars with well-developed consciousness of Arab nationalism, particularly if they were dispossessed Palestinians. Unlike the first immigrants, they identified with nations rather than villages and voiced their opinions about U.S. policies in the Arab/Israeli conflict. Muslim rather than Christian, these immigrants became the fastest growing Arab population in the nation, had less interest in assimilation, and became more visible as a minority.

At first, the two waves had little in common. Second- and third-generation Arab immigrants had quietly become leaders not only in business but also in sports, medicine, education, and politics, as apple-pie American as anyone else, without surrendering their recipes, family ties, and religion. But by the 1970s, the assimilated Arab Americans began to realize that the choice of identity might not be theirs to make.

GROWING SELF-IDENTIFICATION

"Whether they like it or not, the Syrian-Lebanese in this country were forced by circumstances to identify themselves as Arabs since that had become the designation applied by the American mass media to all Middle-Easterners from Arabic-speaking countries," Philip M. Kayal, Ph.D., a sociologist specializing in Arab Americans, noted in 1983 (Abraham & Abraham, 1983, p. 56).

They learned painfully that excellence and celebrity might not protect them against ethnic slurs and began to take pride in a common heritage, uniting against what they often perceived as a pro-Israeli media bias in the United States. Speeding their Arabization was a comment by a Federal Trade Commissioner, speaking to The Grocery Association of America in 1977. He called Ralph Nader, a Lebanese American who was then the nation's leading consumer advocate, "a dirty Arab." The National Association of Arab Americans, founded in 1973, complained, winning an apology from President Carter. The once apolitical immigrants began coming out, identifying as Arabs, and protesting stereotypes.

The number of Arab Americans grew toward the end of the twentieth century through immigration and birthrate. In Michigan, often considered to have the largest concentration of Arab Americans in the country, the population approached 100,000, increasing almost 50 percent in the 1990s. Whereas Arab Americans from Lebanon and Syria continued to dominate the demographics, Egyptians, Algerians, Iraqis, Yemenis, and Moroccans were added to the mix but not to the melting pot.

Greater ethnic awareness and more Arab immigrants did little to lessen negative stereotypes in the United States, which built upon images inherited from Western Europe.

LONG-LIVED MEDIA IMAGES

Mark Twain recast many of the centuries-old stereotypes into American molds when he set off as a journalist on a paddle-steamer cruise of the Mediterranean in 1867. His newspaper dispatches, rare reportage from that part of the world in the nineteenth century, received even broader circulation when published two years later as *The Innocents Abroad,* an immensely popular book that established Twain as a major American writer. Twain introduced his readers to an Arab world of filth, confusion, and violence. He compared one guide to a land-dwelling pirate: "A tall Arab, as swarthy as an Indian...sunbeams glinted from a formidable battery of old brass-mounted horse-pistols and the gilded hilts of bloodthirsty knives" (Twain, 1869, p. 277). Traveling in what was then Palestine was full of dangers, Twain reported. "From Galilee to the birthplace of the Savior, the country is infested with fierce Bedouins whose sole happiness, in this life, is to cut and stab and mangle and murder unoffending Christians" (Twain, p. 278). He found the Arabs "the ugliest, wickedest-looking villains we have seen," a veiled woman with only her eyes exposed looked "like a mummy," and the narrow streets "swarmed like a hive with men and women in strange Oriental costumes" (Twain, p. 255).

Twain complained that the Sea of Galilee and the Dead Sea were not at all as grand as he had imagined. "Neither of them twenty miles long or thirteen wide. And yet when I was in Sunday school I thought they were sixty thousand miles in diameter" (Twain, p. 317). Like most Americans, what Twain knew about the Middle East came through maps in the back of Bibles and home tours by missionaries. Hollywood would later distort reality even more.

As early as 1897, when Thomas Edison made a short film featuring seductive Arab female dancers, movies tapped the visual differences between the cultures to entice and entertain audiences without worrying excessively about accuracy. In the late twentieth century, barbarism, cruelty, and violence were the most common traits associated with Arabs in movies and television. Jack G. Shaheen, who has written widely about the screen image of Arabs, including *TV Arab* (1984) and *Reel Bad Arabs: How Hollywood Vilifies a People* (2001), pointed out that Arabs usually have been cast as villains. If negative stereotypes surfaced only in B-movie action thrillers, the damage would be bad enough, but Arabs also represent evil in films reaching broad audiences and receiving critical acclaim. Consider *Lawrence of Arabia* (1962), with its scenes of cruelty and torture and senseless death over a water hole, and *Robin Hood, Prince of Thieves* (1991), which opens with Crusaders being tortured in a dungeon under a mosque in Jerusalem.

Arab Americans, however, have become more vocal in protesting such negative screen images. In 1993, the American Arab Anti-Discrimination Committee (ADC), which began addressing Arab American issues in 1980, accused Walt Disney's studio of Arab bashing in its Academy Award–

winning *Aladdin.* A less than honest peddler, with a big turban and even bigger nose, opened the movie by singing, "I come from a land, from a far away place. Flat and intense and the heat is immense. It's barbaric but hey, it's home." The ADC successfully protested the portrayal, forcing the movie studio to change the offensive lyric in the video version and to promise to be more sensitive the next time. The ADC returned to Disney to protest anti-Arab stereotypes in *Father of the Bride, Part II* in 1996 and in *G. I. Jane* in 1997. In 1998, Disney's *Operation Condor* received the ADC's "Dishonor Award."

Disney hasn't been the only studio to cast Arabs as the bad guys. Arab terrorists have been challenging Hollywood heroes for the last 30 years. The industry seems to have little room for an Arab hero or lover even when actors have leading-man good looks. Egyptian-born Omar Sharif was nominated for an Academy Award for his portrayal of Ali, the handsome but cruel tribesman in *Lawrence of Arabia,* but his romantic roles in Hollywood were as *Dr. Zhivago* and the Jewish gambler loved by Fanny Brice in *Funny Girl.*

Over the last decade, U.S. military and assorted superheroes have routinely blown away Arab villains on the screen. In *True Lies* (1994), Arnold Schwarzenegger fought high-tech terrorists wearing Arab scarves and yelling commands in Arabic. In *The Mummy* (1999), an Arab character is called "our smelly little friend." In *Rules of Engagement* (2000), American soldiers faced a bloodthirsty crowd of Yemenis in scenes the ADC said, "set a new low for anti-Arab racism and defamation."[2] Closer to home in 1998, *The Siege* revolved around sadly prescient bombings of buses, a Broadway theater, and FBI headquarters in New York City, and the subsequent rounding up of Arab Americans, detained without due process. "This is the land of opportunity," the character played by Bruce Willis tells Arab Americans. "The opportunity to turn yourself in." In his review, Roger Ebert, film critic for the *Chicago Sun Times,* wrote, "Given how vulnerable our lives are to terrorism and how vulnerable Arab Americans are to defamation, was this movie really necessary?" (Ebert, 1998). Following 9/11, moviemakers asked themselves that question, delaying release of some films already completed and indefinitely postponing others, including a sequel to *True Lies.*

What image will Arabs and Arab Americans have in the post-9/11 world? Many journalists immediately sought to present fair and balanced reporting rather than falling back on stereotypes. The Poynter Institute, a training and research center for professional journalists, academicians, and students, began posting reporting and writing guidelines on its Web site the day of the attacks. Three days later, Victor Merina, a Poynter fellow, provided a roundup of how the media had covered Arab Americans, "America's Most Vulnerable," and reported that some media watchdog groups believed balanced news stories had helped avoid serious backlash (Merina, 2001). Drawing upon experience gained in covering its own Arab community, *The Detroit Free Press* issued a guide for journalists that explained the history and culture of Arab Americans and also debunked negative stereotypes. The Society of Professional Journalists passed a resolution urging journalists to take steps against racial profiling in coverage of the war on terrorism and to redouble their commitment to use language and visual messages that inform rather than inflame. The South Asian Journalists Association offered tips on how to cover the conflict and posted examples of fair and balanced reporting on its Web site.[3]

The Internet, in its infancy at the time of the first World Trade Center attack, has become a rich source of information about Arabs, Arab Americans, and the Middle East, not only on media sites but also on sites maintained by Arab and Arab American organizations. One site based in Falls Church, Virginia, announced in 2002: "It is our belief that stereotypes of the Arabic culture continue because of the general public's lack of education about the rich history and modern customs of the Arab peoples."[4]

A more balanced representation of Arab Americans also will help improve the image of Americans and American foreign policy, suggested the Independent Task Force on Public Diplomacy, sponsored by the Council of Foreign Relations in a study related to the war on terrorism. Credible and independent messengers would include Arab and Muslim Americans such as firefighters and police officers who rushed to help at the World Trade Center, well-known sports figures and celebrities of Arab descent, and successful Arab Americans in all sectors of American life (Peterson, 2002, p. 86).

Such concerted efforts will help correct ancient stereotypes and counter the negative images of Arabs that have multiplied since the war on terrorism began. Fear and concern for national security have turned stereotypes of Arabs into a quick way of making judgments that goes beyond marginalization of a minority. Translating stereotypes into public policy abrogates the civil liberties of *the other* and threatens the foundation of a free society. Responsible media portrayals can help address this threat.

Part III

ETHNIC STEREOTYPES

Chapter 11

MEDIA STEREOTYPES OF AFRICAN AMERICANS

Linus Abraham

As Carolyn Martindale noted, "Negative stereotypes of African Americans have been deeply ingrained in Anglo American culture ever since Africans were first brought to this country in chains" (Martindale, 1996, p. 21). The stereotypes predate the mass media, arising in folklore from the slavery period and transferred to and amplified in the modern mass media. At various time points the stereotypes have served various ideological functions. In colonial times, the stereotypes provided a rationale for enslavement of blacks. After slavery, stereotypes served to justify segregation. They have reemerged in contemporary mass media, now functioning to justify differential distribution of resources in a free labor market economy (Dates & Barlow, 1990, p. 15).

Film historian Donald Boggle identifies five dominant mythical character types that have been used to stereotype blacks over time—Toms, Coons, Mulattoes, Mammies, and Bucks (Boggle, 1991). These vilifying images were given full exposure and crystallized in D. W. Griffiths' classic, but racially controversial, film, *The Birth of a Nation.* The character types are subsumed under two mythical character portraits, the sambo and the savage: "sambo—meaning lazy, indolent, carefree, optimistic, and intellectually limited, and the savage—a synonym for sexual prowess, dangerousness, and impulsiveness" (Boskin, 1980, p. 142). The character traits and the stereotypes associated with them are noteworthy for their longevity and tenacity. According to Boggle, the basic types have been repackaged under various guises that deceive people about their origins. In reality, audiences are fed with a steady diet of these same vilifying stereo-types. In the worldview of the dominant Anglo culture, these mythical character types have come to embody all aspects of the black experience.

RESILIENCE OF STEREOTYPES

Taking a look at mainstream media fictional representations, it appears blacks have made considerable progress, moving from token representa-tions to achieve great visibility, some might even say over-representation on the screen (Entman & Rojecki, 2000). Some experts have noted that fic-tional film and TV portrayals have become considerably more positive, and the perception of the mass media as a source of negative images of African Americans "may be more of a historical reality than a current fact" (Messaris, 1997, p. 120). Television dramas, especially from the 1980s, showed African American characters assimilated into the middle class, where they embody the norms identified with bourgeois white America (Dates & Barlow, 1990; Jhally & Lewis, 1992; MacDonald, 1992). The very successful and critically acclaimed *The Cosby Show* was often cited as the epitome of this general shift in television to incorporate positive and cozy images of blacks.

On the surface, film and television may have come a long way in elimi-nating the most blatant stereotypical portrayals. But a deeper examination of representations of African Americans shows that negative images still abound (Entman & Rojecki, 2000). Reviewing the literature on represen-tations of blacks in film, Entman and Rojecki (2000) note the literature is largely critical: "Images of black males and females receive criticism not merely for calling upon stereotypes of irresponsible and irrepressible black sexuality and criminality but for presenting one-dimensional char-acters who lack the rounded complexity of real people" (p. 182).

Arguably, films with narratives centered on blacks, and made by black directors, have in the 1990s experienced the kind of boom that character-ized the blaxploitation boom in Hollywood from 1969 to 1974 (Guerrero, 1993). Unfortunately, most of these films are trapped within the demands of the Hollywood commercial cinema system, which plays to the common denominator, and thus continues "to stock its productions with themes and formulas dealing with black issues and characters that are reassuring to the sensibilities and expectations of an uneasy white audience" (p. 162).

The narrative vehicle that has come to enjoy the most commercial success and seems to dominate the new wave of black studio productions is the " 'ghettocentric,' action-crime-adventure vehicle"(Guerrero, 1993, p. 182)—

starting with the release of films like *New Jack City* (1991), *Juice* (1992), *Boyz N the Hood* (1991), and many others that have followed, such as *Menace II Society, Friday, Baby Boom, Three Strikes, The Wash,* and so on. These films weave narrative tales of adventure in the ghetto, filled with depictions of stunted, wasted lives, black sexual adventurousness, and gratuitous spectacles of gang violence, drugs, and crime. The films co-opt black narratives and social problems and exploit the same ghetto locales and gang cultures to create a crude view of black culture filled with stereotypes of black violence and sexuality. The attractiveness of these films, especially to the targeted youth audience, is often based on the violent depictions of gang culture that serves as the visual, dramatic center of the films. Thus, even in situations where the director's ideological leaning is toward antiviolence, as in *Boyz N the Hood,* which "draws its dramatic visual force from the film's insider depiction of gang culture," the visual violence critical to the film's appeal contradicts and defeats the director's antiviolence message (Guerrero, 1993, p. 185).

The scenario discussed above is not limited to film. Spike Lee, whose film *Bamboozled* reminds us of the degree to which the dehumanization and commodification of Africans that occurred during slavery lingers on in American entertainment, notes that "television is just as bad as cinema.... They've both been guilty" in perpetuating negative images of African Americans. He argues, and rightly so, that "from their birth these two great mediums, film and television, have promoted negative racial images" (Crowdus & Georgakas, 2002, p. 4). Some of the shows on television, especially shows on WB and UPN, are "borderline minstrel shows" that rehash negative stereotypes (p. 6) with blacks "still acting as buffoons and coons" (p. 9).

A look at nonfictional representation of African Americans reveals a picture close to that of fictional representations, but perhaps more disturbing. A number of media scholars have observed that network and local newscasts increasingly focus on lawlessness among African Americans (Dates & Barlow, 1990; Gray, 1989; Jhally & Lewis, 1992; MacDonald, 1992). Blacks are stereotypically portrayed as homeless, underclass, and poor, as drug lords and crack victims (Drummond, 1990; Martindale, 1996). A close relationship exists between the fictional portrayals and the negative images of African Americans arising from television news and infotainment stories on crime (Entman & Rojecki, 2000, p. 183). Jacquie Jones argues:

> The stories that predestined 1991's summer ghetto blockbusters, *New Jack City* and *Boyz N the Hood,* ... first came to the American public in the form of television news. From the advent of drive-by shootings in L.A. and

leather-jackets-for-lives in Detroit, gangs, drugs, and the accompanying violence became an expected fixture from six to seven, and then again at eleven, in American homes. The news became the factory for black mass media imagery in cautious, conservative times. (Jones, 1998, p. 96)

Thus, it appears "distinctions no longer exist between movies, news, television" in their depictions of African Americans (Jones, 1998, p. 97). They all supply a steady diet of negative images that tap into long-standing stereotypic character traits of the sambo and the savage. The predominantly negative representations of blacks in entertainment and news media serve to perpetuate the historical vilification and stigmatization of African Americans.

CONTEMPORARY RACISM AND STEREOTYPING THROUGH IMPLICIT VISUAL MESSAGES

It is not surprising then that numerous studies contend that the mainstream media still manifest bias and prejudice in representations of African Americans (Campbell, 1995; Gist, 1990; Martindale, 1996; Pease, 1989; van Dijk, 1987). What is increasingly worrisome is the fact that racial stereotyping manifests itself in less apparent and subtle forms that are more difficult to detect and therefore to confront. As Entman and Rojecki (2000) note, "The public face of race is now cloaked in chameleon-like form, an ever-changing camouflage that obscures its force" (p. 1).

Contemporary egalitarian trends have made blatant racism passé. Racial prejudice manifests itself in more veiled and indirect ways (Meertens & Pettigrew, 1997), and racial bias in the media appears to be subtler (Campbell, 1995; Entman, 1994b). Van Dijk (1988) argues that contemporary forms of racism are often "expressed by the unsaid"; they are subtly and indirectly implied (p. 18). Thus, a good deal of racial stereotyping now takes place through visual messages, without any explicit or overt reference to race (Abraham, 1998; Mendleberg, 1996; Messaris & Abraham, 2001). For example, Bird (1996), studying a sensational AIDS story that circulated in the Dallas media, comments on how television news coverage of the story did not make an issue of race verbally, but visually tended to reinforce stereotypes of African American sexuality: "Stories repeatedly used the same footage of black people dancing in dimly-lit nightclubs, apparently disregarding the beautiful threat lurking among them" (p. 53).

A number of scholars have noted how news stories make implicit links between blacks and negative thematic concepts such as violent crime, drugs, poverty, prisons, drug-addicted babies, AIDS victims, and welfare by predominantly juxtaposing or illustrating stories with images of African Americans (Entman, 1994a; Entman & Rojecki, 2000; Martindale, 1996). I will give two examples to illustrate how the use of visual messages subtly activates and continuously circulates negative stereotypes of African Americans in the society.

The first example is an opinion piece that appeared in *The Daily Pennsylvanian*—the student newspaper of The University of Pennsylvania (February 28, 1995). The story titled "The Buck Stops Now, Men Must Be Responsible" exhorts all men to take responsibility in helping stop rapes. The written text of the story, which makes no mention of the racial configuration of the men who are guilty of rape and those who should help stop rapes, is illustrated with a drawing of a white man restraining a muscular and menacing black man. The word *rapist* is written across the front of the black man's briefs. The racist propensity of the visual message may or may not have been intended by the writer. Intended or not, one cannot overlook the subtle and indirect racist implications. The resulting racial subtext from the juxtaposition of the visual with the written text creates very powerful racist connotations and activates myths of black sexuality and criminality, though these are not stated explicitly in words; they are rather expressed through the unsaid, that is, through the visuals.

Blackness, as race, in American culture has historically been perceived as synonymous with deviance. In many cases, blackness has become a conventional notation symbolizing abnormality. Its racist symbolic use is so ingrained that, after years of supposed egalitarian trends in the culture, this symbolic notation still appears, albeit subtly, even in arenas where such racist use of language would be most eschewed.

A second example will serve to further illustrate my point. The example comes from an NBC evening news story, broadcast on September 10, 1993. The story is about a program in Cleveland that effectively moves people from welfare to work. The lengthy introductory run-up to the story gives a thematic profile of those on welfare—a profile that explicitly refers to the subjects as "people who have been on welfare all their lives." The visual messages juxtaposed with this introduction are a series of shots of African Americans. The first 14 shots in the story are all images of blacks. None is individualized by name. The preponderance of black images creates a gestalt impression that most people on welfare are black and that the subjects of the story are predominantly black. The text does not state this explicitly; this is a meaning that comes implicitly through visual juxtaposition.

In a similar vein, Entman and Rojecki's (2000) study of the representation of poverty on local and network evening news noted:

> The imagery of television news...suggests poverty is concentrated among blacks, so much so that merely showing a black person on the screen appears to be a code for the involvement of poor people. The concepts of "black person" and "poverty" are so thoroughly intertwined in television news that many whites' perceptions of poverty are difficult to disentangle from their thinking about African Americans. (p. 30)

CONCLUSION

Today, the media may no longer be stating negative stereotypes about blacks explicitly. However, through implicit visual associations of blacks with particular negative contexts, media stories activate mythical character types that have long circulated in the culture. The visual modality, because of its iconic and descriptive nature, provides a rich source of imagery about ethnic groups. Photographic images have a great impact on viewers' perceptions (Lester, 1994). Visuals present physical and behavioral features that affect our perception, often evoking stereotypes (Cowen, 1991). In the presence of a member (or symbolic equivalent—as in media images) of an ethnic group, the stereotypes may be activated automatically, even if unintentionally (Devine, 1989). Visuals therefore can serve very implicit and subtle functions of stereotyping that call little attention to the artifice of construction. And because this practice seldom proclaims itself openly, visual stereotyping can be very insidious and more potent than explicit verbal stereotyping (Browne et al., 1994). The predominant juxtaposition of images of blacks with social problems—welfare, crime, poverty, drugs, violence, etc.—in the news implicitly helps to activate long-existing stereotypes of blacks as sambo and savage. Though verbal references to African Americans may come under tighter scrutiny in news organizations, images may often be taken for granted and go unexamined.

In the largely segregated American society, the images and stereotypes supplied by the media can have profound effects on the dominant Anglo population, which in many cases lacks first-hand knowledge of people of other races. As Carolyn Martindale (1996) contends, "The images send a powerful subliminal message to Anglos that the majority of African Americans are violent, criminal, drug-addicted, and on welfare. And because these images come from the news media, which claim to represent reality and to provide unbiased information about society, Anglos tend to believe the images are true" (pp. 21–22).

Chapter 12

ETHNIC STEREOTYPES: HISPANICS AND MEXICAN AMERICANS

Ramón Chávez

Latino performers burst upon the pop culture scene as the United States entered the new millennium. The popularity of Hispanic entertainers is evidenced by their name recognition: Edward James Olmos, Ricky Martin, Gloria Estefan, Andy Garcia, Shakira, Enrique Iglesias, Christina Aguilera, and numerous others. Thus, it would be inaccurate to state that there has been no progress in U.S. mainstream perceptions of Hispanics through mass media popular culture.

However, media progress, as in all social situations, must be measured over the long term and not simply by current trends or fashion. Many of the more important changes come about as a result of the work of Mexican Americans and other Latinos themselves who have risen through the ranks of media professions into positions of management, production, and decision making. Much, however, remains to be done as these professionals continue their struggle to become a part of the image-making power structure (Perez-Torres, 1988, p. 28).

Media portrayals of Hispanics in general, be they in popular culture such as television or movies or in the mainstream press through newspaper or magazine depictions of the Latino experience in this country, have often been stilted at best and racist at worst. It should then come as no surprise that the term *Hispanic* in itself comes under fire from the Latino community and causes confusion for community at large.

The U.S. Bureau of the Census historically has used *Hispanic* to define a broad range of peoples whose common heritage dates back to their ancestors on the Iberian Peninsula. In the United States, that term has come to encompass three primary groups: Mexican Americans, Cuban Americans, and Puerto Ricans.

A GROWING MINORITY

Figures document the significant rise of the Hispanic population over the past decade. In 1990, the census showed a population of Hispanic origin at 23.5 million, constituting more than 10 percent of the total U.S. population. According to the 2000 census, the U.S. population of Hispanic origin stands at 35.3 million, slightly more than 12 percent of the total population. This past decade marked the first time Hispanics constituted 1 out of every 10 U.S. residents. Because of historical undercounts, however, these population figures are considered quite conservative despite improvements by the U.S. Bureau of the Census to gather information from this group (U.S. Bureau of the Census, 2001).

Mexican Americans make up the largest proportion of this subgroup, conservatively estimated at 20.6 million, or about 7 percent of the overall population and about 58 percent of the Hispanic/Latino population. Younger, more politically active Mexican Americans still prefer to call themselves Chicanos, partially as a result of the 1960s Chicano movement and partially as a show of defiance of U.S. mainstream Anglo culture. The largest concentration of Mexican Americans lives in the Southwest and on the West Coast, where they constitute a numerical majority in some cities. Sizable and significant populations also reside in numerous areas of the Midwest, most notably in the Chicago area.

Cuban Americans, many of who prefer to call themselves Cubans, dominate the South Florida region, primarily Miami, where they constitute a majority of the metropolitan area's Hispanic population. Nationally, their count stands at 1.2 million. Many are exiles from the island of Cuba, whereas a considerable number of second- and third-generation Cubans were born and raised on U.S. soil. However, since the early 1980s the majority of new Hispanic arrivals in South Florida are from Central and South America.

Puerto Ricans primarily reside in the northern states of the East Coast, constituting the majority in many New York City area boroughs and in areas of northern New Jersey. The U.S. Bureau of the Census pegs their number at 3.4 million, or slightly more than 1 percent of the U.S. population (U.S. Bureau of the Census, 2001).

A U.S. territory since 1898, Puerto Rico became a self-governing commonwealth in 1952. Owing to the territorial status of the island of Puerto

Rico, there is a great deal of travel and intermingling of native Puerto Ricans (those residing on the island) and their relatives now residing on the U.S. mainland, all with full U.S. citizenship. This proximity to the island, and the relative closeness of families residing in both the United States and in Puerto Rico, leads to social and political factors that make these Hispanics different from their Cuban counterparts and their Southwestern cousins.

Added to the mix is the latest influx of immigrants from Central America, primarily those from El Salvador and Nicaragua, and South America, the Colombians, Guatemalans, Venezuelans, Chileans, Argentineans, and others. With that influx, the broad term of Hispanic comes to define only the narrowest of commonalities. The picture of Hispanics in the United States is in reality a mosaic, composed of an extremely diverse cultural group.

Not only are the Latino culture and customs diverse, so are the politics. Mexican Americans are traditionalists (read that to mean pro–family values and Catholic) who nevertheless lean toward political liberalism. Mexican Americans have been decidedly pro-Democratic party in elections this past century.

Cubans, slightly more affluent than their Mexican American counterparts and with a decidedly anti-Communist attitude—owing to their economic, social and political experience with a Communist regime in the homeland—are much more conservative and pro-Republican. The existence, for example, of a Ronald Reagan Boulevard in Miami's Little Havana neighborhood is no accident, owing to the staunch support of this community for the former President's battle against "the evil empire."

Puerto Ricans have their politically active Chicano counterparts in the form of the *Boricua*. A lot of political time and effort is still spent on the continuing debate of commonwealth versus statehood status for the island. But many subsequent generations of Puerto Ricans focus more on the inner city politics of their neighborhoods and cities, and their continuing second-class status in the mainstream social and political setting.

This multicultural, multilingual (for example, Brazilians primarily speak Portuguese, not Spanish), multipolitical mix leads many to conclude that the term Hispanic is an unfortunate, unreliable label used by the U.S. government and by mainstream Anglo Europeans to define a group they have never quite understood.

This chapter can only touch upon a small aspect of that misunderstanding by mainstream U.S. culture of the Hispanic/Latino experience in this country. In focusing on the Mexican American stereotype, no disrespect is intended for the other Latino subgroups. But in focusing on the Mexican American experience with media stereotyping, one can unearth the commonalities that lead to the negative stereotyping and overall misunder-standing by the mainstream culture, which has trouble distinguishing the various groups.

MEDIA STEREOTYPES IN A SHIFTING MARKET

Stereotyping by the entertainment industry is the most blatant within the mass media. But the news media are not without fault and will be discussed in the latter portions of this chapter. Still, the primary guilt remains in television and movie portrayals.

Prior to *The Magnificent Seven,* a movie whose plot was actually borrowed from a Japanese tale—*The Seven Samurai*—there were a number of Westerns that carried the Mexican stereotype. The Mexican bandits became the staple bad guys whenever the script called for a change from the usual bad guys in Westerns, the Indians. Rarely was the hero of Hispanic descent, and key roles for Latinos were few and far between. Even when the script called for a Spaniard or a Latino, a Latino actor was not called upon. For example, Tyrone Powers won the lead role to provide a stilted portrayal of the fateful matador in Hollywood's version of *Blood and Sand.*

Even today the trend continues, as if to say that Latino-oriented characters will not sell to a general audience. Hollywood's version of Isabel Allende's popular book, *The House of the Spirits,* was heavily criticized. Although the story focuses on the history of a Chilean family, the main characters in the movie are all non-Hispanics.

The changing demographic profile of the country and the emerging Hispanic market has affected the movie industry greatly. The Motion Picture Association of America's survey data indicate that Hispanics, on average, spend about a third more on movies than does the general population. Although Hispanics now make up 12 percent of the population, they constitute an estimated 13–15 percent of U.S. movie audiences. On average, the Motion Picture Association found that Hispanics go to 9.9 movies a year, compared with 8.1 movies a year for non-Hispanics and 7.6 for African Americans (Ayoso, 2002).

Spanish-language radio is also advancing at unprecedented numbers. In 1993, a milestone was reached when, for the first time, a Spanish-language radio station topped the ratings in the nation's largest radio market, Los Angeles. Radio station KLAX-FM garnered the largest share of the listening audience in the Los Angeles metro service area, or MSA. Of the 44 stations that served the Los Angeles MSA at the time, 9 were broadcast in Spanish (Mendosa, 1993).

Likewise, the Recording Industry Association of America took note of the rise in Hispanic purchases of Latino-related entertainment. It was no accident that the association unveiled the Latin Grammys, which were broadcast in English on CBS in prime time. The association, in a study it commissioned in 1999, found a growing market for Latin recordings. The study revealed that 80 percent of Latino music buyers are under 24 and that 46 percent buy more than 50 CDs a year (Obejas, 2001).

Overall spending habits of Hispanics point to even larger potential. Already established as the fastest growing group in the country, the Hispanic population, at median age 26, is younger than the national average by about 10 years. More than half of all Hispanics are between 18 and 49 years old, the age demographic most desired by advertisers. Additionally, the Hispanic community is experiencing an annual growth rate of 3.5 percent, compared with a rate of about 1 percent for the general population (Obejos, 2001).

With all these changes and the burgeoning Hispanic market, media managers are being careful not to offend their newfound audience. With recognition of the potential of the Hispanic dollar, managers are gaining a new respect for the sensitivities of this audience and attempting to avoid the stereotypes of the past.

NEWS MEDIA PORTRAYALS

The working press, likewise, would do well to learn from these trends. Hispanics remain dissatisfied with news coverage of their community. The low esteem held for newspaper coverage of Hispanics can be attributed in large part to the fact that there simply aren't enough Latino reporters, editors, and media managers on staff to gain the insight necessary for an accurate portrayal of the community. The press maintains sparse and stereotypical treatment of the Latino community. It is an old and continuing problem.

The Hispanic Link news service conducted a national survey in 1990 of leaders of Latino organizations to get their assessment of newspaper coverage. Hispanic Link found that 79 percent of the Latinos surveyed believed newspapers in their communities had not made sufficient efforts to improve coverage of and outreach to Latinos. As quoted in the survey, Elsa Nunez-Wormack, chair of New Jersey's Hispanic Association of Higher Education, said, "There's a lot going on in our communities, but we only see the bad, the stereotypes" (Rodriguez, 1990, pp. 1–2).

In its annual "Network Brownout" report for 2000, the National Association of Hispanic Journalists (NAHJ) examined the nature of newscasts for the three largest networks: ABC, CBS, and NBC. The organization found that out of nearly 12,000 news stories that aired in 1999, only 1.3 percent or 162 stories focused on Latinos or Latino-related issues, the highest total ever. However, of those stories, more than half fell into four categories: the Elian Gonzalez custody battle, crime stories, U.S. Energy Secretary Bill Richardson's oversight in the Los Alamos spy scandal, and health-related issues. Take away the Gonzalez and Richardson stories and NAHJ President Cecilia Alvear concluded that the networks would not have covered any more stories about Latinos than they did in previous years (Torres, 2000).

However, Latinos did appear as interview subjects in 78.4 percent of all stories about them, up from 58 percent in 1997 and 72.8 percent in 1998 (Torres, 2002).

With such low numbers, it is not surprising that America's newspapers and TV networks have not fared well in the eyes of the Latino community in portraying the realities of life, issues, and concerns of Hispanics.

COMMUNITY PERCEPTIONS

In assessing newspaper coverage of their communities on a scale of 1 to 10, with 10 being excellent, respondents gave an average score of 3.4. *The Hispanic Link Weekly Report* said the survey was based on mail questionnaires to 100 opinion makers at local, state, and national levels. Of these, 58 opinion makers in 25 cities responded.

At the beginning of the new millennium, the NAHJ issued reports that focused on two primary areas of media concern: the number of Latino journalists in U.S. newspaper newsrooms and the number of news stories on network television about Latinos. The results were a mixed bag. The annual newsroom survey by the American Society of Newspaper Editors and NAHJ found that Latino journalists working at English-language dailies increased only slightly in 2001. American Society of Newspaper Editors' survey found that Hispanics made up 3.86 percent of all newsroom employees in 2001, an increase from 3.66 percent in 2000. The percentage of Hispanic journalists working in the nation's newsrooms increased only 2.66 percent between 1982 and 2001. This rate is not keeping pace with the nation's overall demographic shift.

NAHJ found other disturbing trends. Among them are the following:

- The number of newspapers that don't employ a single journalist of color increased from 44 percent to 45 percent.

- The number of journalists of color leaving the industry dropped, but the number of new journalists of color hired also declined from 596 to 447.

- While the overall percentage of interns of color increased, the number of interns of color declined from 923 to 870. (Torres, 2002)

A RECENT "DISCOVERY"

But what can one expect when the working press only discovered Latinos some 30 years ago, despite the existence of Hispanics on this continent for more than three centuries?

Renowned Chicano media historian Felix Gutierrez (1978) said the mainstream press discovered the Hispanic community during the turbulent mid-1960s. When news organizations began to wake up to the existence of what the press termed the invisible minority, they often rushed to cover the group with simplistic overviews and facile headlines that revealed more of their own biases than the reality of the people they sought to cover.

"Thus," Gutierrez writes, "*The Atlantic* headlined a 1967 overview article on Chicanos as 'The Minority Nobody Knows,' indicating that if the existence of Chicanos was news to the editors of *The Atlantic,* it must be news to everyone else who mattered" (Gutierrez, 1978).

Gutierrez also cites a *Time* magazine reporter who rode through East Los Angeles in 1967, writing about "tawdry taco joints and rollicking cantinas," the "reek of cheap wine," and "lurid hotrods." Similarly, a 1969 Los Angeles TV documentary was titled "The Siesta Is Over," implying perhaps that the area's two million Chicanos must have suddenly awakened to their own existence.

"Such simplistic approaches glossed over the reality of Chicano life in the United States and played on the preconceptions and stereotypes of those controlling the media and their predominantly Anglo audience," Gutierrez said.

Another observer of the period, journalist Rubén Salazar, became socially and politically active in the 1960s. In a 1969 speech, Salazar said:

The news media is figuratively taking the serape and sombrero wraps off the Mexican American. What it finds under the serape and sombrero, however, seems to puzzle newspapers, radio, and television. The media, having ignored Mexican Americans for so long but now willing to report them, seem impatient about the complexities of the story. It's as if the media, having finally discovered the Mexican American, is not amused that under that serape and sombrero is a complex Chicano—instead of a potential Gringo. (Gutierrez, 1978)

THE 1960s STEREOTYPE OF THE HISPANIC FARMWORKER

News coverage in the 1960s led to one unintended stereotype that left most of mainstream America confused over the plight of the Mexican American. In the press' quest to identify leaders and to rely upon those leaders as quick and easy sources of information, the press painted an inaccurate picture of Hispanic life in the United States. This came with the emergence of Cesar Chávez and his United Farm Workers Union as a symbol of the Chicano civil rights movement.

In Chávez, the press found a likable, articulate and, therefore, quotable folk hero. In his pursuit of decent working conditions and equitable compensation for farm laborers, Chávez expanded the movement to include issues of civil rights. Chávez became more than a union organizer; he became the symbol of the entire movement. In the public mind, Chávez became the Hispanic equivalent of a Martin Luther King, Jr.

Little wonder then that most of America believed that Hispanics were a rural phenomenon. The popular impression was that America's Latinos had arrived via the migrant farmworker stream and that their problems were centered in the rural areas of the nation.

Though many emigrated from rural areas and had ties to the migrant stream, Hispanics in the United States are overwhelmingly an urban population. In excess of 90 percent of them live in cities or suburban towns ("A Melding of Cultures," 1985).

The old, stereotypical images of the Mexican *Bracero* no longer apply. The *Bracero* Program was a short-lived, government-sponsored program of legal importation of laborers from Mexico into the United States to help with a shortage of farm laborers. Recent discussions in Congress have raised the specter of a revival of this controversial program.

To be sure, there are still major problems in the rural areas where migrants still experience the worst of living conditions, the poorest attainment of educational levels, and the health hazards of farmworker life. But the problems of the rural Hispanic are not the same as those of the predominant urban dwellers.

THE NEARLY INVISIBLE REALITY

Two repeating images of the Mexican American emerged out of the 1980s and 1990s and fed into the new century's news accounts. The old image of vast hordes of illegal aliens clamoring at America's gates experienced a revival as a result of the continuing United States–Mexico borderland influx of immigrants and concerns over national security in the wake of the September 11, 2001, attacks. The wetback image of the Latino immigrant as a parasite on society, feeding off food stamps, and living on welfare, enjoyed renewed vigor as politicians sought favor with voters by looking for scapegoats.

The income of all U.S. households remained stagnant in 2000, in figures adjusted for inflation. Income equality also remained essentially unchanged, despite the strongest economy in decades prior to mid-2002. Median income for Hispanic households grew by 5.3 percent. The median household income for Hispanics reached a new all-time high of $33,447 in 2000, up from $31,767 in 1999. However, significant gaps remained between Hispanics and non-Hispanic whites. In 2000, Hispanic households had only 73 percent of the income of whites (Economic Policy Institute, 2001).

About 7 million U.S. Latinos fell below the official government poverty levels in the 2000 census year. Slightly more than two-thirds of the nation's poor in 2000 were Anglo, followed by African Americans at 25 percent. About 23 percent of the poor were Hispanic (U.S. Bureau of the Census, 2001).

Media accounts of the immigration problem tend to be one-sided, giving extensive coverage to the political debate over solutions while inadequately portraying the image of these individuals who come here in pursuit of the American dream. In that sense, these immigrants are no different from any previous immigrants; they've come to pursue a better life for themselves and their families. They take jobs no one else will take, work hard and loyally, pay sales taxes disproportionate to their numbers, and are exploited by a number of people they encounter here. Many avoid the welfare lines, either out of personal pride or for fear that they may become more detectable to the immigration authorities who will deport them.

Yet the press insists on referring to this group by using the double negative, *illegal alien,* to describe the people they claim come here to burden the economic and legal system. Ethnic media groups have made strong recommendations to news organizations that they be more selective in their use of such terms and that they recognize the damage being done by such stereotypes ("Policy statements," 1993). Groups have asked for a change in newspaper and television newsroom policies with respect to the term *illegal alien.* They have asked that alternative terms such as *illegal immigrant* or *undocumented worker* be used where appropriate in news accounts, but news managers have been reluctant to accept the change.

The second image that has emerged is that of the urban criminal—the gang member. In many respects, the gang banger has become the *bandito* of today. Hispanic community members have become the complacent and weak *campesinos* of the past, unable to help themselves in the face of overwhelming odds against their success. The many achievements of Mexican American youth give way to overdramatized accounts of gang members, complete in their attire of baggy pants or shorts, oversized T-shirts, and baseball caps worn sideways. It's the same style worn by the nonethnic kids at the affluent high school across town, but who can explain youthful whims of fashion or the whims of selective news coverage and ethnic-youth portrayals?

To be sure, the severity of violence has increased in the barrios and ghettos of the nation, but so has the severity of violent behavior in all aspects of American life. Gangs are not restricted to ethnic neighborhoods. Drugs are not the sole property of the urban, inner cities; they are a fact of life in Anglo suburbia as well. Drug trafficking is not limited to urban poor neighborhoods. It can also be traced to the posh enclaves occupied by the upper-income professionals who engage in so-called recreational drug use.

Newspaper accounts don't as easily explain the whys and wherefores of these social situations as they highlight the whos and whats of immediate, dramatic incidents. The faces and souls of the immigrant are missing from the front pages. The humanity of the troubled youth is rarely explained in the stories that follow the initial arrest of yet another juvenile criminal. News accounts fail to focus on the community organizations that are fighting the deterioration of their barrios and their families.

News organizations are attempting to overcome inadequate attention to social trends and their subsequent inability to serve the Latino community, but it will take initiative and innovation to overcome past sins (Del Olmo, 1985).

THE FUTURE

The Hispanic population may already have overtaken African Americans as this nation's largest minority. This is a figure that is difficult to confirm because many Hispanics choose to classify themselves as black or mixed race. Nevertheless, by 2025, Hispanics are projected to make up 18.2 percent of the U.S. population (Torres, 2002). With such numbers, it is vital that the media accurately reflect the realities of this population rather than rely on the practices and stereotypes of the past. Without such adjustments, the very survival of some media entities is surely at stake.

Chapter 13

EXOTICS, EROTICS, AND COCONUTS: STEREOTYPES OF PACIFIC ISLANDERS

Tom Brislin

"Watch the hands," the tour guide tells literally millions of visitors a year. "The hula is a gentle dance of the hands—and hips." Maybe that's true at the hotel *luau*. It is, after all, one of the more appealing images that popular media have presented of Pacific Islanders for more than a century: inviting, exotic, and more than a little erotic.

Maybe a few of the tourists will get a taste of more truly traditional hula—active and vibrant, producing a high-intensity sweat and some serious slapping of the soles to the surface of the earth. This is a dance of the feet that unites the dancers with the spirits from the earth. The dancers get their power, their *mana,* from the land.

Land is a significant concern for most Pacific Islanders. Throughout the region there have been recent movements to restore indigenous rights, particularly the return of native lands seized through the nineteenth and twentieth centuries by colonial and occupying nations. But rarely in popular media are we presented an image of a proud people wronged, struggling for a return of their land or in control of their own images.

Barry Barclay, a Maori filmmaker and self-described Media Preservation Activist, has been a driving force behind the First Law of New Zealand. The First Law is an attempt to codify *mana tuturu,* or Maori spiritual guardianship. Barclay (1990) defies the concept that film images are property rights. He argues that thousands of reels shot of Maoris and other Polynesians since Robert Flaherty's *Moana* are not the property of the filmmakers, their estates, or the public domain. Maori culture, Barclay states, insists on spiritual rights over the destiny of those deposited materials and how they may be used in the future. The *kaitaki* (spiritual guardians) and the descendants of those portrayed on film have the only rights to that destiny.

This gap between the Individualist culture of the West that insists on using law to separate and atomize the individual from the group and the Collectivist culture of Pacific societies that values the connectivity of individual, group, and society, is seen in the approach to, and style of, filmmaking as well. Merata Mita (2001), another Maori filmmaker, says the Pacific view of storytelling, whether orally, in text, on tape, or celluloid, goes far beyond entertainment. Stories are an essential part of education outside the classroom, Mita says. They pass on history and genealogy, helping to link families to their history, land, and relatives. They preserve and explain boundaries (land and tribal) and *kapu* (customs). They help to heal and lessen pain. They encourage respect for the Life Force and respect for the gods. They pass on rituals and functional knowledge of the culture—identity and *mana.* Stories don't belong to individuals. They are interwoven in, and inextricable from, the shared culture.

COLORFUL BACKGROUND

Vilsoni Hereniko's *Fire in the Womb,* shot on his home Fijian island of Rotuma, is a powerful tale of the struggles of native culture living under a colonial power. Fijians are the foreground of this film by a native Fijian, who combines mystical legend and harsh reality to tell the tale of the empowering of a young woman to rediscover her culture and identity.

Far from being in the foreground, Pacific Islands and their people have been depicted in Western films and television programs from *Bird of Paradise* on the 1932 movie screen to the 1990s *Byrds of Paradise* on TV screens (as well as stalwarts *Hawaii 5-0, Magnum P.I.,* and *Baywatch Hawaii*) as colorful backdrops to the adventures and exploits of visitors from the Western world. Outside of a few documentaries and the even fewer but growing number of locally made Pacific productions, such as *Once Were Warriors,* we seldom have the opportunity to see the rich textures and structures of Pacific societies and cultures. They have existed only as aberrations of, or adopted adjuncts to, a Western worldview of life as it should be: exotic and not a little erotic—a delightful background where Western man can play out his fantasies.

More than a century of tropical paradise imagery of Pacific Islands has been imbedded in the collective popular culture. Writers such as Robert

Louis Stevenson and Mark Twain laid the foundation in the 1800s. Early films cemented it for the twentieth century. The title of TV's *Byrds of Paradise* was a throwback to *Bird of Paradise,* a stereotype-setting 1932 film that was remade in the same vein in 1951. Both versions portrayed the heroine—Delores Del Rio in 1932 and Debra Paget in 1951—as a promiscuous Polynesian. The story was staple stereotype. Island girl Luana (Kalua in the second version) falls in love with wealthy, worldly *haole boy* (Joel McCrea in the 1930s, Louis Jourdan in the 1950s). But she can't escape the primitive she ultimately is and must appease the angry volcano by taking the big dive into the hot lava.

Now those are the islands we know!

BROWNFACE AND ANYPLACE

The plot device and characterizations of *Bird of Paradise* were lampooned in 1990's *Joe Versus the Volcano,* where the natives of fictional Waponi Woo are the descendants of intermarriages with Jewish shipwreck survivors. (They consider orange soda the nectar of the gods.) The wicked high priest of the Waponi Woos is a comic ringer for the played-for-straight "kahuna" of the 1932 *Bird,* Maurice Schwartz in brownface.

Early films about the islands were marked by the fact that in many cases they had no islanders in them and, in others, no island. Like Del Rio, Paget, and Schwartz, these early adventures in paradise cast white actors to play in brownface—*coconuts,* if you will. Long after the deplorable practice of Anglo actors playing minstrel-like in blackface, Hollywood has continued to cast Anglos in yellowface, playing Asians, or brownface, playing islanders. The controversy touched Broadway, as well, when Asian American actors recently protested the casting of Anglos to play a key role in *Miss Saigon.* It seems to be almost a rite of passage (like playing Shakespeare) for actors to don facial prosthetics, hairpieces, eyepieces, and heavy makeup to play an Asian or islander character. It is, however, not a reciprocal deal. No Asian or Pacific Islander has been invited to adopt the reverse in prosthetics (lowering cheekbones, sharpening noses, flattening eyes, folding eyelids, and donning light-hued makeup) and take a stab at Rhett Butler and Scarlet O'Hara in a remake of *Gone with the Wind.*

Honolulu's legendary detective, the Chinese–Hawaiian Chang Apana, found his exploits translated to film in the early Charlie Chan series. The locale was later shifted to San Francisco, and the acting duties shifted through a succession of players from Warner Oland to Peter Ustinov (whose casting drew a few clouds of protest over the continued stereotype in Honolulu, Los Angeles, Seattle, and San Francisco). But neither a Chinese nor Hawaiian ever played Chan. Unlike the screen Chan, the real-life Apana was hardly one to spout fortune cookie aphorisms while matching criminal wits with his inscrutability. Apana was tough and often two-fisted in his real-life crime solving. He'd still make a good subject for the screen.

Not only were non-island actors substituted for the real thing, but many early films that reflected and reinforced the South Seas stereotype, such as *Wings Over Honolulu* (1937), weren't even filmed in the islands. A few paper leis, potted palms, an ocean backdrop, and the stray stock footage of Diamond Head were enough to create the illusion, as far back as Thomas Ince's *Aloha Oe* in 1915. Bing Crosby enjoyed a *Waikiki Wedding* (1937) without the benefit of Waikiki, and Johnny Downs wooed the local beauties in *Hawaiian Nights* (1939) without ever seeing the sun go down over Honolulu. And there was no Gilligan's Island apart from an artificial lagoon on the Universal Studio back lot.

FOUR IMAGES THAT INJURE

Coconut casting—Anglos in brownface—could do little but reinforce stereotypes of island life from a predominantly Anglo male perspective. So naturally the island women were pliable lovelies, ever willing and ready to serve the visiting *haole,* or Anglo, male needs. The island men were mostly emasculated "heyboys" willing to serve the master, controlled by trinkets, booze, or simply the senior status of being in the shadow of a superior *haole.*

These major stereotypes of Pacific Islanders in popular media can be placed in four categories:

- Pleasant but basically ignorant natives in subsistence social structures. Even after Western contact they cling to their picturesque but primitive customs and mores.
- Savage cannibals who inevitably are overcome by superior Western firepower.
- Shapely, sexy, uninhibited women ever-willing to take a roll in the taro with a Westerner.
- Self-inflated men who preen and strut but are easily fooled by superior Western intelligence—often played comically.

The land itself has similarly been portrayed as ripe and ready for the Westerner's picking. The image of the deserted tropical isle is alluring as the place that will save, support, and nurture the life of the lonely castoff—from *Robinson Crusoe,* to the pair coming of age in the *Blue Lagoon,* to Tom Hanks and Wilson surviving in *Castaway.* The land, like the people, exists only to give—never expecting to receive anything in return.

THE ELVIS INFLUENCE

Post-war Hawaii focused on two things: building a tourism economy to replace the boom of the war years and statehood. They were intertwined. Jet travel, which made the islands accessible to every tourist, and statehood came in the same year—1959. Two years later the fledging state and tourist economy got its biggest boost from the "King of Rock-and-Roll" who chose Hawaii as the site for his post-Army hitch film. The 90 minutes of beaches, babes, leis, and luaus was a Technicolor travelogue credited with attracting tourists by the 707 load.

Blue Hawaii was not Elvis Presley's first brush with the isles. He had performed in concert in 1957—and starred in a special benefit to raise money for the USS *Arizona* memorial. Elvis and Hawaii shared a mutual attraction through the remainder of his professional life. He made three films there and performed his worldwide satellite concert from the Honolulu International Center following another benefit to pay the medical expenses of his friend, Hawaiian songwriter and singer Kui Lee. In his final years, Elvis slipped into Hawaii several times to stay at a remote beach house where local residents respected—and helped guard—his privacy.

Although *Blue Hawaii* and *Paradise Hawaiian Style* layered the screen with beautiful scenery, women, and a carefree lifestyle, the Elvis version of Hawaii fell back on many of the same stereotypes and filming conventions of the 1930s. An Anglo actress in brownface played his *Blue Hawaii* girlfriend. Although Islander actors played his beach boy buddies, they were portrayed as not having jobs or ambition. The island social structure was pictured as a dichotomy between the rich, urban, and Anglo bosses and the rural, happy-go-lucky, and musical local folk.

Paradise Hawaiian Style did a little better. This time Elvis' boss was an islander, but his girlfriends remained mostly the saronged and shaky-hipped hula girls with an appetite for Western boys. Strangely, his third Hawaiian film, *Girls, Girls, Girls,* had nothing to do with Hawaii. Although shot in the islands, Elvis played a shrimp boat captain (an occupation more likely along the southern U.S. coast) and bunked with a Chinese family. There was a hula-luau scene, but not a mention of Hawaii. His adopted family was given little beyond the Chinese stereotype—kids in pigtails with a father spouting the usual fortune cookie wisdom.

SURF'S UP, BUT STILL BLUE

The sea as well as the land has proven a profitable backdrop for surf paradise films showcasing Hawaii and other Pacific Islands (as well as the Pacific island country continent of Australia). Following in the tradition of John Severson's *Going My Wave,* Bruce Brown's *Endless Summer,* John Milius' *Big Wednesday,* John Stockton's *Blue Crush,* and Disney's blue extraterrestrial in the animated *Lilo and Stitch* revisit the myth.

Blue Crush's inventive and dramatic cinematography both on and beneath the waves impressed even hard-core Hawaii surfer audiences. Less inventive and impressive is *Blue Crush*'s revisitation of the standard South Sea formula: land, sea, and people serve as a backdrop for two attractive *haole* (Caucasian folks) to meet, fall in love, and overcome adversity.

Great pains are taken to explain that the lead female character, a talented surfer with a shot at conquering the infamous Pipeline Challenge contest, is a long-time resident who is considered local. But she has distanced herself from the community of local-boy ("we grew here, you flew here") surfers, one of whom is a former boyfriend. Equally great pains are taken to portray this conflict as gender and class based, although an ugly confrontation with the female surfer's new boyfriend, an NFL quarterback in town for the Pro Bowl, can't escape its racial overtones. Once again, island males are presented as brutish and backward, while the visitor from the West is the more reasonable and accommodating—after all, he has two African American linemen he introduces to surfing as well.

The female lead lives with two other surfers, as well as her younger sister, in an endless quest for surf that eschews schooling and is supported by minimum-wage work as maids in a resort hotel (the plot device to hook up the surfer and quarterback). The one actress in the trio who is actually local and is actually a surfer, Sanoe Lake, interestingly has the least relevant role.

The image of the family unit in Hawaii existing without parents is carried over to Disney's *Lilo and Stitch,* where the older surfing sister once again is the only caregiver for a younger rascal one. Into this dyad drops Stitch, a blue extraterrestrial who adds both to the rascal (visual) and Elvis (audio) factor in the film.

Although the local social worker is portrayed once again as the brutish Island male intent on causing havoc and threatening the idyllic image of Island life, *Lilo and Stitch* is generally considered the superior movie in presenting an acceptable version of Hawaiian values (particularly *ohana,* or family) and even Hawaiian pidgin—the local Creole that mixes the plantation languages of Hawaiian, Japanese, Chinese, Filipino, and Portuguese with English in a unique syntax, tone, and cadence.

Part of that success is credited to the use of local actors Tia Carrere and Jason Scott Lee to voice the older sister and boyfriend characters. Chinese–Hawaiian Jason Scott Lee is regarded as a particularly sensitive actor who has done extensive research into cultural contexts of roles he has played, from an Inuit in *Map of the Human Heart,* to an Easter Islander in the more correctly named *Rapa Nui* for that Polynesian island, to martial arts expert–actor Bruce Lee (*Dragon: The Bruce Lee Story*).

It's ironic that it has taken animation and extraterrestrials that spout Elvis songs to produce a film that more closely touches a portrayal that breaks the images that injure mold.

THE TV IMAGE

Baywatch Hawaii was the final version of the phenomenal internationally successful franchise that combined rough water and smooth lifeguards. After years of patrolling the California coast, it joined for two unmemorable seasons the Hawaii/Pacific Islands TV tradition begun with *Adventures in Paradise* in the 1960s—a sort of *Route 66* under sail. Although a few family-oriented TV series have been set in Hawaii (*Byrds of Paradise, Little People*), the bulk of the shows used the islands as a backdrop for crime adventures, beginning with *Hawaiian Eye,* with the sleuths mostly Anglo and the criminals brown. The longest-running and most successful was *Hawaii 5-0*, which presented a Hawaii almost entirely in the control of *haole,* with a few local actors playing lower-level cops. Even when Hawaii had Asian Americans, Hawaiians, and Filipinos in every top position from governor to chief of police, *5-0* gave audiences the images of an island where good local folk took orders and the bad ones got booked by Danno.

But compared with its successor, *Magnum, P.I., 5-0* was a cornucopia of ethnicity. *Magnum* starred a Vietnam vet who solved crimes with his in-country buddies, lived in an absent author's estate managed by a British major domo, and romanced just about every good-looking damsel in distress who got off a United jet at Honolulu International Airport. Occasionally, someone who actually might live or work in Hawaii stumbled onto the set, usually in a bikini on the beach. There was one recurring role for an islander—the police detective who, of course, was always befuddled and a step behind Magnum in solving any case. The show made good use of the scenery, but otherwise could just as successfully have been filmed in San Diego as Diamond Head.

The *haole* hero who moves in to solve the island folks' crimes has continued with several spins. *Raven* featured an American trained as a Ninja in Japan who sought out local bad guys and kicked them into submission. *Jake and the Fatman* presented the rotund William Conrad. *One West Waikiki* is the next series in the lineup featuring a female medical examiner. Another project that vied for network attention but got a pass starred a detective on Maui in tune with the land and spirits who uses his native clairvoyance to solve crimes. A Hawaiian in touch with his heritage? No, a Cherokee transplanted to the islands. With such a steady diet of staple stereotypes, it is little wonder that the mid-1990s *Byrds of Paradise* was considered such a foreign entry in the domestic TV market.

What separated *Byrds*, (an ironic throwback to two earlier films) from its popular media predecessors was that this time the background refused to stay put. The people of the islands kept intruding into the spotlight, presenting images that attempted to defy the stereotypical Pacific Islander. Yes, the women were drop-dead gorgeous. And yes, they did have a tendency to fall for the *haole* fresh from the mainland. But they also showed a resilient streak of independence. Rather than abandoning their own culture to become an adjunct to the Westerner, they were quick to tell the *haole* boy to bag it when he insisted they act less local.

The island social structure, portrayed with fair accuracy on *Byrds,* particularly among the youth, was initially closed to these *haole* outsiders who, among other things, couldn't speak pidgin, didn't know sushi from sashimi, and didn't know that prolonged eye contact with a stranger— *stink eye*—is an invitation to fight.

For the first time the Western stars of an island show were the outsiders—the aliens, the aberration. The Byrd family couldn't float freely through this new culture and win instant acceptance. It was they who had to fit in, who had to adjust. As a professor of philosophy, the head of the Byrd family brought no new and improved Western civilized cure for whatever ailed island values.

The producers (led by one-time TV wunderkind Stephen Bochco) admitted they took some risks by playing a more real Hawaii so close to the front of the stories. They worried they may have scripted too much about Hawaii that is unfamiliar to the mainland (and mainstream) audience, too many island types might have been confusing. The Filipinos were different from the Japanese, who were different from the Chinese and the Hawaiians. And there were too many accents, too. They all sounded different. There was too much pidgin, which forms the seams of this crazy quilt of ethnicities and cultures. And they worried about presenting too much of the sometimes fierce pride and *insiderism* of local culture that lies behind the facade of the tourism industry's promotion of "gentle breezes and gentler people." The Hawaii on *Byrds* wasn't really the Hawaii the audiences knew. And apparently they didn't particularly like it. Perhaps if it had been animated....

LOOKING FORWARD

Finding stereotypical portrayals of Pacific Islanders and Asian Americans is often like shooting fish in a barrel. The challenge, of course, is presenting more realistic images for the future. There are some bright spots. Some are in documentaries, such as Eddie Kamae's *Li'a: The Legacy of a Hawaiian Man,* Stephanie Castillo's *Simple Courage* about Father Damien and the Hansen's Disease (leprosy) colony of Molokai, Edgy Lee's *Waikiki,* and Renee Tajima's *Who Killed Vincent Chin?* Some feature films have spawned cross-cultural versions, such as Ang Lee's Taiwan-based *Eat Drink Man Woman* and the Latino *Tortilla Soup.* Ang Lee has proven his ability to cross cultural lines bringing Western popularity to such films as *Crouching Tiger, Hidden Dragon* and *The Wedding Banquet* and introducing Asian story-telling values in the lyrical *Ice Storm.* Jackie Chan brings his Hong Kong–styled martial arts films to the West with Asian characters as both heroes and villains. As film editor Walter Louie has remarked, the important thing is to get more images of the Asian and Pacific Island experience—positive and negative—onto film and TV screens. "The more images you have," he said, "the less the chance that one will become the overriding stereotype" (Asian American Journalists Association, 1991).

Chapter 14

NATIVE AMERICAN STEREOTYPES

Lucy A. Ganje

One little, two little, three little... going on the warpath... so circle the wagon trains.

Stereotypical portrayals of American Indian people are a consistent theme on our cultural landscape. These misrepresentations are embodied through sports team names and mascots, toys, media entertainment, and corporate iconography for everything from food to clothing, automobiles to alcohol. Preconceived ideas and images of Native people and their cultures are common. Unfortunately, these ideas are often born out of ignorance and old movies.

Since the first accounts in 1706 of "the skulking Indian enemy" (Copeland, 1993), the media have played a major role in fostering fear, hatred, and misunderstanding of Native Americans and inciting public opinion against them. Newspapers often fanned the flames of racial hatred by embellishing and sensationalizing the news of *Indian attacks,* in order to sell papers. But it wasn't just the newspapers that perpetuated this myth. Movies, comic books, cartoons, literature, music, and textbooks all played (and continue to play) a role in what some term symbolic annihilation. Propagated myths include the delusion that America's history began in 1492, that there is only one Native American culture, that American Indian peoples and cultures are becoming extinct, and that they are not part of contemporary society.

THE BLOODTHIRSTY SAVAGE

The media stereotype Native people in various ways—some more obvious than others. Many stereotypes, such as those arising from old Western movies and books, are easy to recognize. These are usually accompanied by phrases such as *Indian Wars, hostile Indians,* or *Indian uprising*. The images are often those of murderous savages with painted faces, yelling war whoops, and descending on the unsuspecting women and children of innocent white settlers. Portrayals such as these, often motivated by social and political factors, were used to justify the inhuman treatment of Native people and the taking of their lands. These stories and images were made popular not only by newspapers but also by nineteenth-century dime novels. Scanning the covers of romance novels, you may see this tradition in contemporary form. At least one white woman can usually be found collapsed in the arms of a Native warrior. Whether the collapse was precipitated by the warrior's savagery or the woman's own erotic desire can only be gleaned by reading the book.

THE NOBLE SAVAGE

Although the savage warrior image is still used, another visual more often seen in advertising and marketing is that of the noble savage.

Stories of Native people who helped the settlers, often at the risk of their own lives and family relationships, were and are also popular. This image portrays America's indigenous population as not only the friend of the white man but also as part of a once great but now dying culture. This is a very subtle form of racism because it usually implies that indigenous people existed to serve Anglo society and were thankful to be civilized by the Anglo Americans. Related to this is the misconception of the stoical Indian, an image that often translates to a perceived lack of humor. Monty Roessel, a Navajo photojournalist, related a conversation with a Navajo woman who wondered why Native people were never photographed smiling. "People must think we don't have any teeth," she laughed. Roessel explained that the unsmiling Indian was usually a set-up shot composed by the photographer, usually an Anglo American, to conform to a preconceived notion.

AMERICAN INDIANS AS SPORTS TEAM MONIKERS, MASCOTS, AND SYMBOLS

Non-Native schools and organizations brand their sports teams through the use of the Indian as both a noble and savage warrior. The Fighting

Sioux of the University of North Dakota, the Fighting Illini of the University of Illinois, the Cleveland Indians, the Washington Redskins, the Atlanta Braves (among hundreds of others) all depend on the stereotype of Native people as proud, warlike, and noble to sell their product and instill fear in the hearts of their opponents. Fans wave toy tomahawks, decorate their faces with war paint, and whoop and holler as they perform their war dances. The Redskins, a term defined as derogatory by Webster's dictionary and viewed by many Native people with the same disgust as the word *nigger*, don't just defeat a team, they *scalp* them, an image that brings with it another violent stereotype. Scalping is a term often accompanied by *Indian* and presents the image of fierceness, savagery, and violence. Most people don't know it was Europeans (not American Indians) who originated this practice in America. In the 1700s, Massachusetts offered bounties for the scalps of Indian people—40 pounds for a male, 20 for a female or young child (Rethinking Schools, 1991).

According to many sports team owners, fans, and university administrators, names like Redskins, Indians, and Fighting Sioux are signs of respect, meant to honor Native Americans. Although some defend the use of Native people as symbols, saying they are meant to honor and not insult Native Americans, others are unwilling to accept as honorable acts that convey a lack of respect for Native cultures and spirituality. Many Native people and organizations continue to condemn this objectification.

Organizations that have formally requested an end to the use of American Indians sports team names and images by non-Native schools include the National Indian Education Association, the National Congress of American Indians, the U.S. Office of Civil Rights, and the Native American Journalists Association.

INDIAN AS SPIRIT GUIDE

Another component of this issue involves the use of spiritual imagery. Many American Indian team symbols and mascots include eagle feathers and pipes. These objects are considered sacred in many Native cultures, and their use in this context may be considered inappropriate and insensitive.

Many Native people object to what they see as the appropriation of their culture and spirituality. Native forms of spirituality, which center on respect for the earth and all its inhabitants, have drawn many non-Native followers. While those seeking "in a good way" inner knowledge and the sacred in their own lives are usually welcomed, those who try to buy or sell spirituality are not.

Tools and fetishes associated with various earth-based religions can be purchased in specialty catalogs. Native images are very often used to sell these items. A sacred medicine pouch, for example, can be purchased along with ceremonial drums and shields. This marketing of American Indian spirituality recently found its way to an electronic bulletin board where a self-proclaimed chief was selling Indian names over the Internet.

Many Native people view this as *cultural genocide,* and the people who contribute to it as "culture vultures" because appropriated ceremonies and ritual elements are not treated with respect and honor. The fact that many non-Indian people turn to Native cultures for help and healing but are unwilling to participate in the ongoing struggle to maintain Native treaty rights is also noted.

INDIANS AS PROTESTERS

Native people themselves are often portrayed in the media as troublemakers, outsiders in their own homelands, as they continue their struggle of autonomy. Besides the obligatory once-a-year powwow story, the most often-seen media images of Native people are usually confrontational. Native Americans are frequently seen opposing or politically challenging a generally accepted stereotype: carrying signs and banners outside a Redskins game, questioning a reduction of sovereignty, or fighting for the return of ancestral remains from museums around the world. Dennis Banks, a cofounder of the American Indian Movement, put it this way: "In the news we're always [viewed as] protesting. Protesting—hell, we're surviving!" (Harjo, 1990).

When people are always seen in conflict, they're often viewed as troublemakers and a threat to established authority. This emphasis on confrontation makes for great images on the evening news; however, rarely is any time given to explain the historical and cultural reasons for the protest and why the event or practice being protested is seen as objectionable.

IMAGING THAT PLACES NATIVE PEOPLE ONLY IN THE PAST

A constant visual diet of Native people in traditional regalia is problematic. (Many Native people, because of its associations with the theater, consider the word *costume* inappropriate.) When all the media give us are images of Native peoples and cultures taken during annual *wacipis* (powwows), it feeds the notion that Native peoples do not exist in the present and are not part of a continuum. This denial of Native people as part of contemporary society is further fostered when we use them as symbols of the past.

OBJECTIFICATION

Turning people into objects, or dehumanizing them, is often the first step in justifying their oppression. While some argue that the use of Native references, such as Redskins, Indians, and Fighting Sioux, signifies respect for Native Americans, author Carol Spindel (2000) disagrees. Spindel said the depth of attachment and the deference shown toward these symbols and names is confused with deference and respect toward real American Indian people (p. 253).

Although *respect* and *honor* are words often used to justify the use of American Indian stereotypes, many Native people and organizations say it is not an honor but an objectification. Several points are made to support these views:

- Consider the fact that Native people are used as names and mascots for teams in the same way as wild animals such as wolves, bears, and tigers. Many people believe this leads to the view that Native peoples are less than human. The following statement by an eighth-grade student talking about her school's mascot is an indication of this: "We simply chose an Indian as the emblem. We could have just as easily chosen any uncivilized animal."[1]
- Mascots for sports teams are often drawn or portrayed in simplistic, belittling caricatures. The fans, following this lead, often paint their faces, wear feathers, and beat drums in complete disregard of the sacred traditions they are mimicking. Some people in the Native community have drawn the following parallel: a sports team called the Christians with a cartoon mascot dressed like the Pope, in long robes and miter, brandishing a crucifix and incense. The fans could wave Styrofoam crucifixes in the air and bring buckets of holy water to sprinkle on each other. That portrayal would be unthinkable, of course, but the same type of insensitivity and spiritual defilement is seen during half-time displays at many sporting events throughout the United States.

NOW YOU SEE THEM, NOW YOU DON'T: THE PROBLEM OF INVISIBILITY

Many people, with help from the mass media, do not see Native Americans as living persons. Some argue the mass media not only refuse to portray Native Americans as persons but also often refuse to see them at all.

When a Native person is in traditional dress, the mass media feel no obligation to identify that person. This lack of identifying information perpetuates the idea that the individual isn't a real person but only an *Indian* or an *Indian-head*. Photos of powwow dancers on a newspaper's front page are often unaccompanied by a cutline—even when the photo is a close-up. A postcard of a person doing a traditional dance is labeled simply, "Indian Dancer." A music group uses a photo of a young child in traditional regalia on its CD cover, without the family's permission. A tourism magazine includes a short story on cowboys and Indians along with two photos. The photo of the cowboy (in contemporary dress) is accompanied by the subject's name, title, and hometown—even her horse's name is included. No identifying information is given for the picture of the Indian, a young man in traditional dress.

These subtle forms of racism send the unspoken message that Indians are not people, that they have no names or identities. Seeing American Indian people only in traditional dress gives media audiences the idea they are simply historical artifacts without significance in today's world. This misconception is often fed by the mainstream media's lack of coverage of Native communities.

NARROW FIELD OF VISION

Unfortunately, most of what people know about Native tribes and cultures is learned through what they read, see, or hear in the media. If all they see are stories about powwows, casinos, or health risks, a reader might assume that such stories are all there is to report. As in other communities, there are well-tended homes, farms, and ranches on the reservation along with modern community centers, clinics, businesses, and colleges. The media have a responsibility, not only to Native people, but to everyone, to portray Native people living in their communities year-round—working, laughing, loving, and crying within the context of their existence as active, productive members of today's societies, both inside and outside the borders of tribal nations.

Giving all sides of the story means understanding that there are more than 500 *sides* to the Native American experience in the United States alone. There are more than 500 separate and distinct tribal nations in the United States, and each nation has its own unique language, customs, beliefs, and history. Along with this knowledge should come the reali-

zation that the terms *American Indian* or *Native American* are generalizations. Using the term *American Indian* to identify someone who is Lakota
or Chippewa or Hidatsa is like describing someone from Germany or
France as *European*. The term is correct but broad and gives readers little
contextual background. By the same token, to say someone speaks Indian
would be the same as saying someone speaks European.

BLURRED FOCUS

One of the biggest misconceptions regarding Native peoples seems to be
that they are all alike, that the tribes in the Pacific Northwest are the same
as the Southwest nations, who are the same as the Native peoples of the
northern plains. Although American Indian students represent more than
50 tribes at the University of North Dakota, the assumption by non-Native
students is often that all Indian people on campus are Sioux because the
university's sports mascot is the Fighting Sioux.

This misconception fuels the notion that there can be one spokesperson
for all Native peoples. This in turn gives rise to the idea that Native peoples all think alike and should all agree on topics ranging from what constitutes a stereotype to school curricula. Often, when Native people or
tribes voice opposing views, non-Native peoples use this as an example of
a lack of cooperation or a sign of infighting. While a unified voice is not
expected from groups in the broader community, it is often expected of
people in underrepresented groups. Of course the Native community is as
diverse as the number of nations, and the nations are as diverse as the number of tribal members.

THE CONSEQUENCES OF MISREPRESENTATION

The consequences of stereotyping in both Native and non-Native communities are far-reaching. According to one Native parent who filed a legal
complaint against the use of school mascots, "By tolerating the use of
demeaning stereotypes in our public school systems, we desensitize entire
generations of children" (Rethinking Schools, 1991, p. 22). Many people
feel stereotyping presents a challenge to self-esteem, that Native children
have the right to grow up believing they're more than mascots for products
and sports teams. They have the right to attend a football game without
standing next to someone yelling, "Scalp the Indians."

Misrepresentations are everyone's concern, and their potential effects
certainly belie the naïve argument that there are more important things to

worry about than sports mascots or advertising images. Children are especially vulnerable, and if their culture is excluded or seen only in a negative way, they may begin to wonder if they're okay. Some critics believe the media are, in part, responsible for the high rate of suicide among Native young people. They believe this high rate reflects low self-esteem based on negative imaging (Harjo, 1990). If we only see ourselves reflected when there's a crisis or only as part of the past, this raises anger, anxiety, and uncertainty. We have difficulty believing we are effective participants in society. All people deserve to see themselves reflected with honesty and balance by the media organizations serving their communities.

Through the efforts of Native people and organizations changes are being made. Offensive advertising is being challenged and in some cases the negative images are being withdrawn. Newspaper organizations like *The Oregonian,* the *Minneapolis Star Tribune,* and the *Kansas City Star* are refusing to print the names and/or images of sports teams considered offensive by Native people. Encouraged by Native activists, enlightened high school and university students, faculty, and staff have worked to remove degrading mascots at their schools. Stanford University more than 20 years ago changed its team name from the Indians to the Cardinals, and more recently Marquette University dropped the name Warriors, eliminating a demeaning stereotype from their school. This type of sensitivity is necessary to provide an environment in which all people are comfortable and made welcome.

Phrases that subtly reference Native Americans are used so often we tend to forget the negative imaging associated with them. Who is excluded when we use the expression "circle the wagon trains"? The battles fought with toy cowboy and Indian figures have another meaning for Indian kids. The children's song that ends "four little, three little, two little Indians, one little Indian boy" was a celebration of racial genocide. The term *Indianhead* becomes an iconic image representing an entire race of people.

The visual stereotyping of American Indian people, their identities, their cultures, and their spirituality is widespread and of serious concern. Many people, when it comes to this topic, know little else. Test yourself on this subject: name five American Indian civil rights leaders. Now name five teams that have an Indian mascot or logo (R. A. Williams, as cited in Elie, 2002).

Which question garnered the most answers?

Chapter 15

JEWISH IMAGES THAT INJURE

Marsha Woodbury

Yes I am a Jew and my father is a Jew.
> Statement from *Wall Street Journal* reporter
> Daniel Pearl before being killed in Pakistan.

As this book goes to press, the global community is seeing jarring news footage from the Middle East. The slaying of reporter Daniel Pearl in Pakistan sent violent reverberations through the world's Jewish population, but this shock is minor compared to the aftereffects of the Israeli/Palestinian conflict.

For years we have seen pictures of heavily armed Israeli soldiers whose power humiliates the Arab populations surrounding Israel. Alas, media coverage has inadvertently fanned a not-so-dormant anti-Semitism (hate of Jews) in Europe and elsewhere. The brutal images of Israeli soldiers are potent, and at times they have been mislabeled or staged for waiting photographers (Keinon, 2002). Negative Israeli images easily overshadow more subtle, positive Jewish images that are not as sensational, such as the Jewish athletes Sarah Hughes and Sasha Cohen, both Olympic ice skaters.

The problem for the media is twofold: first, to be evenhanded in its reporting and visuals from the Middle East; second, to separate Israel—a country that sees itself in a struggle for survival—from Jews in Israel and elsewhere who have been and will be attacked, regardless of their approval or disapproval of Israeli policies. The key point will be separating Israel as a country from people who follow Judaism or have Jewish ancestors.

One tragedy of the intractable Palestinian/Israeli conflict is that it has become a public relations war for the hearts and minds of the global community and a fight for life. This news report on April 19, 2002, sums up the situation:

> In Europe a spate of attacks on Jewish targets from Marseille to Kiev has sparked fears that the tensions in the Middle East are now spilling over into the streets of Europe. The governments of France, Britain, Germany, Spain, and Belgium have appealed for joint European action to combat anti-Semitism, when the EU states meet later this month. Some Jews say they are now suffering the worst anti-Semitism since World War II. In France, police are dealing with around a dozen attacks against Jews each day, and the anti-Semitism has even extended to the Netherlands, which has a long tradition of tolerance. ("Jewish Targets in Europe Attacked," 2002)

Attacks against synagogues include desecrating holy items with human excrement, smashing windows, and scrawling swastikas on walls and lecterns. Such violence foments the growing fear of the world Jewish community, and the seriousness of the current situation makes a chapter about stereotypes even more mandatory. The goal is to heighten awareness of the unconscious assumptions we may hold about Jewish people and to learn where these inner images clash with reality. Thus, this article includes Jewish images in United States entertainment media as well as in the world news. Jewish stereotypes were and are serious and deserve explanation and understanding, particularly in this time of anti-Israeli fervor and the rise of more open anti-Semitism. We begin by describing what a Jew is, and what the images of Jews are.

WHO IS A JEW?

When we talk about images of some minorities, the basic question of who and what they are does not need to be explained. We can quickly spot a child or a woman or an Asian. Jews are harder to identify. Jews are not olive-skinned, brown-eyed, short people with large noses. There are plenty of blonde, blue-eyed, freckled Jews, even in the Israeli Army, and, of course, black Jews, as was Sammy Davis, Jr. Another impediment is that Jewish people or their ancestors have changed their names in order to "pass" under the public radar.[1] Plastic surgery makes distinctive noses disappear, too.

How does a person become a Jew? Why are Jews singled out for hate crimes? By looking at history we can best understand the Jewish stereotypes of our time.

Jews share some distinctive characteristics such as culture, religion, and language. Jewishness comes from birth or religious conversion, and among the Jewish community there is no definite agreement on who is and who is not Jewish. Some insist that being Jewish depends upon a public declaration of faith, while others say that a child's mother must be Jewish for a child to be Jewish.

Hitler's Germany attempted to define Jewishness as believing in Judaism, being married to a Jew, having a grandparent who believed in Judaism, or being the child of a mixed marriage (for example, Catholic–Jewish). Any of those things qualified people for the death camps.

Where did this death sentence come from? About 1,000 years before the birth of Jesus, a Semitic people settled in Judea, having Jerusalem as their capital city. They could have disappeared into history, but their lasting importance is due to their written literature: a world history, a collection of laws, chronicles, psalms, books of wisdom, poetry, and fiction, and political utterances that became what Christians know as the Old Testament, the Hebrew Bible (Welles, 1922).

Throughout their history, Jews have tried to follow their religion, which proved difficult as the Persians, Greeks, Babylonians, Assyrians, and Romans conquered them. The Jews were called a stubborn people for refusing to convert to the religion of their hosts and instead maintaining their own beliefs, rituals, and customs, often at great personal sacrifice. Feelings against Jews have been so strong that, for example, only in the last part of the twentieth century did the Pope recognize Judaism.

Throughout the centuries, invaders or a ruling class have attempted to force Jews to change their religion, and most Jews have refused. Medieval Christianity portrayed Jews as grotesque individuals, ever ready to steal consecrated wafers, murder innocent children, and mock the rituals and the beliefs of the *true* faith (Glassman, 1975).

Because Jews would not convert, countries such as Spain, Germany, and Russia persecuted them and executed pogroms (planned elimination), forcing Jews to seek safety in many lands, such as Poland, and in more recent history, the United States and Israel.

A people without a permanent home, Jews developed skills that were portable, entering into the professions and education. Over the centuries, Jews have been stereotyped as being adept money handlers because in medieval Europe many governments restricted money handling and money lending to Jews and Arabs, believing finance to be morally wrong for Christians. Governments barred Jews from entry into many fields, and competent financiers succeeded in a society where they could do little else (Singer, 2000).

Because Jews believed it best to marry other Jews, their Semitic characteristics remained strong. A German, William Marr, who founded the League for Anti-Semitism, coined the term *anti-Semitism* in 1879. Marr advanced the view that Jews constituted a distinct racial group, a race that was physically and morally inferior. Marr believed scientific evidence proved the Jews were predisposed to be a slave race while the Aryans were the Master Race.[2]

This assertion seems quite strange in 2002 in the United States, where entire Internet sites are devoted to revealing well-known people who are Jewish, because this heritage is so difficult to discern from appearance. That does not imply that Jewish people are not aware every day and everywhere that they are Jewish, it only means that others cannot always identify them. Sometimes a distinctive name or a Yiddish accent is a clue. One way we can tell a Jew from any other person is if she or he wears special clothing. Orthodox Jewish males sometimes wear a yarmulke, a small skullcap, in public.

A stereotype seen in the media is the Hassid. Hassidism is a "family" in the tribe, a small group of devout Jews that springs from Polish roots and holds to very strict observance and worship. They are easily identified by their appearance, for they wear black clothes, with striemels (wide-brimmed, black hats), long beards, and long curly sidelocks. Mainstream Jews often feel uncomfortable about Hassidism. In one of Woody Allen's films, *Annie Hall,* Allen goes to visit Annie's straight-laced, Midwestern family, and he imagines that they are looking at him and seeing a Hassidic with a beard, sidelocks, and a black hat (Kaplan, 2002).

IMAGES THAT INJURE

In today's media in the United States, we do not encounter the more devastating images of the past. On Internet Web sites, we can look at some of the caricatures from the late 1800s.[3] In the drawings, Jews were depicted in English popular culture as they had been since medieval times, as usurious embezzlers, blasphemers in league with the devil, clandestine consumers of roast pork, and seducers of Christian virgins.

In the 1930s, the Nazis widely spread grotesque caricatures of Jews, featuring protruding noses and mouths salivating at the sight of money.[4] Nazi education began with children's books[5] and continued into the community. These images laid the groundwork for the mass extermination of Jews that followed.

Because of the horrific history of Jewish stereotyping and persecution, Jewish people are extremely sensitive to hateful portrayals. The Jewish Anti-Defamation League has fought anti-Semitism for more than 85 years, and today, as a new surge of anti-Semitism washes over Europe and the United States, it remains busy.

JEWISH STEREOTYPES

Films have been criticized for showing Jews as helpless and childlike. Many of us picture thousands of Jews walking passively into the Nazi gas chambers during World War II. In *Schindler's List,* a war profiteer fooled the Nazis into letting him use Jews as cheap labor, rescuing more than 1,100 from death camps. In the film, only one main character is Jewish, the accountant, yet the number of Jews is large, amorphous, all victims. Some Jews complain that films have not told the whole story, excluding the Jews who fought fiercely and perpetuating the image of Jews as helpless victims about to be butchered. The Holocaust Museum in Washington, D.C., attempts to tell the full story of those who died in the camps.

George Costanza sums up the image of the Jewish male on the hit TV sitcom *Seinfeld*—short, bald, aggressive, obsessive, and constantly trying to overcompensate for his profound insecurity. George is a stereotype—always hot for women who are not Jewish, always trying to impress.

The popular TV formula in which male Jews are married or romantically involved with *shiksas* (gentile women) denigrates Jewish women because it makes them appear undesirable and because almost never is the reverse true. *Seinfeld* had an episode called "Shiksappeal," in which the main female character discovered that Jewish men like her because she's *not* Jewish. In *Mad About You,* Paul Reiser's character is Jewish, but his Jewishness is not a topic.

Woody Allen's movie persona is a true stereotype, a male with morose introspection, a fixation upon persecution and the Holocaust, with a restless, questing Jewish intellectuality. His relationships with gentile women are always doomed to fail (Ziv & Zajdman, 1993). Popular novelist Philip Roth's Jewish characters are equally insecure and unsure of their identity.

The *Jew* is the fat kid, the one at the *bar mitzvah,* the boy who finishes last at the footrace. The *Jew* is the indulging, *nouveau riche* father, telling people what to buy wholesale. He is "my son the doctor" or the smart kid in the film *Broadcast News,* the kid the other students beat up after his graduation speech.

The best way to portray Jewish men is as unmistakably Jewish, yet possessing a common humanity and experiencing the joys and sorrows of all people. Oded Fehr, the Israeli actor in *The Mummy* and *The Mummy Returns,* is not the nebbish Woody Allen of the North American subconscious.

The female *Jew* is a JAP, a Jewish American Princess—pampered, demanding, loud, tasteless—or she is the JAM, Jewish American Mother, overprotective, can't let go, the Yiddish mama, loudmouthed, and pushy. The stereotype is so strong that one could joke: Did you hear about the last wishes of a Jewish woman who wanted her ashes scattered on the floor of a fancy department store? She wanted her daughter to visit her at least once a week.

The female *Jew* is Monica Lewinsky, the young intern from a wealthy Beverly Hills family, struggling with her weight and her self-image. She is also young, urban, privileged, and single or intermarried, such as Monica Geller on *Friends,* Grace Adler on *Will & Grace,* and Dharma Finklestein on *Dharma & Greg* (Belasco, 1999).

In the media, few Jewish women are lusted after by gentile men, save Barbra Streisand by Robert Redford in the film *The Way We Were.* And in that film, the two lovers separate at the end. Any Woody Allen film has the same theme.

The Jewish mother has been fairly well carved out by novelists such as Philip Roth. Part of the stereotype comes from the historical roots of Judaism, the closeness of the family, and the struggle for survival in a new country. The Jewish woman had to manage the family while her husband pursued religion, and she consequently developed the strong personality and sharp business skills that are her stereotype. In the process, she also sacrificed herself for the well-being of her children (Ziv & Zajdman, 1993). Other cultures have the same familial bond. Sons and mothers are very close in Asian families, and often after marriage the children move into the family home. In the United States, children move out at 18. The dominant U.S. culture has difficulty understanding foreign relationships and sees them as tainted.

The media could help by highlighting women such as Ruth Bader Ginsburg of the U.S. Supreme Court, whose opinions have consistently leaned toward religious tolerance. Singer Paula Abdul's mother is a Canadian Jew, and her father was born of Syrian Jewish parents (Eisenberg, personal communication, 1994). As B.J. Chakravorty remarked, "See the beautiful things Arabs and Jews can make when they work together" (Chakravorty, personal communication, April 19, 1994).

ERRORS IN COVERAGE OF THE MIDDLE EAST

People believe photos and captions when they come from the *New York Times* or the Associated Press. Among the images that slandered Israeli soldiers and stirred world opinion against Israel was one on September 30, 2000. In the foreground is the bloody face of a young man crouching beneath an Israeli policeman armed with a club. The caption says, "An Israeli policeman and a Palestinian on the Temple Mount." The viewer assumes the policeman bloodied the young man.

However, the young man turned out to be Jewish. Palestinians had just beaten him up, and the picture was taken near a gas station, not on the holy site of the Mount. The newspapers corrected the error a few days later, but by then the photo had appeared in newspapers all over the world, and the damage was done. The Palestinian Information Center[6] incorporated the photo onto its home-page banner as a symbol of the Palestinian struggle and only recently took it off.[7]

Such errors are understandable, because we are caught in a war for public opinion and each side is attempting to spin the news. In a typical photo, Israeli soldiers are shown escorting a young Arab boy who is so scared that he has wet his pants. What the viewer does not see is a photo taken minutes before, where the young boy is throwing rocks at the soldiers. The media want lively, action-filled images. To make the front page, photographers have allowed people to stage "live" photographs.[8] The Israeli government did not ban news photographers altogether, as did the United States in many instances in Afghanistan. However, Israeli Jews now worry that these photos play into latent anti-Semitism worldwide.

OTHER CONTEMPORARY ISSUES

The Internet and Anti-Semitism

The rise of the Internet makes it possible for anyone to be an author and gain a worldwide audience. As much as the Internet helps Jews to connect with each other and share their heritage, it at the same time allows for hate sites to proliferate. Anyone using the Internet may inadvertently be exposed to hate online, and crimes have been traced to Internet use.[9] The images on the anti-Semitic sites are strong, such as the burning World Trade Towers behind a Star of David, with the implication that Jewish people were behind the attacks.

The Internet is not only a way to pass along strong visuals. Sites have made bomb-making information available with the express intent of killing Jews. The Jewish Defense League has assembled a commentary on such sites called "Poisoning the Web: Hatred Online."[10]

Media Holiday Coverage

In many suburbs, Jewish homes are the only houses in the vicinity without Christmas decorations, or perhaps the only ones with a menorah in the window. Kyle Broslofski, from the popular cartoon show *South Park,* illustrated the plight of the isolated Jewish child in the 1997 "South Park Christmas Special," saying, "It's hard to be a Jew on Christmas." Kyle couldn't go to the mall to see Santa, and he missed the small pleasure of catching snowflakes on his tongue. In the episode, the local policeman confirms that Kyle cannot catch "Christmas" snowflakes because he's Jewish (Raphael, 1998). *South Park* helps to explain to children that they may be isolated in their communities, but there are others like them.

Political Cartoons

Jews and Arabs in cartoons often have huge noses. The caricature reflects an historical bigotry and is often a conscious weapon used to isolate and persecute targeted populations. They remind Jews of Nazi propaganda.

Caricatures should be biting and revealing, but there is a difference between exaggerating the observable features of an identifiable public figure (Barbra Streisand's nose, for example) and putting nasty, hate-inducing features on all members of an ethnic group (such as casting all Jews as Shylocks) (Wasserman, 1994). In recent years, political cartoons in Egypt, for example, are similar to those of Nazi Germany.[11] As one editorial writer noted, if "suburbanites have learned to live without lawn statuettes of servile black stable hands, cartoonists can certainly survive without their pictorial counterparts" (Wasserman, 1994, p. 15).

Hiding Jewish Identity

In plays and movies, Jews have been depicted as alienated from society, persecuted, and isolated by their Jewish identity. Steven Spielberg said he made *Schindler's List* for himself, to retake his roots. His relatives were Polish and Ukrainian victims of the Nazis. As a boy in Ohio, "I was embarrassed because of my Jewishness." He was "smacked and kicked around" at high school. "Two bloody noses. It was horrible" ("Critics Leave Schindler Off," 1993).

The alienation of the Jew has led to serious suffering and going under-cover. In many motion pictures, the heritage of characters will be deliber-ately blurred to make the story line more universal.[12] Some Jews have buried their identity to survive. In the United States, the lack of positive feelings and images has caused actors or their families to change their names in part to suppress their Jewishness—some still do. For example, Debra Winger and Winona Ryder often play gentile women on screen. Barbra Streisand presented herself as Jewish from the start, and Richard Dreyfuss said he looked around one day in the industry and noticed, "Gee, no one else is admitting to being Jewish. I will" (Dreifus, 1993). Actors with Jewish heritage include Adam Sandler, Harrison Ford, Goldie Hawn, Lisa Kudrow, and more.

Apparently, filmmakers and actors are damned both for perpetuating the Jewish stereotype and for assimilating and not being proud of who they are (S. Curry, personal communication, 1994).

GENERALIZATION

Some common stereotypes of Jewish people are accurate generaliza-tions. Yes, Jews have been high achievers in the United States. The fami-lies stress education seriously, and their representation in the professions and popular media is out of proportion to their numbers. Jews do flock to professions that are dependent on intellectual talents, such as teaching, medicine, law, and accounting. They often are extremely successful.

Yes, Jews are humorous. Mild stereotyping is combated with humor, for which Jews are rightly famous.[13] "There is a unique tendency—cultural, religious, and ethnic—for the Jew to pick up on the terrible miseries of his life, as well as its absurdities, to make jokes and laugh at them" (Ziv & Zajdman, 1993, p. 82). However, when a joke is generated or repeated to derogate Jews, to spread anti-Semitism, then the purpose, and the humor, is lost.

IN CLOSING

We are in the first years of a new millennium, cursed by the heritage of the old one. Under the surface, or boiling at the top, is anti-Semitism. Reporters, photographers, and media managers need to recognize that today's events are not occurring in a vacuum. Small errors can result in hate crimes, burned synagogues, and overt prejudice. The goal is to look beyond those who want to manipulate us with today's photos to see a larger problem. Nazi Germany was one of the most purely Christian countries in the world, yet we cannot blame all Christians for everything Germany did. Similarly, Israel cannot be equated with Jewishness, whatever Israel's leaders may proclaim.

Jewish people are as complex and varied as any others. To collapse their rich diversity into simplistic generalizations and negative caricatures through poor media coverage and deliberate stereotyping seems most unfair.

Chapter 16

IMAGES OF IRISH AMERICANS: INVISIBLE, INEBRIATED, OR IRASCIBLE

Susan Dente Ross

Once a year, about mid-March, newspapers discover an otherwise neglected segment of their communities: Irish Americans. With the annual wearing of the green and the St. Patrick's Day parades comes a sudden, brief wave of news interest in those Americans whose roots (mythical or real) reach across the Atlantic to Ireland (Cronin & Adair, 2002).[1]

In addition to the rash of parade news and celebration stories marking St. Patrick's Day itself, almost any newspaper content related to Irish Americans in March is tied to this iconic event. So, in a rather typical example, St. Patrick's Day gets the first mention in a Worcester, Massachusetts, newspaper story announcing the appointment of a state representative to the national board of directors of a political action committee devoted to promoting peace in Ireland (Nugent, 2002). The review of a somewhat autobiographical book on the Irish American experience by 1960s radical Tom Hayden appears on St. Patrick's Day and mentions the holiday in the lead, even though the book had been published several months earlier (Nichols, 2002).

Not surprisingly, an Irish American literary and culture fair in San Francisco is slated in March. The *San Francisco Chronicle* denigrates the "weeklong series of panel discussions and readings on various facets of Irish culture" involving internationally known writers, scholars, musicians, and activists by calling it "a warm-up celebration for San Francisco's 150th annual St. Patrick's Day Parade on March 17 and also a pre-emptive strike aimed at deflating the stereotype of clovers and beer"

(Doyle, 2002, p. D1). But rather than present a different image of Irish Americans, the 1,200-word piece opens with a reference to an Irish gangster and quickly touches on Irish poverty, immigration, and broods before ever mentioning the focus of the event: Ireland's literary tradition.

Many St. Patrick's Day stories in today's newspapers stereotype the drunken Irishmen. One New Hampshire reporter comments on the "Guinness-oriented festivities related to the St. Patrick's Parade" (Clayton, 2002, p. 1A). Even the forcedly dour *Wall Street Journal* joins the fray with a St. Patty's Day editorial on the efforts by Guinness to create a "quick pour" creamy head ("Taste," 2002, p. 15W). The editorial flippantly trivializes religious violence in Ireland and then elevates Guinness stout to the official religion of the Irish. As a result, Guinness's new ultrasound pouring system is responsible for alcohol-crazed, fighting mad "Irishmen being set against Irishmen," according to the editorial voice of the *Wall Street Journal.*

Such references are hardly surprising. Indeed, the image of Irishmen as irrationally violent has become so ingrained in American culture that it is now an idiom. As one columnist jocularly commented, "I've got your Irish up!" (Clayton, 2002, 1A). Even without access to a modern-day version of the once-abundant illustrations of Irishmen, caps askew, legs astride, fists aloft, readers get the picture.

During the other 11 months of the year—those months *not* marked by St. Patrick's Day—Irish Americans are largely invisible from newspapers save for the occasional brief mention of Irish bands, brawls, or bars. An example of this coverage is a 50-word piece in *The Patriot Ledger* of Quincy, Massachusetts, announcing a "meat raffle" sponsored by the South Shore Irish American Society to benefit charity and two scholarships (McGee, 2001, p. 4). The virtual absence of Irish Americans from American newspaper pages may reflect a type of acceptance, an integration of the Irish into the white mainstream of American society (Ignatiev, 1995). According to this theory, newspaper reporters and editors feel no need to identify the national or ethnic roots of Irish Americans because this group has been incorporated into the white majority. Newspaper readers don't need labels to identify Irish Americans because readers understand who belongs to the socially constructed group, *us.*

IRISH AS SUBHUMAN

Certainly, invisibility seems preferable to the systematic portrayal of the Irish as inferior and subhuman. Such images can be traced back to the

Middle Ages, when English culture portrayed the Irish as savages and brutes. This view persisted and crossed the Atlantic with the British settlers who continued to use the epithet *wild Irish* and to pass laws overtly discriminating against Catholics, most of whom were Irish. The stereotype flourished in eighteenth century America, fed in part by the fact that the Irish formed the first great wave of white immigrants to help industrialize the growing nation and to build and inhabit its urban slums (Rothman, 1971, p. 254). The Irish had fled the immutable caste system, forced labor, and grinding poverty in England only to become the cheap, disposable labor needed by America's growing factories and railroads. Colonial American industrialists viewed the Irish immigrants as akin to free Negroes who could occupy jobs "where it did not make sense to risk the life of a slave" (Ignatiev, 1995, p. 2).

If Irish labor fueled the industrial revolution, the massive Irish influx to America also presented a social problem whose vestiges remain in contemporary stereotypes of Irish Americans. Irish immigrants occupied run-down tenements and shantytowns behind warehouses and alongside the docks and railroad tracks. They lived amid overcrowding, little or no sanitation, crime, squalor, and disease. The cows, goats, chickens, and pigs they raised to feed their starving families roamed freely among their shacks. The Irish community often abutted or intermingled with that of recently freed Negroes, and the two groups fought, socialized, and "developed a common culture of the lowly" (Ignatiev, 1995, p. 2).

In the nineteenth century, increasingly popular illustrated magazines featured cartoons and caricatures of the Irish as apelike creatures with large mouths, thick lips, protruding lower jaws, jagged teeth, short noses with gaping nostrils, sloping foreheads, receding chins, and dangling arms. The evening before St. Patrick's Day came to be celebrated by "Paddy making." Life-size effigies of Irishmen "dressed in rags, its mouth smeared with molasses, sometimes wearing a string of potatoes around its neck or a codfish to mock the Friday fasting [of Catholics] and with a whiskey bottle stuck out of one pocket" were erected and publicly scorned and jeered in town squares (Potter, 1960, p. 168).

The emergence of the popular so-called science of physiognomy accepted the accuracy of these portraits and justified anti-Irish prejudice on the basis that facial features were believed to reflect mental capacity and behavioral traits. Irish facial features, it was said, indicated the inherent savagery, volatility, drunkenness, and irresponsibility of the Irish. One illustration in *Harper's Weekly*, titled "Scientific Racism," portrayed the similarity of the Irish and Negroes and suggested they both should be extinct.[2] Popular cartoonists including Thomas Nast, Joseph Keppler, and James Wales routinely filled *Harper's Weekly* and *Puck* with racist, anti-Catholic images of apelike Irish. Derisive cartoons condemned Irish social habits, sexual behavior, honesty, cleanliness, employment, and "inclination toward drinking and related crimes" (Solomon, 1956, p. 153). Illustrations depicting the Irish as "ignorant, shiftless, credulous, impulsive, mechanically inept, and boastful" routinely appeared in newspapers, books, and posters.

A cartoon published in *Harper's Weekly* in September 1852 showed an Irishman beating a balking mule, to which he bears a striking resemblance, while two proper gentlewomen look on in horror. A Nast cartoon, *The Day We Celebrate,* shows his typically repulsive Irish immigrants as violent, drunken apes celebrating St. Patrick's Day. Other drawings throughout the period portray Irishmen brawling in the streets during an election; a buxom young Irishwoman surrounded by leering, drunken men telling her employer that all of these men are her "cousins;" and a teeming crowd of gaunt, ragged, filthy, empty-eyed men, women, and children titled *A Court for King Cholera.*

These negative representations became so common, so iconic, that cartoonists could eliminate the traditional Irish symbols once needed to convey meaning. Cartoons of Irishmen with dark-pigmented skin and Negroid characters (Ignatiev, 1995, p. 61) competed with contemptuous portrayals of Irish cops and corrupt Tammany Hall politicians.

These images "had a profound effect on later policy" and upon the Irish self-image (Lebow, 1976, p. 112). Such stereotypes, scholars have noted, are "self-fulfilling and self-justifying images" (Lebow, p. 105). The inability of Irish immigrants to shed the brand of *inferior* stung peasants who had optimistically left their homeland for the chance to improve themselves in America. Many fell into depression. Some escaped through alcohol, and their frequent arrests for public drunkenness and brawling became stock episodes in contemporary theater, illustrations, and cartoons. From this foundation, the stereotype of the lazy, violent, sexually promiscuous, irresponsible, drunken Pat or Paddy emerged.

A MORE COMPLEX IMAGE

By the late nineteenth century, however, the Irish in America had begun to differentiate themselves from the lowliest caste in America. One historian argues that Irish Americans elevated their social status by joining mainstream white America's oppression of African Americans (Ignatiev,

1995, pp. 62–90). Whatever the reasons, by the start of the twentieth century, newly arriving ethnic groups would become the target of American antagonism, and cartoon images of the Irish would soften. The Irishman of the early twentieth century is comic and affable. He is a modern-day leprechaun, full of tricks, "good-natured, fun-loving, and imaginative" (Solomon, 1956, p. 154). Irish drunkenness is presented as an expression of jovial boisterousness rather than violence and bestiality (Greeley, 1972, p. 119). If this Irishman is not taken seriously, neither is he viewed as merely an animal.

This era is perhaps best remembered through satirist Finley Peter Dunne's narrative sketches of Mr. Dooley, a bachelor bartender who directed incisive monologues to the thick-tongued, heavy-drinking Hennessy. For more than 20 years beginning in 1883, Dunne's syndicated newspaper column portrayed Dooley, a first-generation Irish American barkeep, as an informed, opinionated, and critical observer of national and international events. Dooley poked fun at the stock characters of the Irish community, including the policeman who "drinks his beat" and the alderman who does "no work or worry." But Dunne's columns perpetuated the image of the Irish American as a "happy drunk" (Shannon, 1963, p. 145). The drunken characters benefiting from Dooley's sage advice far outnumbered the sober, intelligent barkeep.

Clearly, Dunne's more complex image of Irish Americans actually reflected changes in American society. As Irish American entrepreneurs and politicians escaped poverty and gained respectability, Irish American musicians produced "dozens" of songs glorifying the "good-natured, roistering, and brawling [Irish] individuals who get drunk, meet their friend, and for love knock him down" (Wittke, 1956, p. 245).

HEIGHTENED STATUS THROUGH HARD WORK

By leveling many of the loftiest members of American society, the Great Depression of the 1930s may have served to redeem Irish Americans. Empowered by strong faith, commitment to community, and the positive moral values of the Catholic Church, Irish Americans worked through this economic collapse. Irish Americans became known as hard working. For the most part, the Irish remained stationed in blue collar and service jobs, but they did those jobs well and honorably. At the same time, Irish Americans created community groups, labor organizations, and political parties that elected powerful government officials dedicated to improving the living conditions of middle- and lower-class citizens.

The post-Depression return of jobs to America meant better employment, higher income, and improved status. Emphasis on education aided assimilation and success.

By the mid-twentieth century, Irish Americans had all but disappeared as an overtly disadvantaged or despised group. In 1981, Andrew Greeley noted that the harsh nineteenth century stereotype of the incorrigible, irascible Irishman had largely vanished (Greeley, 1972, p. 5). The Irish American had been subsumed into the American mainstream. "If any immigrant group can be said to have merged into the American social structure to the point where neither they nor the host society any longer cares to dwell on presumed ethnic differences or to limit participation in any area of life because of them, this may be true of the Irish American," historian Marjorie Fallows said (Fallows, 1979, p. 4).

Perhaps. Yet some observers argued that even without overt anti-Irish discrimination, Irish Americans were systematically precluded from achieving true economic success in America. In 1976, Richard Stivers would still assert emphatically that "to the non-Irish world perhaps no behavior is more associated with the Irish than drinking" (Stivers, 1976, p. 75). Historians who argue that the Irish possess more than simply a *reputation* for drink cite early studies showing that the Irish are the ethnic group of Anglo Americans with the greatest tendency for drunkenness and alcoholism (Bales, 1944; Glad, 1947).

OLD MEDIA STEREOTYPES LINGER

An abundance of modern media accounts reinforces such research findings and the stereotype of Irish drunkenness. Database searches of major U.S. newspaper stories involving the Irish document that a preponderance of them deal with revelry and drinking. "Aside from the focus on violence in news stories, the other most common source of the Irish persona is entertainment; movies and television [are] both prone to leaving viewers with fast easy labels of the Irish...either as warring factions or as leprechaun stereotypes" (Feroze, 1994, p. A5).

For example, a 1994 story in the *New York Times,* titled "The Pub: A Center of Ireland in Exile," concentrated on a women's dart championship after which the "women got rowdy,...shook bottles of beer, covering the tops with their thumbs, and sprayed each other until their faces and blouses were soaked and sticky....They climbed up on the bar and ran up and down, shimmying and screaming for joy" (Louie, 1994, p. C1). The story reported that New York pubs bloomed alongside rising Irish immigration to the city and quoted these women as saying that their social life centered on the pub and drink. "The new immigrants," however, "resent the stereotype that portrays the Irish as heavy drinkers," the article said. Yet the only notable difference between this coverage and stories about Irish Americans at the turn of the century appears to be the gender of the joyous inebriates.

In another example, a 1993 *Newsday* column by an Irish American writer presents the excessive drinking, fighting, anger, and eventual police visits that punctuated the life of one Irish American's childhood as "the truth" about Irish Americans (Reel, 1993, p. 81). The columnist then acknowledged that such stereotyped portrayals of Irish Americans were not "politically correct" but should be viewed as one individual's efforts to challenge Irish Americans to achieve a "higher standard of behavior and responsibility."

Violence, cunning, graft, and intolerance also continue as prevalent themes in media stories dealing with Irish Americans. For example, a 1984 *Frontline* documentary, "The Old Man and the Gun," focused on Michael Flannery, who had been acquitted of conspiring to ship guns to the Irish Republican Army. In the rather unflattering and unsympathetic portrayal, viewers hear Flannery compare himself to George Washington and boast that he got away with pulling the wool over the eyes of the jury.

Or there's the 1990s coverage of conflict over the exclusion of gay marchers from St. Patrick's Day parades around the nation. In one such column by Anna Quindlen published in 1991, the author says sponsors of the New York parade have confirmed the stereotype of the Irish as "antediluvian bigots" by trying to exclude the homosexual contingent from the march (Quindlen, 1991, p. A25). This story appeared under the headline, "Erin Go Brawl." Another *New York Times* story, ostensibly focused on the Catholic church's view that press reports of the controversy were "bashing" Catholics, quotes a man who called the opponents of the gay marchers "terminal Donkey[s]" who had "barely risen from the primeval bogs of Ireland" and who epitomized Irish cruelty, stupidity, and hypocrisy (Steinfeld, 1991, p. 27). This is hardly the epitome of fair coverage.

Then there's the Jimmy Breslin column in *Newsday* comparing Irish and Italian Catholics, in which Breslin says Irish Catholicism is epitomized by "hate and meanness" (Breslin, 1991, p. 27).

NONMEDIA STEREOTYPES FLOURISH

Historians Margaret Fitzgerald and Joseph King have noted that American media are not alone in perpetuating negative stereotypes of the Irish.

Omissions and distortions in modern textbooks about the historic role of Irish immigrants to America also contribute to the American view that Irish Americans introduced little of value to American society (Fitzgerald & King, 1990, p. 313). These authors and others have criticized scholars who repeat and reinforce the popular image of Irish drunkenness and violence. "It is distressing that historians...are still parroting nonsense" about the Irish being obsessed and consumed by their unshakeable attraction to alcohol (Richardson, 1961). In fact, recent studies have indicated that alcohol consumption by adults in Ireland is roughly half that of adults in France and Spain. Another study of Irish immigrants to London found they drink no more than their British counterparts.

Yet, to a greater or lesser degree, the stereotype persists. And while it is easy—and accurate—to blame the media, the blame is not theirs alone because the images that injure are within us as well as around us. The stereotype of a drunken Irish American ape persists in magazines, movies, music, and news media certainly. But it persists there because it also persists in our minds.

We both consume and produce media messages. Each of us too often and too readily contributes to the perpetuation of stereotypes by relying on the efficiency of these exaggerated, overgeneralized, unfair, and hostile images to simplify our communications. We too frequently find it far simpler to evoke a stereotype than to engage in the detailed explanation and description necessary to fully and fairly represent the complex and unique individuals with whom we interact. As long as this is true, stereotypes will persist.

Part IV

GENDER STEREOTYPES

Chapter 17

WOMEN AS SEX PARTNERS

Kim Walsh-Childers

They are there while we wait to pay for our groceries, their cleavage spilling out of tight dresses, their taut bellies beckoning above low-rider jeans. They gaze seductively at us from women's magazines, spaghetti straps hugging their prominent collarbones, perfectly toned legs rising from brutally spiked heels or bare feet. In *Sports Illustrated*'s annual swimsuit issue, they display their athletic prowess—the astonishing ability to lounge, wet from saltwater or sweat, in impossibly skimpy swimsuits.

These are the mainstream media's images of women as sex partners. They are available—one might even say inescapable—at the local bookstore, grocery store, discount store, or library. In significant ways, they create expectations about how women should *be* as sex partners, instructing men and women, boys and girls how females should look to be considered desirable sex partners and how women can be expected to respond to men's sexual initiatives. Two types of stereotypes seem to exist, one primarily focused on how sexy women look and the other focused on what might be called sexual response.

LOOKS—WHAT IS SEXY?

First—and almost without exception in mainstream media—sexy women are thin. Whereas slenderness may be healthier than being overweight, the thinness portrayed as *sexy* almost always goes well below healthy body weight. The model in one current Bacardi rum ad offers a perfect example. Dressed in a bra-style top and low-slung jeans, the young woman is so skinny you can see the outlines of her breastbone and several ribs. The same is true of Elsa Benitez, one of *Sports Illustrated*'s 2002 swimsuit models. In one photo, showing Benitez perched on a fire escape, her ribs are prominent enough to be counted. The owner of a dog, cat, or horse that thin would be reported to the Humane Society.

Benitez and the Bacardi model may be somewhat extreme, but research shows they are not out of the ordinary. Owen and Lauren-Sellers (2000) found that anorexia-level body weights were the norm among Playboy centerfolds and other models. Nearly all *Playboy* centerfolds from 1985 to 1997, and 75 percent of female models described on agency Web sites, had body mass indexes of 17.5 or below—the American Psychological Association's criteria for anorexia nervosa.

A corollary requirement of thinness is the perfectly flat stomach—what *Cosmopolitan*'s May 2001 cover called the "Britney-Flat Belly," a reference to teen entertainer Britney Spears. In a May 2001 article touting midriff-baring fashions, *Cosmopolitan* makes the flat stomach requirement explicit with photos of Spears and other female singers and models, all displaying totally flab-free bellies. An information box in the article explains the requirement: "The ab-flashing phenomenon doesn't leave a lot of room for a mountainous midriff."

The second characteristic of the stereotypical sexy woman is cleavage and lots of it. In a February 2002 *Cosmopolitan* fashion spread, the magazine's fashion and beauty director is quoted as stating, "No Cosmo cover look is complete without cleavage" ("Cosmo Cover Style," p. 187). Even *Cosmo*'s dedication to cleavage seems to pale, however, in comparison with the models in *Maxim* magazines "Girl Gallery." In one gallery photo, model Kristy Swanson demonstrates a pose that, in most women, would hide their breasts completely—arms bent at the elbow in front of her bare chest, hands behind her neck—but at least half of Swanson's breasts are still visible. A similar photo of model Christy Taylor takes advantage of both position and water's magnifying effect. The swimsuit-clad Taylor is standing below the photographer in a pool, positioned so the water just covers her breasts. The photo reminded me of the melon-breasted Cream of the Crop character painted on the nose of a World War II bomber my father photographed while he was in the Air Force.

Advertising for breast enhancement products—now nearly omnipresent in women's magazines—claims to make cleavage available to every woman. Typical is an ad for Bloussant breast-enhancing tabs, whose manufacturer claims they will "stimulate your breast glands again, just like when you were a teenager." The ad shows a full-breasted woman in a lacy bra, her shirt unbuttoned to reveal how the product, supposedly, can "Increase Breast Size & Firmness...Naturally." An ad for the Bust Maximizer, which supposedly stimulates breast growth using electrical impulses, is even more blunt: "Because Size Does Matter" reads the headline, positioned across the cleavage of a woman who must wear a D cup or larger.

A third characteristic of the stereotypical sexy look for women is smoothness so extreme that, in many cases, it looks more like plastic than human flesh. In images of today's most popular female models, actresses, and singers, their legs, arms, midriffs, buttocks—in short, anything that's exposed other than their heads—are all free of any visible hair. Recent media hoopla over the Brazilian wax—a procedure in which technicians use depilatory wax to remove all of the hair from a woman's pubic and anal areas—demonstrates the extent to which the hairlessness norm has been accepted (Labre, 2002). Most images in mainstream magazines aren't explicit enough to depict a total lack of pubic hair, but a surprising number of images make it clear the models couldn't have much hair left. For instance, the cover photo for the 2002 *Sports Illustrated* swimsuit issue features model Yamila Diaz-Rahi in a red bikini that reveals nearly as much of her crotch as it does her breasts. She's seated, one foot tucked back toward her buttocks, the other flat on the floor in front of her. No stray hair is visible around the crotch of her bikini. In fact, most swimsuit fashion spreads offer numerous examples of suits cut either so low or so narrow in the front that almost any amount of pubic hair would show. The main photo for one *Cosmopolitan* article on hair removal shows a rear view of four women splashing nude into the ocean. Two have their legs far enough apart that any hair left between their legs would show; there is none.

Labre's (2002) article points out one particularly disturbing feature of the trend toward depicting adult women without pubic hair. As she notes, the growth of pubic hair is one of the earliest signs of puberty in girls; only prepubescent girls have no pubic hair. Articles about the increasing popularity of the Brazilian wax often include testimonial quotes from men acknowledging that having one's sexual partner look and feel like a genitally bare child is a major attraction. Labre cites a Salon.com article quoting a man whose girlfriend had had the procedure: "She made certain the lights were off and when I felt her it was like, oh my God, an unbelievably primal welling of emotion. First from the shock and then from the whole little girl eroticism of it. It's hard to describe. I guess it was like tasting forbidden fruit" (2002, p. 120).

Depicting adult women as children—and depicting young girls as sexual creatures—is one of the most unsettling trends in the portrayal of women as sex partners. Examples, unfortunately, are everywhere. For instance, one fashion photo shows two young girls in short dresses, leaning away from the camera over the top rail of a wooden fence. Their panties are visible in a way that's clearly meant to be tantalizing rather than cute. The same can be said about an ad with the headline "*la vida lactea.*" It shows a girl perhaps 5 or 6 years old lying back on what appears to be a bed. Her arms are stretched wide as if to welcome someone into a hug, and her legs are spread wide, too, showing her underwear below a gauzy dress. The look on her face is serious and intense, not frightened but not happy either.

The look, and the pose, are eerily similar to those in a photo from a *Maxim* magazine article on actress Tara Reid. The entire photo spread features Reid in gauzy, ruffled white lingerie. In one photo, Reid half reclines against a white background, wearing white panties and a see-through blouse that bares her midriff and most of her breasts. Her arms are spread wide, just like the little girl, and her knees are spread. When the two photos are viewed side by side—the little girl posed as a woman, the woman dressed as a girl—the message seems clear: The combination of childlike vulnerability and apparent sexual willingness are meant to make both sexually attractive. In other examples, adult models are shown in sexy poses while holding or surrounded by children's toys. Britney Spears' first *Rolling Stone* cover shows her lying on red satin sheets, wearing low-cut boxer-style shorts and a black halter bra. In one arm, she cradles a stuffed Teletubbies toy.

BEHAVIOR—WHAT SEXY WOMEN WANT

Another common characteristic of the portrayals of sexy women is that they make clear their sexual availability via poses, expressions, and other cues. *Cosmopolitan* cover models, for instance, seem to have a habit of hiking up one side of their skirt to display as much upper thigh as possible. (See the December and August 2001 and February 2002 covers for examples.) One of the models featured in the magazine's "Cosmo Cover Style" article (2002) is pulling down on the unsnapped waist of her low-cut leather pants. The *crotch shot*—a pose in which the woman is sitting or reclining with her knees spread apart so that the viewer's eye is drawn to her crotch—also is common. *Sports Illustrated* chose one for its 2002 Swimsuit Edition cover (described above). In one Bebe ad series, a model is sitting on the back seat of a limousine with her black lace–clad legs spread wide apart, one hand between them on the seat. On another page, the same model, wearing black satin hotpants and fishnet hose, straddles the drive-shaft tunnel. One *Maxim* "Girl Gallery" photo shows model Summer Altice wearing over-the-knee gold boots, knees spread wider than her shoulders. Her hands dangle in front of her crotch so that it's unclear whether she's wearing anything between the boots and the wide gold belt encircling her breasts.

Media portrayals often link images of women as sexually accessible with alcohol. One ad for Chambord liqueur, for instance, shows a woman lying on her side in a black evening dress. Propped up on one elbow, she holds a drink in one hand while the other caresses the bare chest of a man reclining behind her; his hand, propped on her hip, holds a bottle of Chambord. A current series of ads for Hennessy cognac seems to suggest that drinking the product—or buying it for women—will produce ménage à trois opportunities. The ads show two attractive women, a bottle of Hennessy, and the instructions, "Mix accordingly." One of the most offensive ads, for Cabo Wabo tequila, shows just a woman's torso, her hands covering (melon-sized) bare breasts and a large tattoo of the tequila bottle stretching from her low-cut bikini. She's holding a section of a lime between her breasts, so the juice drips down her belly. The headline reads: "Take Your Best Shot." Miller Genuine Draft's two-page *Sports Illustrated* swimsuit edition ad is a close competitor in offensiveness. The left page shows a bottle of the beer with the label ripped off, over the words "Your turn." The next page shows a woman in a bikini.

Linking alcohol to the promise of sex certainly seems problematic, but an even more disturbing trend is linking sexual attractiveness and violence. One fashion photo, for instance, shows a woman sprawled on the pavement in a shiny red evening dress. The color matches that of the blood pooled around her head. Another fashion shot shows a man apparently preparing to throw a woman off a high-rise building. What makes these horrible images most astonishing to me is that each one is a fashion spread for *women's* clothing.

STEREOTYPING WOMEN AS SEX PARTNERS— THE EFFECTS

Even if these images are intended merely to sell products, research suggests that they can create expectations about women's looks or behavior, with potentially serious negative effects. Some of the messages themselves are pretty offensive, it's the effects of the stereotypes that concern me. This section very briefly reviews some of the research about these effects.

Thinness. Numerous studies have linked exposure to thin-ideal media images to body dissatisfaction and eating disorder symptoms in women. Women who are heavily exposed to thin-ideal messages are more likely to accept the thin ideal and to exhibit greater body dissatisfaction and disordered-eating symptoms (Botta, 1999, 2000; Field et al., 2001; Harrison, 1997, 2000; Hofshire & Greenberg, 2002; Stice & Shaw, 1994).

Breast Size. It's surprising how little research actually has examined the relationship between media images of ideal breast size and women's satisfaction with their breasts. It seems fairly clear, however, that many women want larger breasts. Breast augmentation surgery is now the third most popular form of cosmetic surgery in women (Ward, 2001). A survey sponsored by the American Society of Plastic Surgeons showed that 14 percent of 18- to 24-year-old women and 17 percent of those 25–34 would like to change their breast size. In 2001 alone, more than 200,000 American women—including almost 2,600 who were 18 or younger—had implant surgery, 533 percent more than in 1992 (American Society of Plastic Surgeons, 2001). That doesn't take into account the unknown numbers of women who try all the other breast-enhancement products—herbal pills, lotions, pumps, and so on.

Why is this a problem? First of all, the amount of money women spend in the pursuit of larger breasts is considerable—more than $721 million in 2001 for breast implant surgery alone. Some might argue that there likely are better ways women could spend that much money. Second, although the current medical wisdom seems to be that implant surgery is not linked to subsequent diseases, there continue to be questions about implant-related risks, including the possibility that mammogram results will be less clear. Women who have had implants also are less likely to be able to breast-feed their babies successfully compared with nonaugmented women, even considering previous breast-feeding experience (Hurst, 1996; Neifert et al., 1990). This seems particularly ironic when you consider the argument that evolutionary forces have shaped human standards of beauty, in which case larger breasts likely would have been seen as evidence of the ability to nurture children successfully.

Sexualization of Children/Depicting Women as Childlike. Although the problem with this practice seems obvious, there doesn't seem to have been much research on the topic, perhaps for ethical reasons. One very disturbing study, however, found that male pedophiles often generated their own erotica from sources such as television advertising, catalogs featuring children modeling underwear, and similar sources (Howitt, 1995).

Linking Sex with Alcohol. It's not clear that anyone has specifically studied the impact of sexually suggestive alcohol ads on men's (or women's) behavior or attitudes, but it is clear that there are significant links between drinking—or even expecting to drink—and attitudes toward sexual coercion. University of Mississippi researchers have found that college men who listened to an audiotape depicting a date rape after consuming alcohol or expecting to consume alcohol took significantly longer to identify the inappropriateness of the man's sexual behavior toward his date. Those who drank rated the woman's sexual arousal significantly higher the first two times she refused sex (Gross et al., 2001; Marx, Gross, & Adams, 1999). The fact that even expecting to consume alcohol changed men's appraisal of the situation seems to suggest that expectations about drinking are linked to expecting sex, whether or not one's partner is willing. Messages like those in the Miller Genuine Draft "Your Turn" ad may be helping to create these expectations.

Depictions of Violence Toward Women. Again, the problem here seems fairly obvious. Statistics indicate that one woman is raped every two minutes in the United States, and domestic violence is the most common cause of injury to American women ("Violence," 2000). Exposure to media portrayals that objectify women, including those that are merely sexually suggestive, not violent, have been shown to lead to a greater likelihood of seeing women primarily as sex objects (Kalyanaraman, Steele, & Sundar, 2000). Research has shown that college-age men exposed to movies that include graphic violence toward women (i.e., *Friday the 13th* and similar "slasher" movies) express decreased empathy toward rape victims and less willingness to punish rapists (Dines & Humez, 1995).

Taken as a whole, the research seems to indicate about what you'd expect. Although there's no smoking gun proving that these stereotyped images cause women to starve themselves or have their breasts surgically altered or lead men to sexually assault either adult women or children, the studies do suggest correlations between exposure to media portrayals of women as sex partners and unhealthy attitudes and behaviors.

When I first wrote about this topic 10 years ago, I drew heavily on images and ideas I used in presentations aimed at helping women and girls negotiate the often misogynistic media environment. My perspective now is somewhat different, colored heavily by the fact that I've done much of the research and writing with my two young sons, ages three and five, playing in rooms nearby. As I look at these images—drawn from mainstream media, not pornographic Web sites or even the standard skin magazines such as *Playboy*—I can't help thinking about all the messages my husband and I will need to counteract to help our sons grow into men who have healthy, realistic expectations about girls and women.

In a recent focus group session I moderated, one young woman who was seriously contemplating breast implant surgery confessed that her boyfriend had offered to foot the bill. "He says, 'Of course I love you just like you are, but just think how great it would be if your breasts were bigger!' " she told the group. It's impossible to know exactly how much mass media images contribute to the development of attitudes such as this young man's. On the other hand, it's hard to imagine how the media's pictorial definitions of sexy women could fail to reinforce such attitudes, even if they originate outside the media. Parents hoping to raise either boys or girls who don't equate female sexual attractiveness with near-anorexic bodies, ample cleavage, easy sexual availability, and childlike vulnerability have their work cut out for them.

Chapter 18

WE'VE COME A LONG WAY MAYBE: AN ANALYSIS OF THE PORTRAYAL OF WOMEN IN SUPER BOWL COMMERCIALS FROM 1989 TO 2002

Bonnie Drewniany

Super Bowl Sunday is an undeclared national holiday. It's a day when half of America gathers around television sets to watch football and ads. Unlike a typical football event that caters to male viewers, the Super Bowl appeals to men and women of all ages, races, and incomes. Women represent more than 45 percent of the 130 million viewers who tune into the game (McCarthy, 2001). According to Nielsen Media Research, Super Bowls account for 9 of the top 15 shows in the history of American television (Nielsen, 2000). As a result, advertisers are willing to pay a super price. In 2002, advertisers paid $1.9 million for each 30-second spot.

Before the game airs, previews of the commercials appear in national media. After the game is over, media critics offer their views of the commercials. As a result of all of the media hype, viewers have come to expect great commercials and, therefore, don't leave their television sets when a Super Bowl ad comes on the air. In fact, according to a study by Eisner & Associates, a Baltimore agency that tracks consumer attitudes, eight percent of adults who watch the Super Bowl do so just to see the commercials—that's 10 million viewers (Schwartz, 2000). TiVo reported portions of the 2002 Super Bowl broadcast were paused or replayed an average of 44 times per TiVo household. It wasn't the game that saw the most use of the Trickplay feature of the TiVo device—it was the ads (Welsh, 2002).

ABOUT THIS STUDY

For this study, the 1989 to 2002 Super Bowls were recorded, then the games were zapped and the commercials were coded. Local commercials were eliminated to avoid regional bias.[1]

Commercials for movies and television programs were eliminated because they often include scenes from the shows, which would unfairly skew the results. Repeats of commercials were also eliminated. Two coders recorded the product advertised, as well as the sex, age, race, and role of the person shown in the commercial. Any coding differences were resolved by watching the commercial together and discussing the factors used to determine how to code the ad.

Fourteen years of Super Bowl commercials were divided into two 7-year groups, 1989–1995 and 1996–2002, to see if differences existed in the way women were portrayed. A total of 585 commercials were coded—288 in the 1989–1995 period and 297 in the 1996–2002 period.

RESULTS

Men Scored the Most Points in Both Time Periods

Men had major roles in 164 commercials that aired between 1989 and 1995, while women had major roles in only 38 commercials. In the second time period, men had major roles 185 times and women had major roles just 56 times.

Men Score Big with Women in Earlier Commercials, Fumble in Later Years

Women were shown stroking men's faces, surprising men with kisses and hugs, and jumping into their arms in commercials for Gillette that were a staple of Super Bowls between 1989 and 1993. As the Gillette commercials state, it's "the best a man can get." Other early commercials continued the sexual aggression theme. Wearing nothing but a man's shirt, a woman wraps her legs around the back of a cafe chair in a 1989 spot. She whispers to the camera, "If you think I look good in this Van Heusen, you should see Jeffrey." In a 1994 commercial for Norwegian Cruise Lines, a woman caresses a man who is under an outdoor shower. She slides her hands down the man's chest and kisses him as the water trickles over their bodies.

Men weren't so lucky in the 1996–2002 ads. Cedric the Entertainer illustrates men's botched attempts at romance in two recent Budweiser spots. In 2001 Cedric has a gorgeous date on the sofa. He goes to the kitchen to grab a couple of Bud Lights and does a victory dance because he thinks he's about to score with the woman. His dancing shakes up the beer and when he opens the bottle, the beer sprays out and soaks her. It's pretty clear he's not going to score. The next year Cedric helps his buddy Paul find the right words to pick up a hot woman at a bar. Cedric feeds the lines: "My name is Paul. You've got beautiful eyes. I'd love to take you out sometime." Everything is going great until Cedric attempts to pay for his Bud Light and asks the bartender "How much?" Paul repeats this line to the woman who kicks the daylights out of him.

Female Stars Are Starting To Shine

Female stars were almost nonexistent between 1989 and 1995, but have a stronger presence between 1996 and 2002. Sixty-one commercials featured male celebrities, but only nine commercials featured female celebrities in the early years.

Bo Jackson, Michael Jordan, Joe Montana, Shaquille O'Neal, and other male stars appeared in multiple Super Bowl commercials, but only one female star, Cindy Crawford, appeared more than once during the first time period. The male stars were shown bouncing basketballs off of Mount Rushmore, racing up the stairs of skyscrapers, and doing other superhero feats, whereas Cindy was a mere sex object. In her 1992 Pepsi debut, Cindy, dressed in high-cut shorts and a low-cut top, slithered past two awestruck boys, and slowly drank a Pepsi. A glamorous Cindy returned in a 1994 spot, wearing a skimpy red sequin dress and dangling earrings. As she went into a Pepsi deprivation tank she announced, "I'll do anything for science." After she was deprived of Pepsi for one month, she came out of the tank as Rodney Dangerfield. What's the message? Is it, "Drink Pepsi, get respect?" Or is it, "Drink Pepsi, look sexy?"

Female celebrities had a stronger presence in the 1996–2002 Super Bowl commercials. Supermodels Vendela, Naomi Campbell, and Kathy Ireland appeared in 1996 commercials for Baked Frito-Lays. Tyra Banks, Bridget Hall, and Cindy Crawford admire a newborn baby in a 1997 spot for Pepsi. That same year Tyra Banks also appeared in an ad for Nike, and Cindy Crawford donned a postage stamp–size dress for Cadillac. Ali Landry wowed viewers with her acrobatic ability to catch Doritos in her mouth in commercials that aired between 1998 and 2001. Fran Drescher appeared with Donald Trump to hawk the Big New Yorker pizza from Pizza Hut in 1999. Also in 1999 an M&M candy dodged swimsuit-clad Halle Barry's poolside advances. And two Pepsi spots in 2002 featured Britney Spears singing her way through different generations, wearing everything from a 1950s Marilyn Monroe–style wig to a 1990s Madonna-like red leather dress.

It wasn't just supermodels and singers who had super power between 1996 and 2002, however.

Visa showcased female athletes in two commercials that aired in 2000. One featured a female pole-vaulter and the other featured women's synchronized swimmers spelling out VISA to promote the company's 2000 Olympic sponsorship. A Charles Schwab ad, which aired in 2001, showed Sarah Ferguson reading a bedtime fairy tale to her daughter. At the end of the story Ferguson explained to her daughter that if things don't end happily ever after, she'd need to fend for herself. Fergy should know.

Stereotypes Still Prevail

Women love to shop and can be bought with a diamond or a fancy cruise. Guys love football, beer, and women (in that order). A spot for Ourbeginning. com, which aired in 2000, depicted a hair-pulling horde of brides to be in a cat fight over invitations. A 1998 spot depicted a guy stuck in the women's department while his girlfriend shops. He follows power cords under a skirt carousel and finds a bunch of other guys watching football and drinking Bud Light. Also in 1998 a spot for Royal Caribbean reminded guys, "You've watched 22 weeks of football. Better make it up to her. Before you get traded." And in 2001, diamond retailer Zales sponsored pregame programming to plant the seed that Valentine's Day was coming up in two weeks.

Another stereotype found in recent Super Bowl commercials is the notion that women are hopeless romantics and men are hopeless at romance. Two Bud Light commercials in 2002 showed men failing at romance. In one spot, a woman tries to coax her husband to bed by telling him she's wearing a teddy but she gets no response. She tells him she has satin sheets on the bed—still no response. But when she tells him she has a cold Bud Light he rushes up to the bedroom, tears off his clothes, dives for the beer, and slides off the satin sheets, right out the window. Another Bud Light spot showed a woman spending a lot of time selecting the perfect Valentine Day's card while her boyfriend grabs a card as an afterthought as he's buying a six-pack of Bud.

Women as Victors: A Step Forward (Maybe)

Oxygen Media launched its women's Web and TV network during the 2000 game by showing newborn girls tossing their pink hats to the floor. A

2001 Visa ad showed a woman vacuuming her apartment as her couch potato of a boyfriend tells her she's missed a spot. She obliges by sucking him up in the vacuum and then taking out the trash. This Visa spot reflects a genre of *power babe* commercials in which the newly acquired power of women comes at the expense of men (Svetkey, 1994).

Jiggle and Flesh: A Step Back in Time

Victoria's Secret come-hither models busted out all over to promote a live Web fashion show in 1999. That same year a security guard fantasized about his dream jobs in an ad for Hotjobs.com. In one scene he's an executive whose secretaries message his back (and his ego). In another scene, he's a Laundromat attendant and is surrounded by hot, come-hither women. In another scene he's a scientist cloning female go-go dancers.

Even female cartoon characters and puppets flaunt their cleavage and legs. And if they're not sexy, they want to be. Miss Piggy, clad in a low-cut black evening dress, was nearly seduced by a handsome guy until he tried to hog her Baked Lay's potato chips in 1997. Two years later MasterCard featured cartoon characters to illustrate the things a credit card can buy. Mr. Magoo needs contacts, Yogi Bear needs a treadmill, and Olive Oyl needs a Wonderbra. And in 2000, guys whistle at the green M&M candy as she walks down the street and yell things like, "Baby, you are looking swe-e-e-e-t!"

Older Men Continue To Have Power; Older Women Are Starting To Show Strength

Older men were authority figures in Super Bowl commercials that aired between 1989 and 1995. An older chairman was shown giving a speech to stockholders in a commercial for Coopers & Lybrand in 1993. A real chairman, Lee Iacocca, pitched Chrysler in 1990. Another commercial in 1990 featured an older New York Life insurance agent chatting with his long-time customer. Being an older man can even be sexy, as Paul Newman proved when he raced a toddler-sized scooter against a zillion-horsepower dragster in a 1990 American Express commercial and won.

Being an older woman wasn't quite so glamorous, however, in the earlier years. If an older woman was not portrayed as a loving grandmother, there was a good chance she acted weak, senile, or persnickety in a Super Bowl commercial during the 1989–1995 period. A 1989 spot for Toyota featured Margaret, a gray-haired, female driver who confessed, "My palms used to sweat when I had to get on the highway. Now, with my Camry V6, I just punch it." One of Margaret's older female passengers responded, "Yeah. Punch it, Margaret!" as the car pulled in front of a huge truck. Although the commercial showed older women who felt empowered, it played on the fears of older people and made them seem like cute little old ladies. Would the ad have worked if we substituted teenage boys for the older women? Probably not.

In a 1994 spot, a feisty old lady grabs a bag of Doritos back from Chevy Chase. However, Chevy got the last word, "Tough year. Good chip," as he bit into a Doritos chip. And the audience got a chuckle when an older woman got a thrill from a vibrating bed in an ad for Lee Apparel, which ran in 1995.

Older women were no longer the brunt of the joke in commercials that aired between 1996 and 2002. A 2000 Tropicana ad showed an older woman running and doing chin-ups and cartwheels. A woman celebrated her 100th birthday in a commercial for Accenture, which aired in 2001. That same year MasterCard showed 10 older people (men and women) vacationing on a private island. An older female judge starred in a Hotjobs.com commercial in 2002.

Boys Will Be Boys and Men Will Be...Women???

In a 1993 Federal Express commercial, a male boss pretends to be a female secretary on the telephone as he tries to check on the status of a package. That same year Bugs Bunny dons sexy women's clothing and a blonde wig to distract four thugs from scoring points in a basketball game in a Nike commercial. As the players turn their heads and whistle, Bugs flashes a sign to the viewers that reads, "Silly, aren't they?" The next year, Charlotte Hornets' Larry Johnson dressed in drag as Grandmama, complete with pearls and a flowered dress, in a parody of the *Wizard of Oz,* for Converse.

Men continued to wear dresses in Super Bowl commercials that aired between 1996 and 2002. A voluptuous blonde babe at the high-school reunion turned out to be a man in a Holiday spot that ran in 1997. In 1998 Michael Richards (*Seinfeld*'s Kramer) dressed as a society matron in a Tommy Hilfiger commercial. RuPaul, dressed in a blonde wig and low-cut dress, said meetings are a drag in a spot for WebEx.com that aired in 2000. A 2002 spot showed men crammed into little black dresses to sell Docker's pleated pants.

People with Disabilities Play a Disappearing Act

While many commercials featured athletes doing Superhuman feats, few showed people with disabilities. Ray Charles endorsed Diet Pepsi from 1991 to 1993, and, in a 1990 spot that ran before the kickoff, he starred in the "ultimate blind taste test" in which Diet Coke and Diet Pepsi were switched. Only two other spots in the earlier period showed anyone with a disability. A 1991 Nike spot showed a man racing in a wheelchair as part of a montage of athletes. That same year McDonald's showed Americans that people with disabilities can work and be productive citizens in a heartwarming commercial narrated by an employee named Mike, who has Down's syndrome.

Two spots that aired during the 2000 game showed superheroes who have disabilities, and both starred men. Muhammad Ali was shown shadow boxing, fighting against time, to promote WebMD.com. That same year a commercial for Nuveen was set in the future and featured Christopher Reeve walking. Three women walk with Reeve in the commercial, one is walking with a cane, and the others have slight limps. This was the first—and only time—a Super Bowl commercial showed a disabled woman. The following year a male quadriplegic artist was shown painting while holding a brush in his mouth in an ad for Cingular.

Men Are Still the Voices of Authority

One would hope to hear an equal number of male and female announcers, but the power of the male voice came across loud and strong in 196 commercials whereas female announcers were heard in a mere 19 spots in the first period. The second period wasn't much better, with male voice-overs in 186 spots and female voice-overs in just 19 spots. The lack of women announcers is particularly noteworthy when one considers the fact that frogs, lizards, dogs, dolphins, and other creatures frequently talk in Super Bowl commercials.

CONCLUSION

Women have made some progress in the past seven years. Still, we have a long way to go. For every step forward, we take a step back. In 2000 Oxygen's "I am Woman" ad was followed by an OurBeginning.com spot that depicted brides to be in a cat fight over invitations and a World Wrestling Foundation spot that featured beauty pageant contestants wrestling for the Miss Congeniality title.

Although it's great that female stars are starting to share equal airtime with male celebrities, one can't ignore the reality that the majority of these women are supermodels, which seems to give advertisers permission to show human versions of Barbie dolls. But hey, it's not their fault; these women are just naturally gorgeous, right? Yeah, right.

And who can forget the Victoria's Secret babe-o-rama display in 1999? Or the fact that women are rarely used as announcers? And what's the deal with all the men in dresses? Is it a way to show how liberal advertisers have become or is it just a creative way for them to show cleavage and curves?

Bottom line is we may have come a long way, but we still have a way to go.

Part V

AGE STEREOTYPES

Chapter 19

THE CHILD AS IMAGE: MEDIA STEREOTYPES OF CHILDREN

Kathy Brittain McKee

An obligation of any image gatherer—photographer, illustrator, or video-grapher—is to remember that pervasive images portrayed in print and broadcast media foster stereotypes. Whether it is news footage or adver-tising photographs, images on a page or screen become images in a viewer's mind. Because of the power of these images, viewers need to understand that each camera lens sees and defines truth differently, that each photo is, at best, one statement of what may be multiple truths, and that a photo may be an idealized vision held by the one with the lens.

Adults may be taught to discount photos in advertisements, to look at dif-ferent networks' videotapes, and to look at how different photographers shot the same story. But children come to visual messages without learned skep-ticism. Consequently, media images of children geared primarily for chil-dren have a great deal of power to define reality. And certainly media images of children have the ability to establish the *truth image* for children as they see themselves in the images portraying children on screen, on billboards, or on the page. Those depictions may also establish the truth image of children for noncritical adults who look without discernment or skepticism.

HOME ALONE, AND I LOVE IT—THE CHILD AS ADULT

A child is left behind by his parents, forgotten in the bustle of getting luggage, family members, and tickets together and heading for the airport.

A child, who though frightened a bit by the circumstance, suddenly finds himself perfectly able to cope in the adult world—all it takes is a little imagination, according to these films. This is a child who really needs no adult supervision or protection; from what he's learned on television and films, he's ready to face the world on his own, even though he's not yet a teenager. He can outwit skeptical adults who don't quite believe his self-sufficient act or burglars intent on harming him and taking his possessions.

He is comfortable with modern technologies. He can manipulate audio-tape to acquire a usable adult voice and can devise numerous weapons using electricity and household items. He has a thorough understanding of adult patterns; he can check into an upscale New York hotel, order room service, and hail a cab without a problem. Buying groceries on his own or attending a midnight Christmas Eve church service is no challenge. He even overcomes his fear of the frightening next-door neighbor after exercising some adult recognition of the importance of relationships when he's cut off from his traditional family members. Of course, this is all made easier by the upper-class surroundings in which he and his family live.

The child featured in the original *Home Alone* and its sequels (the franchise is now up to its fourth installment, *Home Alone 4,* a 2002 made-for-TV production) offered viewers an opportunity to laugh at the idea of a child alone. But these portrayals echoed an emerging theme: the self-sufficient child who is in charge of his (or much less frequently, her) world, who, while he/she may live with adults, actually functions as the adult in charge by manipulating the unwary and unwise adults into doing his or her bidding. Take the children's roles in the films *Problem Child I* and *II.* Their activities are self-chosen and self-determined. In each film, the adult care-givers are shown as powerless, and the children rule the family.

Within this video environment, the stereotypic portrayal of students again shows them functioning alone as the power brokers in the adult environment. The children, not the parents, run the home, and apparently the adults are unable to establish boundaries. At home or at school, these children operate within self-defined boundaries, supported by the best in material possessions and technology but not supported by adult caretaking. They, too, like the child in *Home Alone,* show a world of childhood in which no harm comes to the children left alone because they are presented as more clever, wise, and inventive than the few adults pictured in their worlds.

This scenario of child in charge is certainly not new to American audiences, but the absence of adults who offer some limits is somewhat disturbing. The world of the *Dennis the Menace* comic strip—not the movie—was seen by parents who could sit their child in the corner for time out and have him or her reflect on obedience. Even in the comically erratic world of contemporary television's *Malcolm in the Middle,* Malcolm's parents are present and offer some guidance. Imagine *The Brady Bunch* children without the omnipresent parents or housekeeper, or the Cleaver household where "the Beav" would be left alone while his parents pursue expensive vacations. A sharp contrast exists between today's film portrayals of the child as adult and the former image of child as dependent.

What's the impact of the new portrayals? Certainly, it is too simplistic to point to a direct relationship between such video images and the child-neglect cases painted by the media as "Home Alone" cases. Yet the fact that media chose to paint these neglect cases with that stereotype offers evidence that a distinctive stereotype of child left to function as adult has been created and accepted as a distinct image within our popular culture. Equating real-life unsafe situations for children with the comic mayhem of the movies illustrates the kind of social and psychological impact such a stereotype can have.

The fallacy of this stereotype is apparent. Children who are left home alone are at risk; children who are expected to act like adults are at risk. Children may believe they can or should be able to manipulate the environments of their home or school in the ways their video counterparts do. And some adults may excuse their lack of nurturing and caretaking of children and the lack of established boundaries by arguing that such nurturing is obsolete and unnecessary. The *home alone and I love it* stereotype can then become more than comic relief; it can provide tragic excuse.

ALL THOSE CARTOON HEROES AND ONLY THREE POWER PUFF GIRLS—THE CHILD AS GENDER STEREOTYPE

Sugar and spice and everything nice.... The formula for a perfect girl? Not when you add a dose of Chemical X, which yielded the Cartoon Network's *Power Puff Girls,* Blossom, Bubbles, and Buttercup. The creations of Professor Utonium, who added the chemical to the sugar and spice formula, are three powerful, flying kindergarten girls who protect the city of Townsville from the evils of villains such as Mojo Jojo, the Amoeba Boys, the Gangrene Gang, and Fuzzy Lumpkin. Though the girls have some resemblance to Charlie's Angels, they more strongly resemble the other legendary superheroes such as Superman and Batman—and creator Craig McCracken allows them to go against the gender stereotypes of cartoon girls. They are the ones summoned by the adult male mayor for help when the city is threatened. They successfully battle male and female opponents—and still find time to attend kindergarten. There is no shrinking violet in this trio.

But contrast the Power Puff Girls with another of the Cartoon Network's popular offerings, *Dexter's Laboratory*. Dexter, a short, square young boy, is a superscientist working in a completely stocked lab conveniently provided in his bedroom. His scientific schemes are most commonly interrupted or damaged by the interference of his sister, DeeDee, who is a tall, willowy ballerina interested only in art and dance—and bothering her brother. Often the plot lines involve Dexter using his scientific knowledge to thwart his sister's wishes, or her desire to torment her younger brother causes her to interfere and damage one of Dexter's experiments. Clearly, in this laboratory, the brother is smart and scientific, and the sister is beautiful and artistic.[1]

Such a gender-stratified world is not unusual within children's entertainment, educational, and advertising media. Nancy Signorielli's *A Sourcebook on Children and Television* (1991) and F. Earle Barcus' *Images of Life on Children's Television* (1983) offer comprehensive surveys of the ways children are depicted in television programs and commercials. Their studies suggest that the world of children on television is primarily a male world. More male than female characters appear (only 16 percent of major characters were female), and the males depicted carry the action as female characters offer support (Barcus, 1983). A more recent study by Thompson and Zerbinos (1997) found that boys and girls are aware of the differences in gender portrayals on cartoons and may make assumptions about appropriate behaviors and careers based on those differences.

The world within children's books was described similarly by a 1972 analysis of characters in Caldecott Medal and Newberry Award winners and Little Golden Books top sellers. The study conducted by Weitzman, Eifler, Hokada, and Ross (1972) found that males were consistently overrepresented in illustrations, titles, and content of these books.

Certainly, things may have changed within the contexts of certain media and certain programs. Some elementary textbooks and *Sesame Street* show a greater diversity of sexual roles and empowerment, although Witt (1997) argues that some bias is still present in elementary readers. Stereotypic gender portrayals still abound, however. Consider the advertisements for children's products. Little girls play with dolls or bake in their ovens. Little boys play with trucks or run in the yard. Little girls want fashion accessories for their doll models to wear in their three-story townhomes; little boys want action accessories to use with their action figures as they conquer villains or battle terrorists. Little girls want to dress like mommy or the latest MTV teen idol. Little boys want to dress like their sports heroes. Female students sit in neat rows and listen while males play on educational computers.

What do these images of male and female children suggest? First, children who watch or view such images learn early the physical and emotional traits traditionally associated with their genders; the packaging of such traits into a 30-second spot, an animated cartoon, or a full-page magazine advertisement merely accentuates the overall message. Having a boy at the computer keyboard while a girl points to the screen tells a different story than if the poses were reversed. Showing boys playing baseball or soccer and girls cooking perpetuates traditional boundaries for gender-linked behaviors, boundaries that have been expanded in society but that apparently have not frequently been stretched within the world of advertising images. Even the ads that show less gender-specific behavior are viewed within the context of sex-typed advertising, which may mute their impact.

The prevalence of male characters or models is troubling in light of the untrue representation of reality it presents. In reality, females outnumber males in the U.S. population, unlike the character world of children's media. In reality, females are not necessarily passive; neither are males necessarily active. Males do not always solve the problems, or females always cause them. The self-image and self-esteem of both male and female children may be affected by the disparity between the pictorial representation and the real world. Perhaps one day it will be the female character in the cartoon—not Dexter or Professor Utonium—who occupies the laboratory, rather than the playroom or the practice hall.

IF YOU'VE SEEN ONE, YOU'VE SEEN THEM ALL— THE CHILD AS VICTIM

The advertisements are always centered around the images: large, dark eyes peering wistfully at the camera, ragged clothing, skinny limbs, swollen bellies, skin of all hues. The text or voice-over speaks of malnourishment, neglect, and war. These are the children of want, used as promotional devices for various charitable groups seeking to raise money for aid projects. They may come from South America, Africa, Southeast Asia, or Appalachia. They somehow represent a vast horde not photographed who also stand in need.

The photographic images offer some truth: some children are victims. Yet the distortion occurs and the stereotype is created when *only* children are represented and when it is the *only* way children of some world regions are photographed and depicted. Repeating the pictorial stereotype of the child as war or poverty victim enables audiences to ignore the problems represented because they either have become desensitized to the horror of the image or too overwhelmed by the frequency of its appearance to believe anything can change. Finding different, even jarring, ways to portray the truth visually may help overcome the problems of stereotyping, and audiences may be willing to respond to the new images with more active viewing, looking beyond the surface visuals to prevent the response of turning the page or flipping the channel to avoid dealing with the real issues.

ONLY A PRINCESS IS VISIBLE—THE CHILD AS SEXUAL OBJECT

Imagine a world where a 15-year-old girl discovers that she is the heir to the throne of a democratic monarchy in Europe. While she ponders whether she will accept the responsibility of the post, her grandmother, the queen, makes it plain that change will be required—and the change does not apparently involve learning a new language or conquering sophisticated political understanding. Is that the real concern prior to any announcement about the royal ties? The adolescent girl has curly, thick hair, bushy eyebrows, and wears dark-rimmed glasses, and socks and clunky shoes with her school uniform. She claims she is "invisible" on her campus to all but her two closest friends, and when her invisibility is threatened, she throws up.

Is there a solution for this political dilemma? The young teen must be redone, complete with straightened hair, thinned eyebrows, nylons, pumps, and contact lenses. Other changes are mandated, too, but they apparently pale in comparison with the physical transformation necessary to become the princess—and, indeed, to gain any attention from her schoolmates. The transformation does succeed, and the beautiful schoolgirl flies off to her new castle home after having gained "leg-popping" kisses from her boyfriend.

This updated Cinderella scenario was depicted in the film *The Princess Diaries,* Disney's Buena Vista Entertainment 2001 release set in contemporary San Francisco. Though the film apparently does seek to satirize the shallowness of the high-school cheerleaders and campus heartthrob by showing their rudeness to the shy teen turned into a suddenly famous princess and to overlay a theme of social responsibility, the underlying message is clear: physical beauty and sexual attractiveness are the key attributes if a girl is to overcome being invisible.

Too often the images of children and adolescents found in film, television, and advertising carry the explicit message that one's worth is equated with one's attractiveness and, indeed, one's sexuality, even as a child. The Barbie generation learned early from commercials and magazine ads that despite the professional costume one might be wearing—a business suit, a doctor's uniform, or an astronaut's suit—it should be worn over a stunning figure. And, obviously, the most important costumes one could choose are a wedding dress or a swimsuit. Commercial viewers learn that the best way to promote a soft drink is to portray young boys on a playground or a sidewalk daydreaming or bantering suggestively with a supermodel. It may even be argued that the waiflike appearance of many sitcom and drama female stars and fashion models suggests a blurring of the line between sexually active adults and sexually attractive children—perhaps to perpetuate the stereotype that beauty can only be found in the young.

Media critics have questioned the depiction of children and adolescents as beautiful and sexual objects for years, and Congress and the Supreme Court continue to grapple with the legal limits that can be placed on extreme portrayals. Little ethical discussion of the involvement of children in soft- or hard-core pornography is necessary—it's difficult to justify ethically any such depiction. Yet the depictions of children in sexual ways in mainstream media are much less certain. Is it necessary to be beautiful to be visible?

Linking the sale of goods or the promotion of attendance to a sexual motif does not rely solely on the use of children's images, certainly. Yet when it does, there is potential for great harm. Elementary-age children are not developmentally ready for sexual involvement, and misleading media images may unwittingly prompt such activity. Sexual exploitation of children reduces them to objects. The features and benefits that combine to make up a successful marketing plan for a product or service should not have to include the sexualizing of a child. Abandoning the stereotype of child as sex object will allow room for more creativity from marketers, advertisers, and writers, as well as from photographers, illustrators, and videographers.

The pictures of children carry a special power when they are geared toward an audience of other children who may lack the training or ability to make critical judgments about manifest or latent meanings. These images also affect the adults who view the images passively, apathetically, or noncritically. For that reason, those who capture the images and plan their use must be mindful of the truth images they are creating, and they must exercise critical judgment about the impacts of those images and the stereotypes they create in light of the inherent values represented by the children within the images. Audience members must also learn to look critically at the images of children, to see behind the stereotypes in order to find more of the reality present and to offer appropriate responses to the stories told by the pictures.

Chapter 20

GROWING OLD IN COMMERCIALS: NOT ALWAYS A LAUGHING MATTER

Ted Curtis Smythe

Using humor in commercials is often very effective, if appropriate to the topic and done well. But some advertisers don't understand that humor can backfire, especially when one uses stereotypes to make the humorous point.

Midas, the auto repair shop company, hired Cliff Freeman & Partners of New York to produce four spots in 2002 intended to use humor to catch the audience's attention. The ads succeeded in getting the audience's attention, more than the agency and advertiser expected, with one spot touting a lifetime guarantee on Midas shocks and struts. The spot featured a manager telling an old woman of the guarantee. She replied, "Lifetime guarantee? That's great! ... What can you do with these?" she asks, removing her blouse to reveal sagging breasts. The suddenly chagrined Midas guy looks down and replies, "There are limits to what we can do" (Garfield, 2002, p. 57).

Advertising Age's Bob Garfield (2002) expressed disappointment with the agency and the spot in his ad-review column. "The whole episode is just plain embarrassing. Not just on taste grounds, or even selling effectiveness. On top of everything else, the spot isn't even funny" (p. 57). But, of course, the editors at *Ad Age* couldn't resist the chance to take part in the poor taste with a headline that read "Innocence Lost: Midas *Sags to a Low With Geriatric Nudity Spot*" (italics added).[1] It's as though the headline writer didn't read the column.

A somewhat similar ad in Scotland also created a furor ("Pensioners," 2000). AG Barr, a soft-drink group, ran an ad in which an elderly woman threatened someone with a kiss if they did not give her their Irn-Bru. The public was not amused.

SHIFTING DEMOGRAPHICS

The Baby Boom is aging. By 2005 those 55 and over will make up 23 percent of the population. Fifty-five years old is traditionally considered the end of middle age, but boomers are changing that; they are transforming old age. "Many of them are doing what might be expected of the most self-absorbed group in history: They are denying that it [old age] even exists" (Hammond, 2001). The thought process involved in this transformation has caused one author to coin a word to describe the perceived state of affairs. "As they reluctantly migrate out of youth, boomers have already begun to engineer a new and vastly extended middle period of life: middlescence," writes Ken Dychtwald, author of *Age Power: How the 21st Century Will Be Ruled by the New Old.*

Lest one think of the older generation as a bunch of consumers indulging themselves without thought for others, though, the opposite seems to be the rule—so far. As one specialist in the medicine of aging has put it, "Another myth about the old is that they only require help, they don't provide help. But older people are contributing . . . not just to families but also to the community. They have the time, the patience and the experience" (Frase-Blunt, 2001). Many of the elderly are volunteers serving community needs, from soup kitchens, to reading programs for children in need, to helping peers who are sick. This last is the most demanding and difficult for seniors, and not all are willing to face up to their own mortality, but for those in good health and who are selfless, it is a valuable option (Frase-Blunt, 2001).

MEDIA PORTRAYALS

Perhaps the Midas ad was an anomaly; perhaps few ads today really portray the elderly in negative terms. Depending upon when studies of media images and of advertising took place, the picture of the elderly is decidedly mixed. Before the mid-1990s, the advertising industry had not done all that well in portraying the elderly in advertising, though some improvement was shown in the early 1990s. More recent advertising seems to be more sensitive to stereotypes of the elderly. Studies of advertising images of seniors before the mid-1990s tend to identify negative advertising portrayals whereas more recent studies show a tendency toward more positive images. Ad images of the aging also depend on where the advertising appeared and what it was promoting.

Three studies conducted in recent years reflect this trend. A study of advertising for financial services between 1997 and 1998 in two national news magazines and financial magazines demonstrated a tendency to portray the services of the companies as a means to prepare for a "life stage of active leisure underwritten by necessary security" (Ekerdt & Clark, 2001). Similarly, a study of travel brochures for middle-aged and older consumers in the United Kingdom revealed photographs of a 50-plus lifestyle in which retirement was a time to be enjoyed with opportunities for new discoveries. The people portrayed were healthy and active (Ylanne-McEwen, 2000).

Finally, advertising images of aging women also reflected positive changes. Advertising portrayals of menopausal women in Canada reflected a 180-degree turn from the sorry plight of such women portrayed in 1980s pharmaceutical literature and the mass media (Kaufert & Lock, 1997). Today "the menopausal woman has well-maintained teeth, hair, and skin, and is shown exercising, playing with grandchildren, and lunching with friends. Usually smiling and glowing with fitness, the women in these pictures suggest a discrete but well-enjoyed sexuality" (Kaufert & Lock, 1997).

EFFECTS OF NEGATIVE PORTRAYALS

Perhaps the improving portrayal of seniors reflects the vision of baby boomer advertising copywriters and account executives who are approaching that age themselves. In any case, what is the problem with negative stereotypes, other than the fact they hurt the feelings of a large class of people? Well, there are three problems created by negative stereotypes of the elderly: they affect people's perceptions of the elderly, which can be life threatening; they affect the elderly's perception of their own mental and physical health, which can have a negative impact on that health; and they cause most advertisers to ignore an increasingly important segment of potential consumers, which can affect both the elderly and those companies.

Stereotypes of the Elderly

Studies show the general population stereotypes older people as handicapped, limited in what they can do, rigid in their thinking, and expensive to employ because of high health-care costs. These images are inaccurate

(Deets, 1994). Though health problems increase with age, insurance expenses do not necessarily climb because most elderly workers have fewer dependents to cover, may have retiree health benefits from earlier careers, and have Medicare if they are over 65. In addition, older workers generally are more experienced and have a strong work ethic (Deets, 1994).

Medical Stereotypes

Stereotypes of the elderly on the part of health-care providers may create life-threatening problems if health-care practitioners misperceive a medical condition as a natural effect of aging. For example, if a dementia caused by AIDS is mistaken for Alzheimer's disease, the effects can be dire. The first condition usually can be treated, but proper diagnosis and early treatment are essential. Dementia caused by Alzheimer's disease, on the other hand, cannot yet be treated successfully.

When doctors in health-maintenance organizations consider the elderly to be too old for life-prolonging medical procedures, another problem occurs. The decision about whether to use such procedures is best left to the individual patient, but many individuals do not get to make that decision because various health-care options are never presented to them.

Inaccurate Self-Perceptions

Stereotypes can be accepted by the aged themselves. Several studies have shown that negative portrayals of aging may affect the elderly by increasing the memory problems that usually are a part of the stereotypes. Even humorous comments that seniors make among themselves, which are ubiquitous on the Internet, can have negative effects (Friedman, 2000). "Seen it all, done it all, can't remember most of it" is one of the lighter examples. Or, "Life is like toilet paper, the closer one gets to the end, the faster it goes."

A group studying the effects of words on the health of the elderly has found that negative messages and stereotypes increase blood pressure in older Americans, which has a deleterious effect on cardiovascular health ("Negative Views," 2000). In contrast, positive images actually reduce cardiovascular stress.

Ineffective Marketing

Many advertisers have ignored the opportunities a growing old-aged cohort means to their products. Obviously, products directed toward the elderly, such as vitamins, medicines, and exercise devices, have often targeted the aged in their advertising. But products that otherwise would be of use and enjoyment to the elderly often neglect this age group in favor of targeting a younger audience.

Advertisers who ignore the vast number of baby boomers (born about 1945 through 1964) now entering old age do so at their peril. Boomers are changing the shape of old age, just as they have changed every other age group as they passed through it. In this case, aging boomers are quantifiably, psychologically, physically, and economically different from the generations that preceded them. "Older Americans today are more affluent, healthier, and better educated than seniors in times past" (Mitchell, 1998). Higher percentages of these older Americans already think their life is more exciting than their predecessors did, and their income is growing, especially as women in the workplace make more money than previous generations.

RESPONDING TO AN AGING POPULATION

Housing developers are already reflecting the changes wrought by the boomers as they moved into their 50s and beyond, and more changes are in the works in anticipation of the large number of retirees who will soon be finding a home where the sun shines most of the days of the year. Del Webb, a builder of planned developments for retirees, has found that many boomers "relocate near their home, [but] half of the ones who move change states for full or part-time living during retirement, with Florida, Arizona and Texas" the most popular destinations (Bryant, 2001, Sec. 5, p. 2). Their homes are larger and include home offices, since many boomers will work part-time in retirement.

Some advertisers also are reaching out to the graying consumer. Chairman/President August Busch III, himself 64, pushed the Anheuser-Busch companies to start marketing to older adults. Why?

> The country's median age and number of people entering their golden years are on the rise; older people drink more than previous generations; many of them have the heavy wallets that make them a marketer's dream. In addition, they have a zest for life, no intention of acting their age, and a social calendar full of events with libations. (Chura, 2002, p. 4)

Perhaps the Midas commercial truly was an anomaly among commercials and advertisements. Still, we may not yet have reached a golden age in advertising, in which images of the elderly are positive rather than negative. As the boomer generation moves further into old age, advertising can be expected to reflect this change in demographics. Advertisers who don't recognize the costs of negative portrayals and the benefits of positive images will miss many opportunities to reach a growing and very viable group of consumers.

Part VI

PHYSICAL STEREOTYPES

Chapter 21

THE INVISIBLE CULTURAL GROUP: IMAGES OF DISABILITY

Jack A. Nelson

Any television viewer knows that when a maimed or hook-armed character shows up on the screen, it's a good bet that he will end up one of the bad guys. At least that's the way it often works out in movies and on the small screen, with villains such as Dr. Strangelove and Dr. No both sporting hands and forearms of black leather. In fact, such evil characters join a long line of media portrayals that show those with disabilities as people to be feared or pitied—and avoided.

Usually persons with disabilities are characterized as victims who possess undesirable social skills and personal qualities. In addition, J. Donaldson (1981) found a conspicuous absence of persons with disabilities in even incidental roles on television, thus giving the impression that disability is not a significant part of mainstream society. When depictions of disability are present, they are usually accompanied by what Donaldson (1981) calls "some sort of stress, trauma, overcompensation, character flaw, or bizarre behavioral tendencies."

Villainy has long been associated with abnormality. Fictional villains of the last century were often marked by physical disfigurement, and we must remind ourselves that even into the last decade one of the most-watched television programs of all time was the final episode of *The Fugitive*. In this finale of the long-running series, the innocent doctor, who had been hounded week after week as a suspect in the murder of his wife, was able to prove that the real murderer was a one-armed man he had been pursuing the whole time. Such stereotypes are burned deeply into the public consciousness by centuries of portrayals of those with disabilities as tainted, with deformity of body usually associated with deformity of spirit.

These stigmatizing stereotypes have persevered through the centuries but now are coming to be questioned and replaced by more realistic representations in the media. Sociologists have examined the effects of such negative television and feature-film representations. Yet it seems obvious that inappropriate and inaccurate presentations of persons with disabilities tend to stigmatize them in the public mind.

The electronic media, of course, are even more powerful than written literature in shaping our views of others. It is perhaps not comforting that the power of television to mold attitudes was shown convincingly in 1978 (Mankiewicz & Swerdlow, 1978). Indeed, the persuasiveness and efficiency of television commercials are by themselves strong evidence that the medium is the most powerful institution in our society today.

A PATTERN OF STEREOTYPES

Observers have noted that stereotypes of handicaps in film and television fit a pattern. These major stereotypes are listed below.

The Disabled Person as Victim: Telethons

Fund-raising telethons are one of the pervasive events on television, which, on a particular weekend, may fill more than 50 hours with appeals for funds to benefit so-called victims of some disease or other. These programs feature tearful pleas from Hollywood stars, along with a mix of heart-rending requests from those with the targeted disability. Most common are wide-eyed children asking for money to support further research of their particular disease or condition.

These telethons are popular, probably because of the star appeal. But disability activist groups have opposed them because they perpetuate the image of those with disabilities as objects of pity. Those featured are usually shown as childlike, incompetent, needing total care, nonproductive, and a drain on taxpayers. It is rare that such telethons feature those who manage to live happy and productive lives despite having the featured disease. They rarely point out the accomplishments of such people. "Disabled people are not characterized [in telethons] as a social minority with civil rights but as victims of a tragic fate" (Longmore, 1985a).

Perhaps the most famous of these telethons is that sponsored by actor Jerry Lewis, the annual Labor Day Muscular Dystrophy Telethon. It is the pity approach to fundraising that most irks those who use wheelchairs to navigate through their daily lives. On May 20, 2000, Lewis told CBS News correspondent Martha Teichner, "I'm telling about a child in trouble. If it's pity, we'll get some money. I'm giving you facts. Pity. You don't want to be pitied for being a cripple in a wheelchair? Stay in your house."

CBS News was criticized when it rebroadcast this interview a week before the 2001 fundraiser without the offensive words contained in the last two sentences. A spokesperson for CBS explained that in light of Lewis' apology and his statement, "I admire people with disabilities," the tape was edited "out of fairness to him." However, Harriet Johnson, a lawyer from South Carolina with a neuromuscular disease, said CBS should have aired the example of "shocking bigotry" because many may believe Jerry Lewis never used the derogatory term "cripple" for those who use a wheelchair (Lester, p. 93).

Journalists are also guilty of using pity in feature stories on occasion. When Mary Johnson, then editor of *The Disability Rag,* a disability advocacy publication from Louisville, Kentucky, visited a journalism class at the University of Minnesota, she reminded journalism students there that reporters who solicit pity for people with disabilities do more harm than good. When shown a text that recommended stories showing the disabled triumphing over great odds, she moaned at one of the examples. "One of the most god-awful 'heartwarming cripple' stories I've ever read," she said. Her point was that maudlin news stories reinforce images of passivity that some disabled people have of themselves, and they reinforce that image in the public mind ("Editor Wins," 1998).

For years Mary Johnson has cajoled and badgered editors about their coverage of those with disabilities. She has had some success in persuading editors to eliminate such demeaning and stereotypical words and phrases as *victim, cripple,* and *confined to a wheelchair* from their newspapers' coverage.

The Disabled Person as a Hero: "Supercrip"

Triumphing over great odds is the theme of one of the mainstays of all the media in portraying those with disabilities. The common heartwarming story is of someone who faces the trauma of a disability and, through courage and stamina, rises above it or succumbs heroically. Television especially thrives on this fare—which on the face of it seems favorable to anyone with a disability. The battles of these people seem heroic, such as *The Terry Fox Story,* the account of a young Canadian who lost a leg to cancer and hopped on one leg across his huge country to raise money for cancer research.

In the disabled community, however, such dramas are regarded as "supercrip" stories that take away from real disability issues. The focusing of public attention on the heroic struggles of a few—the "disability chic" approach—diminishes the much-needed attention to access, transportation, jobs, and housing issues, and to the movement to improve the status of all those with disabilities.

"Sure, Fox's story raised money for cancer, and sure, it showed the human capacity for achievement," says actor Alan Toy, who walks with a brace and has appeared in television shows ranging from *Airwolf* to *Trauma Center,* "but a lot of ordinary disabled people are made to feel like failures if they haven't done something extraordinary. They may be bankers or factory workers—proof enough of their usefulness to society. Do we have to be 'supercrips' in order to be valid? And if we're not super, are we invalid?"

The Disabled Person as a Threat: Evil and Warped

Conflict and suspense are central to most movies and television shows. Usually, this means a threatening, evil character whose very presence implies danger for the protagonist. Modern screens abound in portrayals of villains whose evil presence is exemplified by some obvious physical limitation—a limp, a hook for a hand, a black patch over the eye, a hunchback. One of the most recent examples was the character played by Samuel L. Jackson in M. Night Shyamalan supernatural thriller, *Unbreakable* (2000). Jackson plays Elijah Price, a mysterious and ultimately evil art gallery owner who uses a wheelchair. These portrayals play on and reinforce subtle and deeply held fears and prejudices. It would be naive to think these attitudes, which have been nurtured through the years by Hollywood portrayals, do not carry over into attitudes toward others with similar limitations in real life.

The Disabled Person as Unable To Adjust: Just Buck Up!

In recent years television programs have often featured the person with a disability who ended up maladjusted, unable to handle the trauma of his or her problem. Simply put—and the shows put it very simply—these people are bitter and full of self-pity because they have not yet learned to handle their disability.

Most of these shows feature a confrontational scene in which the protagonist, usually a friend or family member, sets the pitiable character straight. "Just buck up and take control of your life" is the usual message. There is no mention made of social prejudice or the role of social programs in helping alleviate the problems. Almost always the nondisabled person is shown to understand the problem better than the one with the disability. For instance, in an episode of *Night Court* during the 1980s, the young judge, Harry, is asked on a date by a young woman who has lost her legs. When he turns her down because he is too busy, she is devastated, so he naturally sets her straight. The problem, he tells her, is all in her attitude, not in her legs. A few minutes later she walks in on artificial limbs that she had with her all the time, smiling now. All she needed, it seems, was Harry's insightful advice.

Such messages imply that persons with disabilities don't really understand their own situations. Others provide these insights. Therefore, says this myth, those with disabilities need guidance because they are unable to make sound judgments themselves.

The Disabled Person as One To Be Cared For: The Burden

One consistent portrayal of those with disabilities is that of the frail person who needs to be cared for, the burden on family and society. Foremost is the view that this is a duty that needs to be faced. At the same time, the implication is that a burden is difficult to bear and must be avoided. Thus the portrayal dehumanizes those with disabilities. As a dramatic device, this depiction is often used to show the noble intent and generosity of those who furnish the care, which makes the disabled person little more than a prop rather than a human being capable of interacting with others to the profit of both.

This treatment is familiar from Johanna Spyri's 1881 novel *Heidi*, whose title character is hired as a companion to the "rich little cripple" Clara. Through the loving attention of Heidi, Clara gets well. In reality, Clara's role exists to show the virtues of Heidi. Tiny Tim in Dickens's *A Christmas Carol* serves the same function.

The Disabled Person as One Who Shouldn't Have Survived

One of the most sobering portrayals of those with disabilities comes under the heading of the better off dead syndrome. This reflects the attitude that those with a serious disability would really be better off if they hadn't survived. It echoes the belief that anyone with a serious physical impairment cannot live a fulfilling and happy life and, therefore, might as well not be alive.

During the 1980s, several dramas reflected this attitude: the play and movie *Whose Life Is It, Anyway?*, the television movie *An Act of Love,* and the play *Nevis Mountain Dew.* In each of these, quadriplegics and paraplegics beg to be assisted in suicide because they say their lives are not worth living. A rather frightening subtext in these dramas is cost efficiency: in a time of spiraling medical expenses, it costs a fortune to keep people alive who would be better off dead anyway.

This portrayal also deals with the fear and loathing some people feel for those with handicaps. For many, the sight of serious physical disability is an unpleasant reminder of their own mortality and vulnerability. Longmore (1985b) suggests that this view is reflected in dramas that show disability alienating a person from society and depriving the individual of self-determination. Death is shown as preferable, partly because it relieves society of the problem of dealing with the long-term needs and rights of those with disabilities. The chilling implication is that this attitude is a step toward justifying euthanasia for those whose lives—in someone's judgment—are unworthy of existence.

These distorted portrayals appear over and over in dramas that fill our living rooms almost every night. Only in recent years have attitudes changed to balance the stereotypes with more accurate and individualized depictions.

TELEVISION PORTRAYALS

One of the interesting findings of sociologists is that on television the lives of people with disabilities are obviously empty. People with disabilities are excluded from important roles as husbands and wives, as fathers or mothers. One survey showed that two-thirds of television characters with disabilities were single, even childlike, often victims (Zola, 1985). Thus, power and strength were denied them. Their lives centered on their disability.

Another study of 85 half-hour prime-time television shows noted that, although what were called handicapped characters were sometimes seen in major roles, they seldom appeared in incidental roles (Donaldson, 1981). In fact, in the entire study not one handicapped character appeared in a minor role except in juxtaposition to other handicapped characters. None were visible in groups of shoppers, spectators, jurors, customers, or workers. Handicapped people were thus invisible among the thousands of people in the background. Indeed, considering how often disabled people have been shunted out of sight, it is not remiss to call them *the invisible minority*.

In the above study, Donaldson (1981) found that positive portrayals appeared less often than negative portrayals. In the rare positive portrayals, those with a disability were shown valiantly struggling against a dominating facet of their life such as blindness or paralysis. In a sense these portrayals are somewhat positive, but they also strengthen the stereotype that the disability is the central focus of a person's life. What was absent was the portrayal of a person who lived a full and rich life in which a disability was an incidental facet—a successful lawyer or professor who happened to use a wheelchair, for instance.

Just as important, Donaldson (1981) reported those with disabilities were seldom shown living their lives in interaction with those who did not have disabilities. The absence of positive portrayals that belie stereotypes and depict comfortable interaction between handicapped and nonhandicapped people suggests that prime-time television is not exerting a significant influence in shaping positive societal attitudes toward individuals who are handicapped, nor is it facilitating comfortable relationships by providing models of interaction (p. 415).

As might be expected, Donaldson (1981) found that those with disabilities were often shown in extremely negative roles. When they were shown as evil threats to society, the negative portrayals of the handicapped presented their disabilities as only incidental to the plot. In other words, their disabilities were not shown to dominate their lives, as was the case in the positive portrayals.

One recent example that perhaps goes against the stereotype is the character of Stevie in the Fox television comedy, *Malcolm in the Middle*. Stevie is one of Malcolm's genius classmates, has asthma, uses a wheelchair, and is involved in Malcolm's misadventures just as any of his friends. Craig Lamar Traylor, who doesn't use a wheelchair in real life, plays Stevie. Ironically, he "loves gymnastics and hopes to one day be a gymnastics teacher."[1] But before too much praise is heaped on the writers of the situation comedy, it should be noted that when Malcolm first resisted getting to know Stevie, Malcolm's mother exclaimed, "You're going to be friends with that crippled boy, and you're going to like it!" (Peyser, 2000).

THE RISE OF THE MEDIA ACCESS OFFICE

One positive influence at work for the disabled is a group known as Media Access Office (MAO), which has operated since 1978 on the Hollywood scene to exert quiet pressure in favor of the disabled. Made up of approximately 250 actors and actresses with varying disabilities, the group advocates the use of actors with disabilities to portray characters with disabilities and more normal treatment of people with disabilities by writers, producers, and directors of movies and television. They particularly encourage roles in which the disability is seen as incidental. For instance, former MAO Chairman Alan Toy recalls a commercial he made in which he portrayed an ordinary businessman carrying a briefcase and walking on crutches, which is how he normally gets around. "If only we could get that image of normality projected more," he says, "the more audiences would get used to seeing us as human beings, and the less aghast they'll be when they meet us in the street" (Wood, 1989).

MOST IMPORTANT INFLUENCES: STEREOTYPES IN THE MIND

Of all the stereotypes about the disabled that plague the public, none is so insidious as the one that dwells inside the mind as a result of being exposed to all the media stereotypes. That is, the accumulation of all the movie portrayals, the television characterizations, and the real-life experiences that all of us are exposed to during our lives results in expectations of how those around us will act, given certain signals.

The signals of disability, such as a wheelchair, an unsteady gait, or a tremor, elicit reactions that one might expect from some unenlightened people. Take the example of someone portraying a person with cerebral palsy, for instance. In preparing to star in the film *My Left Foot,* Daniel Day-Lewis strove to get inside Christy Brown's head. To accomplish this, Day-Lewis used a wheelchair, was lifted in and out of cars, spoke with impaired speech, and had someone feed him in some of Dublin's best restaurants.

"It's strange what happens, even though everybody knew who I was and what I was doing," he explained later. "When people see someone in a wheelchair, their attitudes change. . . . They start treating you like a child." He found that people talked around him instead of to him. He had become one of the invisible disabled (Longmore, 1990).

The average person walks around with certain expectations—the pictures in his or her head—and changes come slowly. But changes are taking place in how society treats the disabled and how they are portrayed in the media. These improvements are partly fueled by the Americans with Disabilities Act of 1990 and by a growing awareness that those with disabilities are first of all people and only secondarily defined by any impairment they might have.

CHANGES GOING ON

The past two decades have been times of monumental social change in American society. The growing awareness of the rights of minority groups has been one of the hallmarks of this century. Granted, deeply held archetypal fears and attitudes do not shift 180 degrees in a few years, but it has become apparent in the last two decades that attitudes toward those with disabilities are undergoing some major shifts. The culmination, of course, came with the 1990 passage of the Americans with Disabilities Act, which guarantees a new deal for those with disabilities, particularly in such matters as access to public accommodations and employment. Perhaps what is most important is that passage of this act signals a change in public expectations and attitudes regarding this important group.

Media signals also indicate that the traditional stereotypical treatment is no longer acceptable. Major changes have occurred that reflect new attitudes. Indeed, new attention is being given to the representation of the disabled in the media. For instance, in the fall of 1991, NBC's *Reasonable Doubts* broke new ground by featuring a deaf actor, Marlee Matlin, as a deaf district attorney who delivered some lines in sign language. Later, Matlin went on to appear in the popular NBC series, *The West Wing*. Most importantly, in both roles her character was not predominantly a disabled person, but a professional who incidentally was deaf. Similarly, in the popular, early 1990s ABC series *Life Goes On,* the central character was acted by a young man with Down's syndrome. Perhaps most noticeable was the growing number of users of wheelchairs who showed up on television ads in the early 1990s as normal people doing the things that normal people do. In the growing catalog industry more and more models are appearing in wheelchairs for retailers such as Eddie Bauer and Nordstrom.

Since the early 1980s, ads featuring disabled people have appeared on television, but by 1992 the roles were more frequent and more varied. Many of these showed workers in law offices and high-profile places such as newsrooms carrying out routine tasks without fanfare like everyone else in these offices. In other words, the message is that those with disabilities have a place on the job like everyone else. Similarly, in an ad for Target discount stores, a photograph of a child in a wheelchair was included in a sales circular. This occurred at the suggestion of a vice president of marketing whose daughter was born without a left hand. He approved the ad with some trepidation, but the reaction of the public was enthusiastic. The company received more than 2,000 letters of praise, he said ("People Gain," 1991).

A new spirit of self-identification and activism has emerged among the disabled community to describe those with disabilities. In recent years, disabled people have recognized themselves not as victims of disease and disablement, but as members of a stigmatized cultural group, discriminated against, segregated, and denied the opportunity to participate equally in the good life of normal society. In an effort to change perceptions inherent in traditional pejorative language, they have fashioned neologisms such as *differently abled, physically challenged,* or *handicapable.* In 1991 the National Cristina Foundation announced a $50,000 prize for the best word that put a positive spin on describing those with disabilities. From 50,000 entries, the winner was "people of differing abilities," which brought hoots of derision from those in the disabled community (Johnson, 1987). While none of these terms has won wide acceptance, the growing move among the disabled to describe themselves proudly as an in group is suggested by the trend to describe others as TABs (temporarily able bodied) or ABs (able bodied). Such emerging language is a sign of the refusal of those with disabilities to accept the role of a stigmatized group who are only marginally recognized as human beings.

At the turn of this century, there is promise of vast improvements for the disabled community. New public attitudes seem to be building, but many of the prejudicial attitudes of the past that view the disabled as invisible or unworthy of notice remain. The influence of television and movie portrayals of disability can hardly be overestimated when we consider the huge audiences they draw. The impact of these images in changing stereotypes in the public mind cannot be overstated. But in a world where the information superhighway is taking a more and more central role in people's lives, there is also vast promise of what these powerful institutions can do to alter attitudes.

Perhaps most encouraging of all, those in the disabled community have emerged with stronger images of self-empowerment. As they view themselves differently, the world may follow.

Chapter 22

THE BLIND IN THE MEDIA: A VISION OF STEREOTYPES IN ACTION

Lee Wilkins

The human animal is distinct from other mammals in many ways. One of the most profound is the neural capacity of the human occipital lobe, or visual cortex—the portion of the brain that processes visual information. Metaphors of vision have imbued the capacity to see with qualities of myth and mental acuity. Presidents are expected to have vision; Cassandra saw the future and was cursed. These cultural understandings provide multiple meanings to an important symbol: the seeing or blind eye. Sight is fundamental to what and who we are as people.

The media, of course, are symbol transmitters. That is the focus of this chapter. Common themes about the blind drawn from Western literature and art will be applied to a selected sample of the more than 200 films in which the blind have been major characters. News accounts from the print and broadcast media from 1993 and again in 2001 will then be examined to determine if and how journalists use these same culturally based symbols in reporting the news. The chapter concludes with suggestions for improving journalistic performance.

THE CULTURAL MEANING OF BLINDNESS

"In the popular mind, the concept of blindness simultaneously juxtaposes two contradictory notions: that the loss of sight dooms most of its victims to lifelong dependence, but that it also rewards a few of them with super human powers. Out of these twin beliefs have grown the stereotypes of the blind beggar and the blind genius" (Koestler, 1976, p. 7).

Blindness is one of Western literary culture's most common dramatic conventions. The Egyptians were the first civilization to try to medically treat sightlessness, and the Greeks introduced the metaphor of blindness into Western literature. The blind poet Homer wrote that Odysseus was deprived of sight for his cruelties. Oedipus tore out his eyes to atone for his patricide and incest. References in Western religious tradition link blindness with evil or sin. Lot's wife was blinded when she looked back at Sodom. The Talmud and other Hebrew commentaries refer to the blind as the living dead (Koestler, 1976). Although some Eastern cultures found an economic niche for the blind (for example, in Japan they worked as masseuses), almost all ancient Western civilizations sanctioned euthanasia for the physically deformed. The Romans borrowed from the Greeks the tradition of putting blind children by the side of the road in specially constructed baskets where they were left to die.

However, not all of the fallacies and fables about blindness are negative. Positive images also are interwoven into its mystique.

> These positive stereotypes include the notion that other senses can compensate for sightlessness, that blind people possess the desirable character traits of spirituality, patience, and cheerfulness, and that they have superhuman command of the non-visual senses. Humor by a blind person is often interpreted as an example of extreme fortitude or an attempt to hide sorrow. (Monbeck, 1973, p. 10)

These stereotypes are sometimes accepted by blind people themselves.

Helen Keller, who is discussed more extensively later in this chapter, noted the logical inconsistency of such persistent cultural views. She found "a medieval ignorance" concerning the blind.

> They assured me that the blind can tell colors by touch and that the senses they have are more delicate and acute than those of other people. Nature, they told me, seeks to atone to the blind by giving them a singular sensitiveness and a sweet patience of spirit. It seemed not to occur to them that if this were true it would be an advantage to lose one's sight. (Monbeck, 1973, p. 4)

Stereotypes of the blind are among the most evocative in contemporary culture and many are laden with visual messages. Among the most common are as follows:

The blind are deserving of sympathy and pity. Buddha taught that mercy should be extended to the deformed, and the Koran makes some exceptions for the blind. Christ asks for pity for the blind.

The blind are miserable. Seeing double or having to squint are common motifs in folk literature. Think of the animated cartoon character Mr. Magoo. The Greeks considered blindness the worst of misfortunes, and the Bible and Greek literature curse people who misdirect the blind. Kipling, Conrad, and D. H. Lawrence all developed blind characters that were miserable.

The blind live in a world of darkness. Milton linked blindness with darkness, as did Dickens. However, many medically blind people report a grayness of vision, while many legally blind people retain some useful sight.

The blind are helpless and useless. Perhaps no better encapsulation of this stereotype can be found than in Deuteronomy 28: 28–29. "May the Lord strike you with madness, blindness, and bewilderment; so that you will grope about in broad daylight, just as a blind man gropes in darkness, and you will fail to find your way."

The blind are fools. Deception or trickiness by the blind is a concomitant stereotype that Shakespeare, in *King Lear,* and Milton, in *Samson and Delilah,* employed.

The blind are beggars. The blind as unfortunate homeless people is a recurring motion picture stereotype. Few motion pictures, however, feature blind homeless people in significant roles. However, in 1991, Juliette Binoche played a young homeless woman going blind and struggling to survive in *Les Amants du Pont-Neuf* (*The Lovers on the Bridge*). In 1999, the little seen *Bobby G. Can't Swim* featured a character, Popeet, a blind street peddler.

The blind are compensated for their lack of sight. That the blind have the gift of prophecy is part of the mythology of Turkey, Korea, and Russia.

Blindness is a punishment for past sins. Traditional Christian teaching has linked physical disability with original sin. Folk literature in India, Sweden, Finland, Greece, Spain, Brittany, and among some Native American peoples repeats this view.

The blind are to be feared, avoided, and rejected. Psychologist Gordon Allport notes the image of a blind man is a linguistic "label of primary potency" (Monbeck, 1973, p. 83).

The blind are immoral or evil. Stagg in Dickens' *Barnaby Rudge* and Pew in *Treasure Island* typify this stereotype. Paradoxically, an evil person is neither helpless nor useless.

Thus, blindness represents a complicated cultural stereotype simultaneously including strong positive and negative elements. Research suggests many of these stereotypes are "cross-cultural in nature, indicating some commonality in man's experiences with and reactions to blindness and blind people" (Monbeck, 1973, p. 63). Their universality makes it more difficult to counteract them.

THE BLIND IN FILM

Blind people have been major characters in more than 210 films, and their dramatic qualities have enhanced and puzzled critics for as long as the medium has existed. For example, in the film trilogy of *Star Wars,* fighter pilot Hans Solo loses his sight as a result of carbon freezing–induced hibernation. He regains his sight off camera, a plot irregularity that was noted by many critics of the wildly successful series. Cinematic renderings of the blind have also borrowed liberally from stereotypes developed in literature. Gene Hackman's hilarious portrayal of the innocent blind hermit in Mel Brooks' *Young Frankenstein* owes a debt to the dramatic rendition of the legend in James Whales' *Bride of Frankenstein.* In *Oh Brother, Where Art Thou,* the late 1990s adaptation of the *Odyssey,* the Cyclops (acted by John Goodman) is portrayed as a malevolent salesman who is blind in one eye.

Scholars and critics agree there are certain touchstone films about the blind worth examining. Two of the earliest films to employ blind characters, Charlie Chaplin's *City Lights* and W. C. Fields' *It's a Gift,* illuminate opposing stereotypes. Two other films from the 1960s, *The Miracle Worker* and *Wait Until Dark,* demonstrate an evolution in dramatic technique and in cultural understandings. Two more recent films, *Scent of a Woman* and *Contact,* provide insight into contemporary thinking.

Although the era of sound motion pictures had begun when Chaplin made *City Lights,* the director and star chose to keep the film silent. This decision, which has been critically acclaimed, gives even more power to the imagery Chaplin, as the Little Tramp, chose to capture on camera. The plot itself focuses on two cultural understandings: traditional stereotypes of the blind as innocent and an enlightened view of blindness as a curable malady.

The Little Tramp falls in love with a beautiful, blind flower girl. The young woman, with encouragement from the tramp, believes him to be wealthy, a delusion Chaplin encourages as he attempts to raise money for an operation to restore her sight. He succeeds, and much of the comedy in the film centers on the travails Chaplin must endure or overcome in his fund-raising endeavors. In the final scene, the girl discovers the identity of her benefactor, producing one of Chaplin's most poignant on-screen moments.

Innocence is one of the major themes of many Chaplin films. The blind flower girl embodies an almost ethereal quality, enhanced by her beatific expression and her total acceptance of the Little Tramp at all stages of the plot. She is better than most other people, has qualities of patience and spirituality, and seems to divine the Tramp's innocent core. Yet, she is helpless and must rely on others. Her occupation is superfluous in American culture, and she is so trusting that the actors and director had a delicate line to tread between enhanced perception and foolishness. The blind flower girl in *City Lights* represents ethereal beauty coupled with helplessness and emotional insight. Her character employs multiple stereotypes for dramatic effect.

If Chaplin used this film to discuss the concept of innocence, then W. C. Fields' work represents experience, using a bumbling and irascible blind character to further the plot of *It's a Gift*. Small-town grocer Harold Bissonette (Fields) is harassed by family and customers alike. In a memorable five-minute encounter, Fields must wait on a blind man who enters the audience's frame of vision by smashing a glass window with his cane. The character wears a bowler and dark glasses, walks hesitantly and only with assistance, and stereotypically breaks glass, upsets store displays, and is generally cantankerous. In addition, he's hard of hearing, a disability that also renders him foolish. It is only as the blind customer, Mr. Merkle, is leaving the store—again smashing another glass window with this cane—that Fields tells another customer that Merkle is the house detective at a local hotel. Fields then guides the blind detective to the street, assuring him there is no traffic. The audience's last glimpse of Merkle is a long shot where he wanders across the street, dodged by multiple emergency vehicles.

Fast-forward three decades to Broadway, where two successful stage plays were adapted equally successfully for the screen. *The Miracle Worker,* starring Patty Duke and Ann Bancroft, re-created the play to critical acclaim. The film, and particularly Duke's portrayal of Helen Keller, provides one of the least stereotypical portraits of the blind in popular culture. In fact, one critic reacted so badly to the lack of stereotypes—he would not accept that Keller had been as stubborn and as difficult as the film suggested—that as part of his review he read both Keller's and Sullivan's books about their experience. He wrote, when "I got around to looking up the sources...I find that the movie is accurate literally, that Helen was indeed a holy terror and a spoiled brat" (The miracle worker, 1963).

It is difficult to estimate the impact Helen Keller, popularized in a Broadway play, a film, her own books, and her life's work, has had on popular understanding of the blind. She remains a heroine to many for whom blindness represents an obstacle overcome by enormous personal courage, tenacity, and a fine intellect. The underlying issues of Keller's struggle for self-sufficiency, her grasp of the power of an idea, and her stalwart individualism also resonate deeply in American popular culture. Myth resonates within myth. Keller, who also overcame deafness, may embody an almost unachievable ideal, representing as she does values far outside the traditional thinking about physical disability. But like the real life it was based on, *The Miracle Worker* also provides an antidote to negative stereotypical thinking.

Wait Until Dark was equally influential, but within the filmmaking community. In this 1967 psychological thriller, Audrey Hepburn plays a blind woman who, for reasons the plot leaves completely unclear, becomes trapped in her New York apartment with three murderous thugs and a doll filled with heroin. Hepburn levels the playing field by knocking out the apartment lights. The resulting action is filled with visual messages of blind people tumbling over furniture, the thugs groping and stumbling through the apartment, and camera work where weapons seem to flash out of nowhere, playing upon the audience's perception of blindness as blackness and as filled with unpleasant surprises. Hepburn eventually foils her attackers, primarily through trickery. Some critics wondered why such an intelligent woman would not have thought to send for help earlier in the incident (a problem with the plot of the play, as well).

Wait Until Dark plays stereotype against stereotype. Hepburn is alternately helpless and capable, quick thinking yet groping in an environment she should know well, clearly a better person than the thugs who attack her, yet able to succeed only by tricking them.

The blind also became protagonists in several films in the 1990s, among them *Sneakers,* Disney's *Wild Hearts Can't Be Broken,* and *Places in the Heart.* Two of the most successful were *Scent of a Woman,* which earned star Al Pacino an Oscar, and *Contact,* a film based on astronomer Carl Sagan's book by the same name, in which a research astronomer played by Jodi Foster befriends Kent Clark, a blind colleague.

Scent of a Woman gains dramatic force by playing off traditional stereotypes. Pacino portrays a dissolute and depressed former Marine officer who, through his own bull-headedness, blinds himself. He has saved his disability checks to fund one extravagant weekend at New York's Plaza Hotel, which includes wine, women, and suicide. The tension in the film is provided by the high school military cadet Pacino finagles into accompanying him to the city. The young man objects to Pacino's plans to end his life and spends the weekend convincing this unpleasant and often unfeeling character that death is not a preferable option to living sightless.

The character Pacino plays represents many of the traditional stereo-types. He is maladjusted, he is useless in terms of earning money, he needs the help of a sighted person to get around, he is unpleasant, and, depending on individual interpretation of his interactions with his family, could also be considered evil. Blindness has rendered him morose. Even the film title borrows from stereotype: Pacino can no longer recognize women visually but he can sniff them out.

Three visual messages dominate Pacino's performance. First the actor appears blind without many awkward physical cues. Second, while Pacino does need a cane and an arm to walk around, his bearing is that of a former military officer. Third, there's the tango, perhaps the most writ-ten-about scene in the film. Pacino, having smelled out a lovely young woman, dances a forceful tango with her, never missing a step, never letting his partner out of reach, and never letting on that he is doing this as a blind man. In this one scene, Pacino's character contradicts the stereo-types that dominate the plot. The tango provides the filmgoer with a vision of what Pacino might have been, a reason to be sympathetic with him, and a visual message of what the blind can accomplish that is star-tling for its similarity to what viewers would expect from the sighted (and coordinated).

It is this vision of normalcy that pervades *Contact*. Here the audience sees not the idealized vision of Helen Keller but rather the normal accom-plishments of a character whose blindness takes second place to intellect, friendship, and the ability to contribute in a world where accommodation is accepted but does not replace individual effort. Some stereotypes linger. For example, it is the blind character, Dr. Clark, based on real-life physicist Kent Cullers, who first hears (the stereotype of one sense com-pensating for lack of sight) the encrypted message woven into the televi-sion signal from outer space. But the script also makes it apparent that this sense-based acuteness is linked to intellectual achievement. Both *Scent of a Woman* and *Contact* provide the culture with an image of what can be.

These films, of course, do not reflect all of the portraits of the blind in film. But they represent trends. The more recent films edge toward a view of the blind that is multidimensional and capable. As important, female blind characters often assume qualities of helplessness and surreal good-ness whereas male characters are more unpleasant or evil. In film, stereo-types of women and men dramatically infuse stereotypes of the blind. It is difficult to tell which dominate.

This analysis of the characters in film is intended to be illustrative rather than exhaustive. The cultural myths that have dominated literary portraits of the blind are definitely part of the dramatic vocabulary on the silver screen. They form a cultural matrix that includes visual, behavioral, and verbal cues. Audiences cannot be expected to forget those cues when they turn to the news. Journalists, as members of a culture, may also have a difficult time framing news without them.

THE BLIND IN THE NEWS: GROPING FROM CLICHÉ TO REALITY

No one medium can represent all news organizations; however, several are taken to be indicative of national trends. The *New York Times* often represents the elite press; *USA Today* epitomizes every person's newspaper. The three national television networks provide most Americans with most of their news as well as a collection of visual messages. Examining how the blind are portrayed by these news organizations provides a sketch of what journalists are doing.

The Lexis/Nexis full-text database of the *New York Times* and *USA Today* were examined for any story that used the words blind, blinded, or blindness in 1993 and again in 2001. The individual story was the unit of analysis. Network news coverage was examined using Barrell's database. A similar methodology using the same key works and a full-text search netted the television database. It is worth noting that the search process itself contains a conundrum. If blind people were the subjects of news stories and blindness was not mentioned, the articles would not be included. Such stories might not rely on stereotypes. Yet, searching without the key word *blind,* for example substituting *physical disability,* yielded an unusable database. Traditional news values suggest that blindness is likely to be mentioned in news accounts, but it is impossible to determine whether every story that included blind people is part of this data set.

In 1993, there were 1,081 stories using the key words in the *Times,* 338 in *USA Today,* and 107 in nightly network newscasts. Eight years later, in 2001, there were 219 stories in *USA Today,* 256 in the *New York Times,* and 13 on the network news. While this initial data set suggests both a great deal of coverage and a change over time, it also merits a caveat. In both years, the vast majority of stories used blind as a cliché or colloquialism, for example, duck blind, blind trust, blind love, race-blind admission, etc. If these uses were eliminated, in 1993 only 160 stories in the *New York Times* and 131 stories in *USA Today* used the term to mean physical disability. In 2001, there were 45 mentions of *blind* with this meaning in the *New York Times* and 44 in *USA Today.* The networks reflect the same variance. Thus, in both years, between 70 and 80 percent of the news stories used the word blind as part of a cliché or colloquial phrase.

There was one other important similarity. In both 1993 and 2001, the most frequent use of the word *blind* to mean physical disability was in connection with the two terrorist attacks on the New York World Trade Center. In both years, news accounts mentioning the blind, diabetic, Muslim cleric Sheik Omar Abdel Rahman, who was convicted of the 1993 attack, were the predominant news story using the word *blind*.

Most stories were not illustrated, and those stories most likely to be illustrated appeared on the sports pages or on network television news accounts of sporting activities, such as when blind mountain climber Erik Weihenmayer attempted Mount Everest in 2001. These visual messages portrayed the blind as physically vigorous. Personality profiles sometimes included mug shots, photos of people playing musical instruments, or photos of works of art. These photos certainly ran counter to many of the negative stereotypes associated with blindness and reaffirmed some of the more positive ones.

Though photos were not common in news accounts of the blind, the images that words evoke certainly were a part of news accounts. Furthermore, these word images followed some predictable patterns. Blindness was used as a label most often in association with terrorism. The second most common way of portraying blindness was in medical news, either as a symptom of specific diseases, for example multiple sclerosis, or as the focus of new treatments, from computer chips to vitamins, designed to reduce or cure blindness. An understandable preoccupation with curing blindness infused medical stories, emphasized the disabling aspects of blindness, and more subtly suggested blindness could only be surmounted medically.

In 2001 more than in 1993, stories about the blind focused more on accomplishment, particularly athletic accomplishment. Blind people were depicted as happily married, raising families, and achieving in their chosen professions. This shift in news coverage parallels, to a certain extent, the shift in depictions of the blind in film during the 1990s. This is a welcome movement, however small, away from stereotypical coverage. It may reflect the media's role as mirror of a society that has adopted and implemented the Americans with Disabilities Act.

In summary, news organizations, while providing less stereotypical coverage over time, also appeared to follow some cultural patterns. When blindness was not a cliché, colloquialism, or label, it appeared most often in the news as a disease to be cured or a disability to be endured. The blind too seldom were portrayed as active, contributing members of society. When they were portrayed that way, it was often in the stereotypical realm of giftedness compensating for lack of sight, primarily in the realm of athletics or the arts. This view of blindness is particularly significant because the disability itself occurs relatively infrequently in the population. Most people, including journalists, may not have much first-hand opportunity to know blind people. What people know about blindness, then, becomes a mediated reality unchallenged by experience.

SOME ETHICALLY BASED CRAFT SUGGESTIONS

Journalists can strive to provide readers and viewers with a vision of the blind that provides a depth of understanding not found in cultural stereotypes. To that end, I suggest the following:

- Eliminate, as much as possible, clichéd uses of the word *blind* from news copy. Don't allow hackneyed analysis to crowd out the original.
- Stop using the word *blind* as a descriptive label unless it is essential to understanding the story. Journalists need to understand that visual messages can serve as descriptive labels.
- Continue to cover medical advances, but do not include, as part of that coverage, word pictures of hopelessness and despair unless they are appropriate. Such images may (and may not) be appropriate when writing about multiple sclerosis or end-stage AIDS. They are far less appropriate when the issue is diabetes, cataracts, physical trauma, or aging.
- Cover blind people as whole human beings—an end in themselves, not as the unfortunate result of one physical trait. Incorporate them into daily news coverage in the same way that women and ethnic groups are now being incorporated.
- Finally, be sensitive to the richness of cultural perceptions of the blind. Understand that blindness has both positive and negative elements associated with it, and that it has allowed us to ask some profound questions about ourselves as human beings. Asking those questions is appropriate, but it is the quality of the answers that matters most.

Part VII

SEXUAL ORIENTATION STEREOTYPES

Chapter 23

RECAPTURING THE ARCHETYPE: AN INCLUSIVE VISION OF SEXUALITY AND GENDER

Marguerite Moritz

I really believe that the pagans, and the abortionists, and the feminists, and the gays and lesbians who are actively trying to make that an alternative lifestyle, the ACLU, People for the American Way—all of them who have tried to secularize America—I point the finger in their face and say, "You helped this happen."

The Rev. Jerry Falwell, September 13, 2001

Two days after the attack on the World Trade Center and the Pentagon, this statement was made on the popular religious program, *The 700 Club* Within hours, those words had traveled far beyond their original audience and were being widely reported in the mainstream media. A host of gay rights groups, including the Gay and Lesbian Alliance Against Defamation (GLAAD), denounced the remarks. George W. Bush, hardly a gay-friendly president, soon echoed that sentiment. Reverend Falwell backpedaled as fast as he could, issuing an outright apology and going on national television to attempt some damage control.

Good Morning America host Diane Sawyer, herself a graduate of the Nixon White House, was not exactly receptive. During a live interview, she replayed the *700 Club* videotape and excoriated Falwell for the remarks. At first, he attempted to argue that his statement had been taken out of context. "Tell me," she demanded, "any conceivable context that could redeem those words." As Falwell stumbled, the outraged Sawyer said she wondered if he wanted to create an American Taliban. And, she said, his claim of being misread by the media "defies credulity."

It was a small moment in the weeks of extended 9/11 coverage, but a noteworthy one nonetheless. After all, 10 years earlier Falwell's remarks would have been considered fair comment. Twenty years earlier they might have gone unchallenged, and 30 years earlier...well, who was talking about gays then?

With the widespread denunciation of the Falwell remarks, many wondered if the so-called culture wars were one more thing that would never again be the same after 9/11. It is indeed true that in both news and entertainment, representations of gays and many other marginalized groups have undergone dramatic changes in recent years. But, as the events of 9/11 themselves demonstrated, the culture wars may have shifted focus, but they are far from over.

GAYS AND TELEVISION

From films to books to newspapers, gays—a term I use to include gay men, lesbians, bisexuals, and transgendered people—have a long history of being excluded from mass media representations. This chapter looks most particularly at television portrayals because of television's reach and power. As critic Caryn James put it, "Anyone who does not watch television cannot possibly understand mainstream American culture. That may be disappointing news to art collectors who wish we lived in Renaissance Italy, but there it is. We have a messy society and television mirrors who we are in all our contradictions, complexities, and uncertainties" (James, 2000).

Or does it? These are endlessly debated questions: Does TV reflect our realities or create them? Does it mirror the entire culture or only that part of it that is white, straight, and economically advantaged? In the case of American television, the answer may be that it both reflects and creates cultural expression as well as political, economic, and social realities. And certainly in looking at representations of marginalized groups, the reflection conveyed by television may be just as important as the reality that people experience and live. In twenty-first century life, television has the power to define who we are because "...even as the explosion of channels creates a more fragmented television universe, what we know and how we know it is shaped more than ever by television" (James, 2000).

In its early years, television told us, its audience, that gays did not exist. In news, entertainment, talk shows, and public affairs programs, gays were rarely seen, heard from, or even referred to. In the wake of the civil rights movement for blacks and the women's movement, an initiative for gay rights began to gather strength and coalesce. One of its first goals was to gain media visibility, an effort aided in large part by a social and political climate in which many long-established norms and values were being aggressively challenged. By the 1970s, gays were beginning to get some media attention, although most early portrayals and discussions showed gays in negative or stereotyped ways (Gross, 1991). For gay media activists, the issue moved increasingly to questions of *how* gays were being represented rather than *if* they were being shown. And it was in this context that the complexities of visual representation began to gain significance.

THE VISUALS OF NEWS

In its most basic terms, television consists of sounds and images, audio and video. Audio includes spoken words as well as sound effects and music tracks. Video includes all the visual elements contained on the screen. In the case of a fictional portrayal such as a situation comedy or cop show, the visual elements refer not only to the actors but also to their costumes, facial expressions, mannerisms, and movements, the sets in which they are shown, and the camera shots, angles, framing, and editing that are employed in photographing all of this. In the case of news, visual elements include these elements as well: the arched eyebrow of the anchor, the look of pain on the face of the eyewitness, the look of panic on the face of the corporate executive who is ambushed for an interview. When we begin to examine the television visual itself and then add the interaction of the visual with various sound elements, we quickly see that representation is a highly complex matter.

A news story as a San Diego television station reported it provides a case in point. The San Diego station was one of several across the country that used hidden surveillance cameras to obtain footage of male sexual encounters from men's rooms at rest stops, department stores, libraries, and other sites. The stories created a furor among gay viewers and gay advocacy groups. Since late 1996, when KENS-TV in San Antonio aired graphic hidden-camera footage during the November sweeps, GLAAD has actively criticized this kind of "gay-baiting and sleazy journalism" (GLAAD Alert, 1996). "It is high time for a larger discussion within the media profession of the social costs of this kind of hardcore hidden camera hype and sweeps month sleaze."

The National Lesbian and Gay Journalists Association's Karen Boothe said,

Depicting such images, homosexual or heterosexual, becomes suspect when
highly promoted as investigative journalism. Public sex is as foreign to the
lives of most gay people as it is to most straight people. Males who engage
in this practice with other males are usually those whose fear of societal condemnation makes them afraid to frequent clubs and bars where they risk
being identified. (NLGJA news release, 1998)

Boothe said such stereotypical stories rarely examine the societal pressures that push people to have anonymous sex. What's more, day-to-day
coverage on these stations often fails to present an accurate portrait of gay
people living healthy and productive lives.

The National Lesbian and Gay Journalists Association convened a panel
at its annual meeting to examine whether the reporting was fair and accurate. The TV report out of San Diego was one of several screened at the
panel session. While no consensus emerged (some said the San Diego
story was both fair and accurate, others said it was accurate but unfair
because it reinforced negative stereotypes about gay men), one of the most
salient critiques involved the highly stylized photography used in the
piece.

In news depictions, it is standard practice to employ a level horizontal
plane in setting up the camera on a stand or a tripod. In fact, professional
video cameras have a built-in level bubble so the photographer can know
precisely when the shot is square to the ground. The result is that shots typically look very stable: buildings sit at right angles to the ground, and people traverse a flat plane when they walk across a street. If the horizontal
plane is tilted dramatically away from this norm, let's say by 45 degrees,
then buildings suddenly will look like they are falling over, and people
will look like they're going uphill or down. The result is a noticeably atypical shot, which can feel unconventional, dramatic, or simply disconcert-
ing: Something is wrong when the world is titled on its side.

In the San Diego news story, almost every shot was done in this atypical
style. What was the visual message? I would argue that, literally and
metaphorically, the viewer was being told that this is not a story about the
straight world where stability is the order of the day. Instead, the visual
message conveyed was that this story is about a world where everything is
askew and hence not at all as it should be. With the employment of that
single photographic device, a visual commentary was attached to the story
that was particularly powerful precisely because it was not part of the verbal text that audiences are adept at analyzing. Visuals require an interpretation of their own. Indeed, it is somewhat common for students from

grade schools through the university to have classes in what is often called visual literacy.

Understanding the content of a still photograph is a complex task that can be complicated further by issues of gender and sexual expression. This is something that became profoundly clear to Deirdre McCloskey, a college professor who is transgendered (D. McCloskey, personal communication, April 2002). At the time of the surgery, Professor Donald McCloskey was on the faculty at the University of Iowa, had written a number of economics books, and was a "fairly prominent person in my community." Her story was reported in the Iowa press as well as in the *New York Times* and *Fortune* and on National Public Radio. It "got a lot of media attention," and newspapers "always wanted a photo" to print with the written text.

"It is a story with a visual aspect," Professor McCloskey correctly points out, "but there is a rhetoric in the photos. Photographers wanted all kinds of sexy poses. For example, they would want to show me putting on my makeup. I said no. It's sexualized." In contrast, she says, the *New York Times* covered her 35th college reunion in June 1999 and "I wasn't asked to pose." The writer and the photographer, she says, did not sexualize the story.

Today we live in a visual culture. A shift started in contemporary media with the hugely popular photo magazines: *Life, Look,* and *The Saturday Evening Post.* "The shift these photo magazines represented from preponderant text to preponderant pictures was a subtle kind of revolution that has had immense consequences. Today—when visual messages are as ubiquitous as oxygen—or smog—it is not easy to imagine it was ever otherwise." Images became "crucial communicators of information and entertainment . . . ," something that today is manifested in the "pivotal position of television" in our popular culture (Goldberg, 2002, Arts p. 25).

In analyzing the rhetoric of news photography, it is essential to understand that for most audience members, "the still photograph and the moving image have become synonymous with reality." While we have tools for determining the subjectivity of word choices and oral inflection, images are usually accepted as "unmediated representations, a true rendering that is not subject to debate or interpretation. In short, news consumers have been conditioned to believe that pictures equal reality, that they are documentation that is irrefutable, and that news simply holds up a mirror to the real world" (Moritz, 1996).

Yet, as the two examples above both demonstrate, the creation of visuals is itself a highly selective process that involves obvious and subtle distinctions with enormous implications for how reality is depicted. What pictures are taken, how they are framed, lighted, posed, and positioned all have implications for the visual message being conveyed. In addition, the ways in which television pictures are edited together and combined with various sound tracks will always have a primary role in shaping the visual message.

THE VISUALS OF FICTION

In 1978 television producer Norman Lear offered one of the first prime-time portrayals of a lesbian character and storyline on his enormously popular situation comedy, *All in the Family*. The "Cousin Liz" episode revolved around the death of Edith's cousin, a lesbian whose long-term sexual relationship with her roommate, Veronica, had been kept secret from the family for years. With the death of Cousin Liz, Edith and Archie inherit a valuable silver tea service, which they intend to collect when they attend a memorial service planned by her surviving partner, Veronica. As the plot unfolds, Veronica tells Edith that she herself would like to keep the silver service as a reminder of the quiet, peaceful, and loving times she and Cousin Liz had shared over tea every afternoon. In an effort to explain the importance of this, Veronica finds it necessary to reveal to Edith the true nature of her relationship with Cousin Liz. In the scene where the coming out takes place, the nervous Veronica takes Edith into the privacy of her bedroom and carefully closes the door lest anyone overhear her revelations. The two women sit on the bed Veronica once shared with Cousin Liz. In this very private setting, Veronica makes repeated, awkward attempts to explain to Edith that she and Cousin Liz were not just roommates.

Veronica: Edith (long pause). Your Cousin Liz and I were (long pause). Very fond of each other (pause). Extremely fond of each other.

Edith: Oh, I know. We was too.

Veronica: No (pause). You see, we, we, we (pause) loved each other.

Edith: I know. We loved each other too. I can remember when we was kids in school, we was like sisters.

Veronica: No, this wasn't like that. We loved each other in a different way.

Edith: What way?

Veronica: Well, this was more like a marriage.

Edith: A marriage? Well, it couldn't be. I mean you and Cousin Liz was both g.... (look of recognition and horror).... OOOOH. You mean you and Cousin Liz (pause).

Veronica: Yes.

Edith: OOOOOOOH!!!! (as the camera zooms in for an extreme close up of her wide-eyed astonishment.)

A 1990 episode of *Designing Women* offered a very different kind of coming out scenario. In this story, the character of Suzanne is reunited with Eugenia, a friend from her beauty pageant days. Eugenia is now living in Atlanta and working in a television news department where she does the daily weather forecasts. The reunion takes place in the living room where Suzanne and her costars have their fictional interior design studio, and when Eugenia arrives no one suspects she is a lesbian. But that quickly changes when Eugenia announces that since she broke up with her lover a few months ago, she hasn't done much socially: "Seems like the only places I go anymore are to work and of course my Sisters in Sappho meetings." She also reveals that "everybody else from the pageant circle won't have anything to do with me since I came out." After a brief visit, Eugenia thanks Suzanne for being so accepting, and dashes off. Despite the forthright revelations, Suzanne obviously does not realize that Eugenia is a lesbian.

Suzanne: Isn't she a sweetheart! You know, if all the women in the world were like her, I'd have no trouble finding girlfriends.

Mary Jo: I'd say that's the understatement of the decade.

Anthony: Suzanne, you do realize that Eugenia swings the other way, don't you?

Suzanne: What's that mean?

Julia: He means Eugenia is a lesbian.

Suzanne: Oh I can't believe you people. You just met the woman and already you're bad-mouthing her.

Julia: When she said "coming out" she didn't mean at a cotillion, she meant from the closet.

Mary Jo: What did you think she meant when she mentioned Sappho?

Suzanne: I didn't know. I thought it was a detergent.

When Suzanne finally realizes that Eugenia is a lesbian, she is not so accepting after all, and thus the dramatic problem is set in place to await narrative resolution. After considerable soul-searching prompted by her friends, Suzanne ultimately decides she can accept Eugenia as a friend despite her lesbian lifestyle. In the final line of the script, however, Suzanne reiterates her continuing belief that Eugenia would be better off straight than gay. "If we can put a man on the moon," she says to Eugenia, "we can put one on you."

The "Cousin Liz" episode ends in a similar fashion with Archie finally accepting Veronica and agreeing to give her the silver tea service. Yet the final lines of the script reveal his belief that Veronica can and should simply stop being a lesbian.

Archie: You're a good-looking woman. Why don't you go out and get yourself a good-
    looking guy and turn yourself around?

    Veronica smiles, then gives Archie a hug.

Archie: Well there. Didn't you get something out of that?

I use these two episodes to introduce the discussion of visuals on network entertainment television because they illustrate a number of the critical points that involve visual representation and its interaction with the
narrative story line and structure.

Given that the *Designing Women* episode appeared 12 years after *All in
the Family* first broke the cultural ice with its lesbian story, and given the
increased visibility of gays and lesbians in society generally over that time
period, one might expect some significant differences in fictional depictions of lesbians on prime-time network television, and indeed there are.

Norman Lear's 1970s lesbian is quite ordinary looking, even frumpy. Her
hairstyle, makeup, and dress are all distinctly understated and conservative.
She might just as easily have been cast as an old maid. In the script she is a
schoolteacher. By contrast, the 1990s lesbian is a former beauty queen who
has become well known around Atlanta as a television celebrity. She is
markedly glamorous, fashionable, outgoing, self-confident, and sexy.

If the characters are polar opposites, so are their moments of self-
revelation. While schoolteacher Veronica seeks out a totally private space
in which to attempt coming out, TV star Eugenia is quite unconcerned and
open in announcing her sexual status to a room filled with strangers. The
1970s lesbian expects to be sanctioned for admitting her sexual identity;
the 1990s lesbian expects to be accepted.

On one level, lesbianism in 1990 is framed very differently from the
way it was in 1978, and that difference may be seen as highly significant
in terms of prime-time television's understanding of the place lesbians
occupy in society. This is to say that for a variety of complex reasons, producers and writers now apparently realize and want the programs that take
up gay topics to reflect a broader range of representation than media stereotypes of the past presented. In the case of lesbians, they are not all war-
dens in women's prisons; they do not all want or need to hide their sexual
identity. Gay men are not all hairdressers and cross-dressers.

On another level, however, production and narrative strategies remained
somewhat more consistent with past practices. Gay characters were often
episodic and not members of the regular cast. Often they continue to constitute the narrative problem that the regular, straight cast members must
struggle to understand and resolve. Thus gayness was presented in the nar-

rative as abnormal from the perspective of heterosexual normality. In this significant matter, the 1978 character and the 1990 one are positioned identically by the narrative.

As the 1990s wore on and cable increasingly pushed the boundaries of acceptable viewing fare and brought in huge numbers of viewers along the way, the networks were under pressure to respond. In terms of gay representation on prime-time network television, the door was pushed open ever wider. The 1990s saw the emergence of several recurring and regular gay characters on hit shows such as *Roseanne, Friends, Spin City, Will & Grace,* and *NYPD Blue.* The most noted event in this respect came in April 1997, when the central character in the situation comedy *Ellen* declared she was gay. The fact that comedian Ellen DeGeneres, who played the part, also came out in real life as gay made for a news event of major proportions, "the biggest gay media event of that year" (Moritz, 1998, p. 399). With cable outlets such as HBO and Showtime pursuing younger, hipper, and gayer audiences, twenty-first-century television got underway with far more permissive and progressive programming strategies.

THE AUDIENCE

Examination of television as a visual text can reveal a great deal about television's depictions of gays and lesbians; there are, however, other important levels for analysis beyond the visual and the narrative that should not be overlooked in an attempt to understand how these video portraits are drawn in the first place and what meanings they may convey in the second. Again returning to our two examples, it is no mere coincidence that both of these lesbian characterizations were presented on long-established programs that had achieved top 10 television ratings for several seasons running. The requirements and constraints of production, what I will call the context of production, have a profound, and in some cases determining, impact on the text being produced.

The very emergence of Norman Lear's Tandem Productions as a major series supplier in the 1970s, for example, is directly related to specific changes in the industry triggered by changes in government regulations. Lear's ability to take on social topics that had not been touched by network television ties into an emerging interest in urban audiences at that time, as well as the creation of new ratings measurements to track that audience.

As to the issue of meaning, we must also recognize two critical points. First, writers and producers may build ambiguity into their texts and thus open up the possibility of varied readings. Second, the messages encoded in a text—ambiguous or not—may not be what certain audience segments decode from that text.

To return to the examples above, I showed these episodes to a group of college students studying representations of women in mass media. I argued that the ending for the 1978 episode and the ending for the 1990 episode both suggested a desire to identify the lesbian characters as needing to be returned to heterosexual normality. A student who said she saw both of these endings as reiterations of the main characters as obtuse, unsophisticated, and therefore comic, immediately challenged my reading. The final lines, the student argued, make us laugh at Suzanne and Archie, not at the lesbians they have failed to really understand.

The point here is that television texts, precisely because of their structural, narrative, and visual intricacies and interactions, will generate diverse and sometimes contradictory readings. For an understanding of this diversity of readings we can go beyond both the text and the context of production by turning to the audience itself. In short, I am arguing here that a comprehensive examination of gay depictions should locate and examine this topic on the following three levels: context, text, and audience. To uncover the production processes that impact most directly and profoundly on texts we must look at industry practices. After identifying these practices and their textual implications, we may turn to the texts themselves to explore the meanings that are inscribed in them. And finally, in an effort to see how encoded and decoded meanings may differ, we turn to the audience.

Through this stratified approach we can begin to understand and perhaps change the central reality of gay depictions on prime-time network television, which is that they are still a remarkable rarity.

CONCLUSION

The cultural invisibility of gays in the most powerful and pervasive of our public arenas for discussion denies gays status and hence power in society. It deprives them of cultural heroes and role models. In addition, it denies the culture at large the opportunity to explore the goals, needs, definitions, aspirations, and contributions of gay people. It further isolates an already isolated group.

It is my hope that examining television's treatment of all minority groups will reveal much about how the industry and the groups with which it interacts (including its many audiences) function and why. This may uncover strategies for change that could benefit all marginalized groups who have also been symbolically annihilated by television for decades.

Chapter 24

THE AVOCADO AND THE ASPARAGUS: SEARCHING FOR MASCULINE AND FEMININE ARCHETYPES WITHIN THE STEREOTYPING THEATER OF SEXUALIZED MEDIATYPES

Julianne H. Newton and Rick Williams

> And the avocado hangeth from the tree bow, ripe and swollen, holding within it the seed of life. And the asparagus riseth from the earth, firm and erect, tapering to a tender tip of daring thrust. And together they honor the archetypes of human expression: the primordial feminine and masculine. (Newton, 1996)

Through a confounding oversimplification, perpetuated through cultural, personal, and media imagery, we have come to view human beings through *either* masculine *or* feminine filters. We misrepresent the masculine and feminine aspects of archetypes as separate, physical manifestations of male and female. The problem is that we stereotype women as embodying only the characteristics we associate with the feminine archetype—nurturing, compassionate, and relational—while we stereotype men as aggressive, dispassionate, and independent—characteristics we associate with the masculine archetype.

These images injure by misrepresenting the integrated character of the masculine and feminine archetypes, supporting our misguided determination to categorize one another by gender and sexual orientation. Archetypes are inclusive, rather than exclusive, and represent the unified ideal of the individual, embodying the power of both masculine and feminine characteristics.

Stereotypes, on the other hand, dichotomize and diminish the power of the archetypal ideal. Media imagery often categorizes individuals though stereotypical sexual behavior that perpetuates the misapplication of the concept of archetypes. This chapter argues that, rather than confuse masculine and feminine characteristics with sexuality and gender as oppositional, dichotomous variables, we need to contextualize masculine and feminine as archetypes that prescribe the unique energy that composes every human being, female and male. These archetypes manifest through an infinite continuum, limited only by the imagination and creativity of the human psyche. Focusing on masculine and feminine as archetypes within all human beings, regardless of gender or sexual orientation, frees us all of culturally imposed, stereotypical boundaries on the human capacity to feel, understand, interact, and dream.

As archetypes, masculine and feminine are attributes all people experience through their genetic encoding, through psychological manifestations and intrapersonal intelligences, through cultivation of personal attributes, through social interaction and socialization, through dreams and myths, and through literature, the arts, and the media. A problem at the core of studying masculine and feminine attributes from an archetypal perspective, however, is that the archetypes have been confused with gender and sexual orientation. As such, they have been stereotyped as separate sexual entities rather then as integrated parts of each individual. So, in their most stereotypical form, men are left without grace and women without power, in turn leaving each person and thus whole cultures out of balance. A stereotypically *masculine* man, therefore, must have a large penis and large testicles, must exhibit virile strength and aggressiveness, and must be both attracted to and attractive to not just one woman but many women. A stereotypically *feminine* woman must have large breasts, must exhibit gentleness and sensitivity, must be attracted to and committed to one man, yet must be attractive to many men.

ARCHETYPES ARE NOT STEREOTYPES

Archetypes versus stereotypes versus mediatypes. What do they mean? An *archetype* is an emergent pattern that helps explain complex and often contradictory human behavior. Carl Jung (1964) considered archetypes primordial remnants of ancient humans before evolution into contemporary species.

Stereotypes, on the other hand, are constructions imposed on groups of individuals who are viewed as having similar characteristics or attributes in common. The key issue in distinguishing archetypes from stereotypes is that stereotypes too often lead to negative social interactions that deny the complexity of human behavior and communication, even among those who share attributes. Stereotypes are not archetypes. Archetypes shift, converge, turn, and interweave in the manner of a Mobius strip, emerging within and without the human psyche and body. Stereotypes impose crude, reactive filters through which one human being can categorize another almost reflexively, with neither conscious thought nor interpersonal interaction. In the case of masculine and feminine, stereotypes impose definitive boundaries for sexuality, behavior, personality, and gender roles. Because they are exclusive, stereotypes feed everyday interactions, providing for the exclusion of various groups of individuals based on ethnicity, nationality, race, gender, sexual orientation, age, class, club membership, neighborhood, education, profession, religion, and all the other human characteristics discussed throughout this volume.

The term *mediatype* refers to stereotypes purposefully constructed and repeatedly enacted and disseminated via media. Although their potential to influence our understanding of humans and how we live has yet to be measured adequately, we suspect their most powerful effect is the undermining of human diversity through repeated homogenizing imagery. By *media,* we mean any form of communication external to individuals. That includes clothing and possessions, gesture and handwriting, architecture and art, as well as the more commonly perceived forms of television, publications, film, and the Internet. Whether a medium communicates on a mass level is not as important as whether a medium is part of a meaning system shared among individuals. When referring to media stereotypes in this chapter, we will use the term *mediatypes* or *mediatypal.*

Stereotypes operate within systems of discrete categories rather than systems of continua. A dominant group stereotypes a subordinate group to establish distinctions that not only separate one group from the other but also help maintain the power of one group over the other. Stereotypes objectify by depersonalizing the individual. Stereotypes are disintegrative, divisive by design. Their objectifying divisiveness is the source of injury because it separates not only the groups from one another but also the individual from the uniqueness of her or his own humanity. Through stereotyping, human beings become less than human, objects of scorn and ridicule separated from the supposedly mainstream culture by the barriers of stereotypical norms. This disintegrative separation makes stereotypes the antithesis of archetypes.

Such simplistic misapplication of the unifying archetypes of masculine and feminine underlies public discrimination of homosexuals, providing misguided ammunition for oppressing anyone who does not fit stereotypical sexual molds. Such misunderstanding of archetypal patterns, our primordial imprint, imposes false, polarized, gender stereotypes that abuse all humans, regardless of gender or sexual orientation. The confusion of gender, sexuality, and sexual orientation with masculine and feminine archetypes has prohibited—or at the very least discouraged—us all from engaging the full complexity of what it means to be human. Furthermore, such thinking has led to the oppression of ambiguity, as well as to the oppression of the lively, multidimensional spirit within us all.

From an archetypal perspective, no barrier exists between the individual and all of the complex human characteristics that he or she may possess in unique combination. Archetypes integrate and embrace the unique and complex character of each individual human being, who is unique by genetics and experiences. In this unity, manifest both in the individual and, subsequently, in culture and society, the fear generated by differences is erased, and the threat of integration that is the basis of stereotyping does not exist.

ARCHETYPES AND MEDIA

One of the most pervasive misapplications of archetypes is the way in which they have been translated into male and female sexual mediatypes. These incarcerating stereotypes have been made explicit in media, and in much of art and literature through time, in ways that have established them as the norm for masculine and feminine behavior. To vary from such stereotypes is to be labeled *alternative,* a relatively new and kinder term for nonheterosexual or nonconformist within conventional heterosexuality.

Most media help create and sustain stereotypes and the boundaries they imply. The most obvious stereotypes that media promote include a culture in which people are mostly white, heterosexual, flawlessly beautiful or handsome, and upper class. They overly value material possessions and live beyond the means of most real-world people. Though these characteristics are not inherently demeaning to a particular group or individual, when repeated with only occasional exceptions, they are exclusive, establishing stereotypical norms for an imagined dominant culture. If one does not fit the norm practiced by this mediatypal group, one is excluded. It is interesting to note that even most individuals who come closest to fitting the dominant mediatypal norm rarely share the actual lifestyles or attitudes portrayed by the stereotypes.

Mediatypes are counterfeit archetypes that exist only in the virtual culture created via media. Because mediatypes are consciously constructed and are disseminated to mass audiences via mass repetition, they are likely to have more influence on and be more destructive to mass culture than more localized stereotypes.

EXPANDING THE BOUNDARIES

Rather than use our limited space here to focus on examples of mediatyping, we want to discuss briefly a few examples of the occasional exceptions that push the boundaries of stereotypes. You will note that the ways these exceptions push boundaries can be confusing to the point of ineffectiveness, even reinforcing the stereotypes they were meant to expose.

For instance, when a look between Ally and Ling on *Ally McBeal* unexpectedly stirred sexual curiosity in each woman, they openly explored the possibility that one or both were lesbian. Each determined that she was, indeed, heterosexual. In other episodes, a male attorney in McBeal's firm came to terms with his love for a woman who turned out to possess a penis. These brief forays into alternatives did raise significant questions about human sexuality but quickly settled back into the status quo. Yet when Ellen DeGeneres came out as lesbian on prime-time television, her emotional and occasionally physical intimacy with her same-sex lover were interpreted by the network as more than many viewers—and therefore sponsors and therefore the network—could handle. Such examples suggest that, at the time, it was acceptable for heterosexuals to explore homosexual curiosity briefly, but it was not acceptable to be gay.

In the NBC television sitcom *Will & Grace,* Grace exhibits mediatypal, heterosexual feminine characteristics—long, flowing hair, slim body, bumbling but sensitive interactions with others, a career in interior design (ironically countering another stereotype of the gay interior designer), and a constant search for her counter-mediatype, the male rescuer on a white horse (whom she encountered in the last episode of the 2001–2002 season). Her less-than-huge breasts are recurring subject matter for jokes. Jack, long-time friend of Will and Grace, exhibits stereotypical gay male gestures, mannerisms, omnipresent manifestation of sexual desire for men, and phobias generally associated with men who are viewed as effeminate, and, by default, gay. Will, however, exhibits a more complex set of characteristics that includes neither stereotypical mannerisms nor obsessive expressions of desire for men. Will's character longs for emotional as well as physical intimacy with a male partner.

On rare occasions the show's mediatypal characters are allowed to exhibit a broader range of characteristics, such as when Jack demonstrates he can be a good father to his son, apparently despite his mediatypal personality characteristics. The fourth main character, Karen, is perhaps the most complex. As the alcoholic wife of a wealthy, imprisoned executive whom we imagine but do not see, Karen exhibits racial and sexual bigotry, even as she occasionally succumbs to erupting bisexual desire. Ironically, her nonsensical character is free to exhibit practically any behavior usually considered unacceptable in stereotypical society. Is it because she uses mainstream culture's approved drug of choice, alcohol, reinforcing yet another stereotype of the alcoholic who is outrageous but benign?

Talking with individuals about *Will & Grace* offers interesting anecdotal evidence of the cultural conflicts and confusion evoked by mediatypes. One heterosexual viewer could hardly watch the program. She saw the sitcom as portraying classic negative stereotypes of gay people, as well as of women in general. On the other hand, two gay viewers reported that they rarely miss an episode, saying they enjoyed what they considered the sitcom's subversion of stereotypes through its appropriation of one type of gay male, its revelations about another type of gay male, and the bisexual innuendoes manifested in interactions between Karen and Jack.

So, broadcasting *Will & Grace* does not necessarily push boundaries regarding media portrayal of sexual orientation; rather, it may reinforce stereotypes viewers already have adopted. It was interesting to see hints of more complex character development in the opening episodes of the show's 2002–2003 season.

The exponentially more complex HBO series *Six Feet Under* offers a significant counterpoint to mainstream television's portrayal of human sexuality. The show fully and uniquely develops characters and relationships from season to season. During the show's first season (2000–2001), for example, we learn about David, the designated head of the family business, who runs it with strong, masculine authority and dispassionate business acumen. At the same time, he struggles to accept his homosexuality and resolve his internal conflict with externally imposed expectations of heterosexuality. As the show ended its second season (2001–2002), David struggled to maintain his live-in relationship with Keith.

A stereotypical interpretation might view David's character as exhibiting more relational—and therefore feminine—behavior toward Keith's niece and the couple's would-be adopted daughter, as well as a desire for emotional intimacy with Keith. Keith, on the other hand, could be viewed as exhibiting mediatypal masculine propensities for detached sex, emotional distance, impatience, and violence. Shift now from stereotypical interpretations of the media characters to archetypal interpretations. By using *both/and* (rather than *either/or*) thinking that incorporates the idea that all human beings, regardless of gender, sexual orientation, or personality characteristics, possess masculine and feminine archetypal components, one can interpret both David's and Keith's behaviors and internal struggles as the evolving maturation of unique human beings, each of whom is drawing upon both masculine and feminine parts of himself.

Does that mean that Keith has not realized his full masculine/feminine potential? Or that David was not a whole person because he exhibited so-called feminine characteristics? Not at all. That is a key point of this discussion: masculine and feminine archetypes are more complex than overt characterization makes them out to be. Other *Six Feet Under* characters exemplify this point. In one scenario, David learns that a priest he had assumed was gay because of his overt personality characteristics was, indeed, heterosexual. The two characters actually discuss the idea that effeminate men often are assumed to be gay. In another ongoing saga, David's brother, Nate, rejects unwed fatherhood, exhibiting behavior characteristic of ignoble heterosexual men, even as his female fiancée explores a suppressed part of herself by having sex with strangers.

Unbelievably complicated? If we're thinking stereotypically through conventional mediatypes, yes. However, if we consider the complexity and diversity of the lives of real human beings, no.

This suggests another consideration about stereotypes. Can mediatypes be used in a prosocial format to encourage discussion of sexual orientation and gender roles? Both media comedy and drama have a way of allowing human beings to consider ideas they otherwise would reject. So much depends on the eye of the beholder. Someone who disapproves of effeminate men will watch Jack in *Will & Grace* with condescending, derisive judgment of Jack...and yet laugh at Karen's obsession with alcohol. Someone who likes men who happen to exhibit so-called feminine characteristics will enjoy Jack's character with great affection, laughing with him instead of at him.

EFFECTS OF STEREOTYPES AND ARCHETYPES

The distinction made above is significant and requires a clarification about the potential prosocial effects of mediatypes. Although mediatypes can be used to stimulate prosocial discussion, most mediatyping promotes objectification of human beings in a way that maintains so-called cultural norms. Mediatyping usually reinforces stereotyping, thus dehumanizing the individual by suppressing his or her own unique qualities of character and personality beneath qualities that are considered to be characteristic of a group. As noted earlier, this process typically diminishes the depth of human character, limiting the complexity of behavior and communication, and imposing conscious, definitive boundaries, such as ethnicity, race, gender, sexual orientation, and other human characteristics, that are the bases for exclusion from the dominant cultural group. The norms established by these stereotypes are rigid and have the effect of objectifying the individual as a threat to the norm or status quo. Objectification is the first step toward unprovoked violence directed at groups and individuals who exist outside of constructed, perceived norms.

Stereotypes are delivered in many ways, but the most pervasive and effective system is visual media. Thus, mediatypes that are promoted visually are the most damaging—for several reasons. We know from research that concepts derived through visual information are more readily remembered than concepts delivered by words (Graber, 1990; Madigan, 1983; Paivio, Rogers, & Smythe, 1968; Sargent & Zillmann, 1999; Schultz, 1993). So, the fact that mediatypes almost always are visual on at least one level makes them particularly significant in terms of learning and memory.

Perhaps even more significant is the way that visual information is processed in the brain to create learning and develop memory that directs decision making and behavior. The human brain operates from systems of distinct but integrated cognitive processes (Sperry, 1973) that, in many ways, reflect the same dualistic model of masculine and feminine archetypes. As this suggests, there are two primary cognitive processing systems that operate independently but that are integrated as part of the whole system. One system, the one with which most of us are familiar, processes information using logic and reason to understand and know the world and the self. We call this the *rational cognitive system.* Linguistic and mathematical intelligences are the two primary rational intelligences used by this system. The other primary system, which is equally complex and significant to whole-mind cognition, processes information directly, through synthesis, without the need for reason. We call this system the *intuitive cognitive system* because intuition means attaining knowledge directly without the need for reason. Visual and intrapersonal intelligences are two primary intuitive intelligences (Williams, 1999).

The significance of this dichotomy to our discussion of mediatypes' influence on the perception of sexual orientation lies in the unique way visual information is processed into long-term memory. Visual information takes a primary and separate route from rational thought through the brain (LeDoux, 1986, 1996). It is cognitively processed into knowledge on unconscious levels that guide decision making and motivate behavior. When an instantaneous decision is needed, this visual knowledge directs behavior before the information is even transmitted to the rational processing center of the brain. Furthermore, the visual knowledge is stored as unconscious, long-term memory in the hippocampus and the prefrontal lobes, still in preconscious, prerational formats to be used in future decision making as the standard of reality against which other information is judged (Bechara, Damasio, Tranel, & Damasio, 1997).

So, when stereotypes are manifested as visual mediatypes, their messages and characteristics are stored in our unconscious long-term memory and help shape our perceptions of reality and the decisions that guide our subsequent behavior. The divisive and negative connotations of these mediatypes influence our future decision making, limiting our choices in even more profound ways than we might imagine because they operate on preconscious levels of knowing. This is not to say that the information cannot be brought into consciousness and rationally considered in prosocial formats. However, that conscious process requires awareness of the existence of these unconscious cognitive processes and of techniques to access them. In a culture that is as rationally biased as our own, few of us have even been taught that our unconscious minds are significant to our behavior, much less that there are techniques to access and rationally consider the unconscious mind's contents and their effects on our lives (Williams, 2000b). This task is made even more daunting by the fact that the average U.S. citizen consumes between 4,000 and 5,000 media-generated images every day.

LONG-TERM BENEFITS OF ARCHETYPES

How do stereotypes of masculine and feminine alter our understanding of ourselves as male and female, and more importantly, perhaps, our understanding of our sexual selves and of gender roles?

Is it possible that Jung's archetypes of *anima* and *animus,* the expression of masculine and feminine characteristics Jung believed all humans possess, have been misunderstood through time and incorrectly used to channel the tendencies of humans to love and/or be attracted to someone? Recent developments in neurobiology and the study of dreams challenge critics of Jung's theories and confirm much of what Jung suggested as they uncover the critical role of dreams in helping humans develop strategies for living (Winson, 2002). Defining masculine and feminine as parts of all human beings, sometimes in opposition, sometimes in harmonic wholeness, can help us evolve to be more inclusive and accepting of a broader diversity of both interior and exterior manifestations of humanity. As Hopcke (1989) wrote, "Jung and Jungians have had a great deal to say about homosexuality over the years and much of it is of great help in deepening and broadening our perspective on homosexuality and heterosexuality" (p. 2).

What if heterosexuality is only a constructed concept with origins in ancient survival-based prescriptions for masculine and feminine exterior characteristics and survival of the species? If we cannot even ask that question, we are not really trying to understand what makes us human creatures. We are just falling in line with conventional (and stereotypical) wisdom.

If we turn to so-called nature, we find a remarkable symbol system of feminine and masculine: avocados and asparagus, apples and bananas, peaches and cucumbers. We also can find androgynous symbols: flowers with both stamen and pistils; watermelons with huge, swollen, elongated bodies filled with many internal seeds and a basic yoni shape; bell peppers; trees with long, rigid trunks and rounded, erupting, flowering greenery. People may scoff at such references in comparison to human sexuality, but few can scoff at the ways human beings have persisted in moving beyond imposed existence. Some fashion models are known for their androgyny. Humans have moved beyond the relatively rare appearance of hermaphroditism through cross-dressing and daring to convert their sexes physically through surgery to match their outsides with their insides, becoming what some view as a third sex.

Not only masculine and feminine, but also maleness and femaleness are now beyond either/or categories. The ancients expressed the integration of masculine and feminine through such concepts as yin and yang, recognizing both were necessary for wholeness. Contemporary humans, however, have misunderstood the archetypes, assuming they are discrete, oppositional, and physically manifested. Is this akin to early misinterpretations of left-brain, right-brain theory: that the left brain, representing traditional masculine characteristics (which also happen stereotypically to represent Western-European, North American—and therefore dominant—traditions), handled such functions as linear, logical, hierarchical thinking, and that the right brain, stereotypically representing traditional feminine characteristics (which also happen stereotypically to represent Asian, African,

Latin American, and American Indian—and therefore subordinate—traditions), handled such functions as visual, creative, and multidimensional thinking? Just as pre-Galilean humans believed the earth to be the center of the universe, the stereotypically rational mind became the center of our understanding of human cognition. Yet we were wrong on both counts.

What else have we misinterpreted? Consider an early McLuhan work, *The Mechanical Bride* (1967). Long before such media and cognitive theories were formalized, McLuhan warned us with clear examples that media were constructing our realities. McLuhan later would assert that the twenty-first century global village would need *both/and* thinking in order to prevent destructive conflict between eastern and western cultures (McLuhan & Powers, 1989). Yet we continue literally to buy into media abuse of our bodies, our sexuality, our minds, and our psychological composition. The media have for years played on heterosexual fears of the vital masculine/feminine components of ourselves and on homophobia in general, encouraging the promulgation of masculine/feminine stereotypes. In so doing, we have abused masculine/feminine archetypes almost beyond recognition. We have forced our very bodies and souls into a new category beyond archetype and stereotype—the mediatype, the nonorganic, posthuman, mechanized, commodified, and consuming self that categorizes, homogenizes, and dehumanizes the most precious, holistic, universal, healing parts of our being—our basic selves—that which is original and diverse in our sexual, soulful, physical, and spiritual manifestations.

Here is where contemporary humans, though somewhat more willing to admit openly the complexities of humanity and human sexuality, have lost their way. We see women's bodies as uncharacteristically tall, thin, and without blemishes, and their character as sexually available, frail, submissive, infantilized, objectified, brutalized. We see men's bodies as super muscular, taller than average, and appropriately dark (but not too dark), and their character as athletic, aggressive, violent, sexual, dominant, powerful, and often brutal. These are the limited, counterfeit characters of the *anti-archetype,* the stereotypes media portray as normal. And, of course, the pervasive, redundant message of billboard sexuality is that all the products associated with these mediatypal caricatures will convey mediatypically desired male and female physical attributes that will lead, in turn, to unlimited heterosexual opportunity—if only we buy, drink, drive, dress, and pose accordingly.

The dehumanizing, mediatyping portrayal of the human body, character, and spirit is not limited to gays and lesbians. Stereotyping is the norm in television, film, advertising, video games, the Internet, and print media throughout our culture. The misappropriation of archetypes to promote a divided, always struggling, never good enough self who seeks wholeness through the attempt to live the stereotyped, sexualized, product-consuming lives of characters of the media is the benchmark of normalcy in our culture. There we see the constant portrayal of women's and men's bodies through mediatypes and lifestyles condensed into restricted caricatures of mediated normalcy that reflect little of the complexity or diversity of actual human character. When we buy into this limited portrayal of humanity, adapting our own thinking and behavior to the mediatypal image of reality, we lose the very essence of ourselves—the integrated, uniquely diverse beings that we are.

THE ANTIDOTE

In the last 20 years, integrative studies in neuroscience, cognition, and visual theory have revealed how significant the consumption of repetitive visual stereotypes is to formations of perceptions of reality, influences on behavior, and the development of cultural norms. To address the dilemma of the misrepresentation of archetypes through mediatyping, visual theorists have developed techniques to help us understand and reformat those effects. Examples of creative new tools for understanding and reframing visual media include Lester's six perspectives (2003), Williams' omniphasic theory of cognitive balance (1999), Barry's visual intelligence (1997), and Newton's visual ecology (2001). With conscious effort, we can move not only toward a clearer understanding of visual communication but to applications of visual intelligence that help reinstate archetypal character in the primordial spirit symbolized by the avocado and the asparagus.

We propose five postulates for consideration:

1. Society and popular media regularly misinterpret the instinctive patterns identified as masculine/feminine *archetypes*.

2. This misinterpretation manifests through overly simplistic male and female *stereotypes*.

3. Masculine/feminine archetypes have been (mis)appropriated as *mediatypes* to promote products and ideology, which, in turn, promote stereotypical thinking.

4. The stereotyping of human sexuality and gender roles into a misapplied masculine/feminine dichotomy has oppressed humankind, whether homosexual, bisexual, transgendered, transsexual, or heterosexual.

5. We need to reframe this stereotypical misapplication of masculine/feminine as the infinitely variable archetypal bases for being within all human beings.

CONCLUSION

Isn't it fascinating that we witnessed a sexual revolution, almost to the point of anarchy (Showalter, 1990), in the last part of the twentieth century—right at a time when we figured out how to be whatever sex we want—through lifestyle, dress, surgery, chemistry, technology, or virtuality—and to have sex with whomever we want because it is no one's business but our own? Would we truly rather see billboards using sexual mediatypes, mere caricatures of human beings, to sell us "deatharettes" and "deathahol" and "sexemup" trucks and "spend all your money on them 'cause then you'll look sexy and like you've made it" things than be exposed to honest, sensual, sexual, traditional, radical, middle-of-the-road people who may look like what we have constructed as regular men or women, or look like neither, or both, or even a third sex? Society can influence us through every external form imaginable. Why not take charge of our most private selves—our own identities, our own sexualities, our own physical and psychic connections with other human beings?

It seems to us that one of the gifts of strong minority figures, of powerful women, of sensitive men, of gayness, of lesbianism, of bisexualism, of transsexualism (Stone, 1993, 1995), of cross-dressing, of androgyny, and of anyone deemed *alternative* to so-called mainstream society, is *freedom*

- from convention,
- from logical, linear either/or-ness,
- from being locked within a socially acceptable body,
- from a life of masks and constant theater,
- from a life of stereotypical constructions, and
- from a life exemplified by mediatypes.

Through stereotypes, we appropriate masculine and feminine archetypes into external male and female biological forms within heterosexuality rather than draw upon the archetypes to foster honest communication and authentic representation of self. Adherence to these media-reinforced and media-generated stereotypes often leads to a lonely, counterfeit, and ultimately impossible archetypal search for wholeness and self within a rigid structure of corrupted, acceptable expressions of the masculine and feminine.

This is a call to humanity to strip away the false mediatypes and stereotypes that constrict our rights to define our own identities based on our individual, interwoven expressions of the masculine and feminine archetypes. Our goal is psychological and physical freedom.

Part VIII

MISCELLANEOUS STEREOTYPES

Chapter 25

DRAWING BLOOD: IMAGES, STEREOTYPES, AND THE POLITICAL CARTOON

Keith Kenney and Michael Colgan

Stereotypes are the lifeblood of political candidates. Politicians frequently rely on stereotypes to define themselves and their platforms. Stereotyped images can function as visual shorthand for political candidates. Think of any recent political campaign, on any level, and you will probably remember the candidate in visual stereotypes: the self-made businessman, the lying scoundrel, the all-American patriot, the caring intellectual, the incompetent boob, or the mean-spirited mudslinger.

POSITIVE, POPULIST IMAGES: NEWS PHOTOGRAPHS

Especially during political campaigns, photographers take positive pictures and editors select positive pictures of politicians. Cliché pictures convey excitement, public involvement, and dynamic, attractive personalities. Upbeat imagery of candidates so permeates visual campaign coverage that many assume the pictures were crafted by the media handlers who used the picture press like putty to shape candidate imagery at will.

Most campaign photographs look similar because politicians have learned to manage press coverage of their campaigns: "Candidates and their staffs have become the ultimate journalistic gatekeepers, deciding what is and is not news by allowing access only to those events which they wish to publicize" (Schlagheck, 1992, p. 57). As *New York Times* political reporter Maureen Dowd (1988) noted, "Now the press are led like cattle to one perfectly controlled event after another" (p. 44).

It is true that politicians and their staffs try to control photographers, but they do not always succeed. Without special access, Arthur Grace has been able to show candidates looking small and vulnerable against an expanse of sterile walls and empty stages. The usual grins and forceful gestures are absent, as are the adoring crowds. Grace provides glimpses of the reality available to any news photographer wishing to capture them rather than stereotypes.

But the dominant media images are pervasive, and they arise from a long political tradition of populism. Andrew Jackson's election in 1828 symbolized the triumph of the common man (Grob & Beck, 1970, p. 163). In his veto of a congressional rechartering of the privately held Bank of the United States, Jackson noted that the rich and powerful "bend" acts of government to become even more rich and powerful, while "the humble members of society—the farmers, mechanics, and laborers—who have neither the time nor the means of securing favors to themselves, have a right to complain." A stand must be taken, he said, "against any prostitution of our Government to the advancement of the few at the expense of the many" (Handlin, 1960, p. 314).

The idea of populism remains in the 1990s, especially during political campaigns. Politicians like to be photographed with farmers, blue-collar workers, police, and cowboys. These are *real* people, not elites. In contrast, suburban, white-collar workers are rarely pictured with politicians because they do not fit the populist ideology. Viewers of photographs also rarely see the political players who truly influence the political process— major contributors and well-financed special interest groups. Instead, the press follows the populist ideology that the people have more influence and involvement in government than they actually do.

Populist Stereotypes: With the People

Four different stereotypes of politicians follow the populist ideology. First, there is the "glad-to-see-you" politician. We see photographs of a politician waving, shaking hands, or giving a thumbs-up sign to common people. The politician shows his or her enthusiasm and concern for ordinary people by visiting a bakery, factory, day-care center, or other facility where he or she can ostensibly learn about workers and issues that affect their lives. A variation is the classic photograph of a politician with tie loosened, hair tousled, coat off and slung over one shoulder, wearing a blue (not white) dress shirt. This projects an image of a hard working man of the people. Rarely do photographs show the politician visiting the kinds of nondescript offices where most business and bureaucratic work takes place. Never do politicians appear sad, pessimistic, or distressed.

Of the People

Second, stereotyped photographs show politicians as athletes or outdoors persons. Politicians throw balls, pitch horseshoes, fish, hunt, bowl, and run in order to tap into the nation's obsession with sports and to convey energy, health, strength, and a competitive spirit. Some sports, however, are more suitably populist than others. During the 1992 campaign, aides discouraged President George H. W. Bush from "manic rounds of his favorite elitist pastimes, golf and boating" because such pictures "reinforce the image of an aristocratic president out of touch with the common man" ("Can We," 1992, p. 6).

Connected to the People

Third, the politician appears as a father figure. Contrary to popular belief, politicians rarely kiss babies, but they do hug them and hoist them into the air. By appearing with a child, politicians are cast in a glow of reflected innocence and they project a concern for education and the future. Father figure pictures are so common they create the false impression that politicians spend a disproportionate amount of their time wooing people who are too young to vote. A study of the 1992 campaign found more pictures of candidates with children and youths than with representatives of business and labor combined (Glassman, 1994).

Exemplar of the People

Related to the father figure role are the many photographs showing a candidate with his/her spouse, children, or parents. The fourth stereotype, that of family figure, is used to convince voters of the politician's respectable and virtuous character. Politicians appear as human as we are. For men, the politician's wife also must play a stereotypical role for the cameras. The press supplies photographic evidence of a warm and loving wife who wants nothing more than to support her husband. Cliché photographs of Nancy Reagan and Barbara Bush were inevitable. With Hillary Rodham Clinton, photographers and editors had a choice: they could follow the stereotype or portray Ms. Clinton as the tough, independent lawyer she was in reality. In its 1993 year-end retrospective issue, *Life* magazine chose a shot of the Clintons in front of a huge American flag. Ms. Clinton is demure and slightly in back of her husband. Her eyes are raised skyward in a boys-will-be-boys look of girlish charm (p. 10).

THE HISTORICAL BARB: POLITICAL CARTOONS

Stereotypes are also the lifeblood of political cartoonists.[1] The editorial cartoonist, much like the editorial writer, wants you to see the world in the same way that he or she sees the world, but instead of relying on words, the editorial cartoonist relies on images—often stereotyped images. Author, Roy Paul Nelson (1975) describes the political cartoon as "a figure of speech in graphic form" (p. 4).

The term *cartoon* was originally used to refer to an artist's preliminary drawings for what would eventually become a painting, mosaic, or tapestry. Today's editorial cartoons are usually, but not exclusively, single-panel drawings. They represent the cartoonist's view of political issues, current events, public personalities, and contemporary social mores. When you read a political cartoon, you are exposing your mind to the cartoonist's perspective; you are seeing the world as the cartoonist sees the world. Although primarily humorous and only occasionally sentimental, editorial cartoons stereotype and exaggerate by design to make a point and to influence the reader's opinions. Sometimes cartoons are subtle and evasive, but often they are obvious and provocative. As newspaper editor Martin Tolchin said: "Political cartoonists are the court jesters of modern society" (Freedom Forum, 1997).

It was during the nineteenth century that the cartoon first earned its independent significance as a form of commentary. In France, the periodical *Le Charivari* (founded in 1832) featured caricatures drawn by Honoré Daumier (1808–1879). In 1841, England's first comic weekly, *Punch*, began publication. *Le Charivari* and *Punch* became powerful media for social and political criticism ("Cartoons," 1993, Sec. 2, p. 1). In 1843 the cartoon sketches of England's new Houses of Parliament were exhibited in London. When the comic magazine *Punch* then satirized these drawings under the title "Punch's Cartoons," the word cartoon began to signify pictorial humor, satire, and parody.

Evidence of the use of pictorial drawings and caricatures can be found in caves and pyramids, as well as in the pottery of ancient Egypt, Greece, and Rome. These drawings are records of historical events, political biographies, and legends. They represent ideas and opinions. Even the ancient

Chinese caricatures depicted in J. P. Malcolm's 1813 work, *An Historical Sketch of the Art of Caricaturing,* looks like a primer for the novice political cartoonist.

Cartoonist Syd Hoff (1976) has said:

> All present-day cartoons and caricatures have their roots in what the primitives did many thousands of years ago. Even then, society was ridiculed or glorified by those pioneer satirists. We see proof of this in the most ancient stone chiseling or wood carving...kings and chiefs who look ridiculous or magnificent, slaves and commoners who appear crushed or alert.... [I]t is as though someone had already laid down the ground rules for political cartooning, or as if a kind of international school for comic art was already in operation. (pp. 16–17)

In the Middle Ages hand-drawn illustrations were often a part of book texts. In eighteenth- and nineteenth-century Europe, cartoons were called caricatures and were sold as single sheets instead of as an element of a publication (Nelson, 1975). The Bayeux tapestry is a particularly significant work that depicts William the Conqueror's invasion of England ("Cartoons," 1993, Sec. 2, p. 1).[2] This tapestry contains captions that flow from scene to scene describing the invasion in much the same way that a comic strip would illustrate an event today. After the invention of the printing press in the fifteenth century, the general public gained access to many illustrated flyers and pamphlets that described political and social happenings and that often contained early forms of the editorial cartoon ("Cartoons," 1993, Sec. 2, p. 1). The development of pictorial humor and caricature—as a means to influence public opinion—can be seen in the work of William Hogarth (1697–1764) and Thomas Rowlandson (1756–1827). James Gillray (1757–1815) and George Cruikshank (1792–1878) became famous political satirists who took aim at George the III and Napoleon.

Political cartoons in the United States can be traced to colonial times. Early American cartoons focused on political and social events, just as they did in Europe. Although most of the early American cartoonists or engravers remained anonymous, Benjamin Franklin generally receives credit for creating the first American political cartoon. Thomas Nast (1840–1902), creator of the Republican elephant and Democratic donkey, is regarded as America's first significant political cartoonist (Nelson, 1996).

Technological improvements in the reproduction of drawings led to wider dissemination of political cartoons. In the early nineteenth century,

Americans' strong opinions about the presidency of Andrew Jackson meant that American cartoons focused largely on partisan politics, government policies, and historical events ("Cartoons," 1993, Sec. 2, p. 1). As time passed, cartoons evolved and took a number of different paths. However, the basic reliance on stereotype and satire, which political cartoonists use to make their point, has not changed much over hundreds of years.

DRAWING BLOOD: THE TOOLS OF CARTOONING

Art Spiegelman, a cartoonist and contributing editor of *New Yorker* magazine, pinpoints the essential form of the cartoon when he writes: "Cartoons echo the most fundamental processes of cognition.... Cartoons are an especially effective and basic language" (Walker, 1994, p. 45). It is this very simplicity of communication that often raises cartoons to a higher level of expression: art.

Caricature

Caricature is an essential element in the political cartoon's makeup. According to *Merriam-Webster's Collegiate Dictionary*, 10th edition, *caricature* means a "distorted representation to produce a ridiculous effect." The exaggeration and ridicule found in caricature is actually the cartoonist's mechanism for representing his perceived truth. Sixteenth century Italian caricaturist Annibale Caracci observed: "A good caricature, like every other work of art, is more true to life than reality itself"(Garland, 1989, p. 32). The cartoonist's goal is to use caricature and humor to force the reader to see that the emperor is not wearing any clothes. By manipulating stereotypes, the cartoonist conveys a viewpoint that he or she hopes will ultimately change your opinion. So, by nature, editorial cartoons are biased; they intentionally are drawn with extreme prejudice. Using stereotypes is, quite simply, the means to an end.

Political cartoonist Nicholas Garland (1989) describes what he believes to be the three essential elements of the political cartoon:

> First, caricature[,] the humorously or maliciously distorted representation of politicians; second, the actual political comment, criticism, or stance communicated in the drawing; and third, the vehicle or image chosen to convey the political point. When brought together, the effect—at its best— is formidable.... In its directness and simplicity, caricature... has an awful bluntness.... Caricaturists... pursue a different kind of truth. (p. 32)

In an effort to describe the essence of the editorial cartoon, Garland (1989) writes that though caricature lies at the heart of political cartooning, the idea and the image that carries that idea, are inseparable.

> "Getting an idea," therefore, is finding the right vehicle for an opinion, one that simultaneously expresses and illuminates it. On good days an "idea" pops up complete with cast, props, and setting. On a difficult day, the political thought has to be struggled with in order to find the right image to convey it, which involves a search for analogies.... The best, the most striking cartoons can be read at a glance.... The idea contained in a political cartoon must not only be easily understood but even be already widely established *before* the cartoonist uses it. It could be reasonably argued that political cartoons are merely telling people what they already know in a highly simplified form. But the paradox is that cartoons express very simple ideas or attitudes through a medium that allows them to be extremely complex. (p. 33)

Ironically, it is the very form of the political cartoon that sometimes draws the most severe criticism for the cartoonist. Cartoons are commonly thought to be a form of expression targeted specifically toward children. The desire to somehow purify what is historically a very sophisticated—and sometimes mean-spirited medium—reflects the average reader's naiveté about the function and form of the cartoon.

Humor

Syndicated cartoonist Mort Walker (1994) defends the use of stereotypes in cartoons.

> Most cartoons deal with stereotypes and universal truths so that readers can see themselves in the gag and relate. Humor is also based on human failure. Success is not funny. Therein lies the rub. Certain people don't like to be made fun of.... [P]eople are more sensitive about a subject when it is treated humorously than when it is discussed seriously. (p. 48)

When it comes to the political cartoon, theories about what is funny and what is not funny go back hundreds of years. Because the foundation of the editorial cartoon is built on caricature, it is fundamental to understand that caricature distorts representation of an image in order to produce a ridiculous effect or joke. The hostile and aggressive nature of caricature is the essence of its purpose and therefore an essential element of the political cartoon.

In the 1980s, comedian Steve Martin released a comedy album. A close-up picture of Steve in full makeup appeared on the cover of the album. His lips were painted in a particularly bright shade of red lipstick and he feigned a sexy pout. The title of the album: *Comedy Is Not Pretty.* According to research psychologists, social scientists, and a number of scientific studies, Steve was right.

In a study of aggressive cartoons, McCauley, Woods, Coolidge, and Kulick (1983) state that there are at least eight different theories that try to explain why something is funny and why it is not, and that three of these theories can reasonably predict why aggressive humor is funnier than nonaggressive humor.[3] One of the three theories is Freud's concept of *tendentious wit,* which explains humor as a pleasurable expression of sexual and aggressive urges that were repressed in childhood (McCauley et al., 1983). In short, Freud postulated that the repressed sexual and aggressive urges from childhood could be safely released through sexual and aggressive jokes in a far more effective manner than through nonsexual and nonaggressive jokes. This theory indicates that aggressive and sexual jokes are simply funnier than other kinds of jokes (McCauley et al., 1983, p. 817).

The second is D. E. Berlyne's *arousal theory.* This theory posits that something is funny when heightened arousal is quickly relieved: a joke releases tension caused by anger, fear, sexual urges, etc. (McCauley et. al, 1983, p. 817). Aggressive humor is initially more arousing than nonaggressive humor, and so the release of tension is stronger; the joke is funnier.

The third theory that postulates aggressive humor to be funnier than nonaggressive humor dates back to 1651 and Hobbes' *Leviathan.* Hobbes' *superiority theory* suggests that laughter is an "expression of triumph over another person" (McCauley et al., 1983, pp. 817–818). According to Hobbes, aggressive humor should be funny because it demonstrates personal superiority over another person or group. A more modern approach to this theory, put forth by LaFave and Mannell in the 1970s, extends the superiority theory to people's ability to laugh at themselves (McCauley et al., 1983, p. 818). Although this may at first seem to be a contradiction to Hobbes' original theory, the modern approach suggests that aggressive superiority humor allows individuals to celebrate a weakness or inadequacy within themselves. So, even if the joke is directed at another person or group, it is funny because it allows the release of feelings of personal inadequacy.

What do you think is funny in an editorial cartoon? Surprisingly, your answer may depend on how much testosterone you have flowing through your body. Humor is in the eye, and possibly the sex, of the beholder. Men and women perceive what is funny in different ways. Take the Three Stooges. There is a common perception that men love the wacky antics of Larry, Moe, and Curly, whereas women just don't get it. Aggressive and sexual cartoons have been shown to have a higher perceived degree of funniness among diverse and generalized groups of males and females. According to Zillman's *predisposition theory* and the LaFave, McCarthy, and Haddad *group identification theory,* an individual needs to identify with the aggressor, not the victim, in order to appreciate aggressive humor (Love & Deckers, 1989, pp. 649–50). If the individual reader identifies with the victim in the cartoon, the cartoon just isn't as funny.

How does perception of humor break down along gender lines? A 1989 study by Love and Deckers attempted to eliminate uncontrollable variables and "determine if significant relationships existed between the degree of cartoon sexism, sex, and aggression, the subject's and experimenter's gender, and funniness" (p. 650). This research revealed that when the level of sexism in cartoons increases, females find the cartoons less funny. For males, on the other hand, as the level of sexism in the cartoon increases, the funnier the cartoon is perceived to be.

These results, when interpreted through Zillman's social predisposition theory, indicate that women are more likely to identify with the cartoon victim and so, as a group, women find sexist cartoons to be less funny. This may result from the fact that females are more likely to have been victims of sex discrimination at some point in their lives (Love & Deckers, 1989). A Zillman interpretation further suggests that men, because of their social history and experience, do not identify as closely with the victim (Love & Deckers, 1989). Men are also more aware of the sexual aspects of the cartoons, and this makes the cartoons funnier for them as a group. While this research does not propose that men are a bunch of sexist, drooling comic-book readers, it does indicate gender differences in the funniness ratings of cartoons (p. 653).

Audience Sensitivity

What does all this mean to the political cartoonist and the manipulation of stereotypes? Differences in the gender funny bones have significant implications for the cartoonist who decides to tackle any editorial drawing, particularly one with sexist or aggressor/victim overtones. With the information from these studies and a little self-reflection (not self-censorship) the cartoonist may be able to use stereotypes to produce a more effective piece of art that opens more minds than it closes—both male and female.

Quite simply, the cartoonist must recognize that many individuals are unable to enjoy humor when it cuts too close to home. This aspect of humor perception suggests that cartoonists who want to change someone's opinion about a political, social, or contemporary event must balance the aggressive nature of caricature and the manipulation of stereotypes so as not to completely offend the reader.

The aim of the political cartoon is to make a point through ridicule, sarcasm, or pathos. The fundamental nature of the political cartoon is to simplify and reduce complex personalities to easily identifiable labels and caricatures. By doing this, cartoonists often create media images that remain long after the details of the specific event fade from memory (Ammons, King, & Yeric, 1988, pp. 79–80). This can have profound influence on the intuitive perceptions that readers develop about their government, culture, and social structure. This powerful effect provides an incentive for consumers of cartoons to recognize and understand the history, use, and purpose of stereotypes within the form of the political cartoon.

Political cartooning is, by definition, unfair. It is supposed to be unfair. It is supposed to hit you over the head with its candor and insight—and with its manipulation of popular stereotypes. In so doing, the cartoonist is following a long line of artistic tradition. When the cartoonist causes you to think about an issue, the cartoonist is doing his or her job. When the cartoonist causes you to change your opinion about an issue, then he or she is succeeding at that job. The pen can be mightier than the sword—especially when it is used to draw an opinion.

Chapter 26

TRANSFORMATION OF A STEREOTYPE: GEEKS, NERDS, WHIZ KIDS, AND HACKERS

Olan Farnall

From 1939 to 1941, on the tiny campus of Iowa State University, John Atanasoff and Clifford Berry created and perfected the first electronic digital computer. The Atanasoff-Berry Computer, or ABC as it was called, weighed 750 pounds and was a mass of rotating drums, vacuum tubes, and circuits (Jolivette, 2002). Atanasoff was a professor of physics and mathematics at Iowa State and Berry was his graduate assistant. Their respective biographies describe both men as having been precocious children, preferring school and the pursuit of knowledge to more typical childhood activities. Both ultimately received a Ph.D. in the hard sciences, and, although married, both limited their social lives during early adulthood as a result of commitments to work.[1] In short, these two distinguished and honored men could have been poster children for the computer nerd stereotype that would arise some 40 years later.

The stereotype of the computer nerd is an interesting example of the evolution of harmful professional images. What once generally was acknowledged to be a derogatory reference to a less than masculine male who possessed high intelligence and a mastery of modern technology recently has become an almost desirable badge of honor among young, and not so young, men and women (Schorow, 2001). The shift can be traced in part to changes in the way Hollywood has presented the nerd, particularly the underdog turns to hero scenario carried out in the *Revenge of the Nerds* films of the late 1970s and early 1980s.

But a perhaps stronger impact on the nerd stereotype came from real-life examples of nerd power presented in national headlines at that same time. People who began careers working on computers in their garages were becoming rich and famous. Names such as Steven Jobs, Bill Gates, and Steven Wosniak were being touted in the press as examples of what every man dreams of: wealth and power coming as a result of some personal passion and special knowledge. If social-learning theory has taught us anything, it is that young minds will imitate the behaviors of those who are presented as successful and admired. It is no surprise then that today young computer nerds take pride in their association with others who possess advanced computer skills.

In the past decade the computer nerd reference in the media also has mutated into a reference with a darker meaning. The computer nerd of yesterday sometimes becomes the computer hacker of today. The world of the Hacker, Cracker, or Phreaker is quite different from the 1980s and 1990s image of a nerd and will be explored later in the text, but first a more historical look at the computer nerd stereotype.

FROM INNOCENT BEGINNINGS

The *American Heritage College Dictionary* traces the origin of the word *nerd* to a character described in the Dr. Seuss book entitled *If I Ran a Zoo*. Dr. Seuss's nerd is a humanoid creature that looks like an angry, thin cross (*American Heritage*, p. 915). One suggestion of how the Seuss nerd reference came to be applied to the stereotype presented here is that young readers of the Seuss story passed the label on to their older siblings, who, by the late 1950s, applied the term to the most comically obnoxious creature of their own class, the square.

Another history traces the American nerd to the early radio amateurs of post–World War II (Eglash, 2000). Dr. Ron Eglash of Rensselaer Polytechnic Institute identified the first nerds as the "electronic hobbyists" of the time. Fused together by their interests in science fiction, model trains, stereophonic sound, and other nonmasculine pursuits, these early nerds were the "ham radio operator, Boy-Scout merit badge in chemistry, Radar O'Reilly's" of the world, according to Eglash (2000).

NOT A GIRL'S CLUB

Regardless of the origin, one thing the early stereotyped nerd was not was female. All the early references to nerds in both movies and television are male. The stereotype in part reflected reality. As Myra Strober and Carolyn Arnold observed, "Computer-related occupations were sired by the fields of engineering and mathematics, both strongly male-dominated fields. Therefore, the computer engineering and electronic technical work employed very few women, whereas the data processing field, much akin to clerical work, became almost exclusively female" (Strober & Arnold, 1987, p. 171).

When one searches for early media images of women using computers, the few examples portrayed women as incompetent and confused. Even today, relatively few women are portrayed as computer experts on TV and in the movies ("Cultural Stereotypes," 2002). Among the rare but prominent exceptions are Demi Moore's less than completely positive role in *Disclosure* in 1994. Another is Ariana Richards, who plays Lex in *Jurassic Park*. Lex saves the day by restarting the computer security system in the dinosaur park. Arguably the strongest reference to a female computer nerd is found in the 1995 movie, *The Net*. In this film Sandra Bullock plays a program system analyst who works from her home in Venice Beach, California, for a big software development company. Bullock's character, Angela Bennett, is a prototypical nerd; shy and isolated, she never leaves her apartment and is cut off from human contact except through her computer.

The scarce and less than completely positive media images of women and computers affect women's perceptions as well as their choices. As Kathryn Weibel (1977) wrote in her book, *Mirror Mirror: Images of Women Reflected in Popular Culture*, "Women have eagerly sought reflections of their lives and concerns where these have been available in popular media....Never seeing women in some roles and seeing women playing other roles poorly reduces the likelihood that a woman will attempt such roles herself" (p. 24).

The net result of these images, or more accurately the absence of positive media images of women using computers, may be to limit women's role in the field of computer technology. In fact, a recent report from the American Association of University Women found that "girls today have reservations about the computer culture, particularly in the ways computers are used, the products used on them, and the way classes about them are taught." The report goes on to say that girls participate far less in computer labs, computer clubs, and advanced programming classes than boys ("AAUW Report," 2002). A UCLA study separately found that men are five times more likely than women to seek careers in computer programming ("First-Year," 2001).

DEVELOPMENT OF THE COMPUTER NERD IN FILM

Images and portrayals in magazine ads, television shows, and the movies have guided the development and transformation of the computer nerd stereotype. This discussion focuses on the development of the computer nerd stereotype in film because an examination across media indicates that film offers the most prevalent media images of the computer nerd. In addition, studies have shown that individuals most often attribute their mental images to exposure to stereotypical character portrayals in movies (Farnall & Smith, 1999).

Dr. Strangelove, Fail-Safe, and most Bond films of the 1960s serve as examples of the typical character portrayal of individuals associated with computers prior to the introduction of personal computers. The entertainment industry depicted computer programmers and operators as white-coat technicians, adults working in a laboratory-type setting, whose lives were square.

By the mid-1970s the term nerd was regularly applied to reoccurring figures appearing in movies and TV shows dealing with teens. The screen nerd was usually an intelligent but socially inept male. He could be either skinny or fat but not muscular or stereotypically masculine. He wore glasses, often held together by white tape around the nosepiece, and ill-fitting clothes that did not match the style of the time. He exhibited little physical prowess and a complete social ineptness.

Examples of the 1970s nerd in the media include Charles Martin Smith as the smart but inept nerd in George Lucas's 1974 classic *American Graffiti* and Stephen Furst as the freshman pledge nicknamed Flounder in National Lampoon's *Animal House* released in 1978. Actually, an entire collection of nerd types appears in the Lampoon movie. Early in the story a mixed bag of young men was herded into a group and isolated from the rest of the guests during a fraternity rush party. In that one scene the definition of a nerd was expanded to include anyone outside the in crowd.

Fueled by the personal computer revolution of the early 1980s, the association between nerd and computer began to surface in movies and television. Movies such as *Weird Science, War Games,* and the classic *Revenge of the Nerds* series firmly implanted the stereotype of the computer nerd as someone who spent an inordinate amount of time with computers and was extremely skilled in computer usage. In the case of the *Revenge of the Nerds* films the computer nerds also displayed the traditional nerd characteristics. As reconceptualized, the 1980s media nerd "includes aspects of both hypermasculinity (intellect, rejection of sartorial display, lack of feminine social and relational skills) and feminization (lack of sports ability, small body size, no sexual experience with women)," according to Kendall (1999).

Though Kendall's description holds true for the media images of computer nerds in the 1980s, it fails to consider one additional important element. The computer nerds portrayed in films during this period usually persevered through the ridicule and taunts of the jocks and fraternity bad guys to ultimately prevail, many times as a result of their computer skills. In the first *Revenge of the Nerds* movie, the nerds got revenge on the Alpha Betas (the football fraternity that burned down their house and humiliated them during a social) and the Pi's (the sorority that rejected an invitation to a social from the nerds) by using the very skills that labeled them as nerds. Chief among these skills was a mastery of computer technology. The nerds were able to spy and photograph the Pi sorority girls through a system of high-tech cameras tied to a computer monitor. They bettered the Alpha Betas at the carnival with the assistance of computer technology and music synthesizers.

REAL-LIFE NERDS MAKE IT BIG

The transformation theme from underdog to hero present in all three Nerd movies reflected the real-life success stories of garage start-up computer entrepreneurs such as Steve Jobs and Stephen Wozniak (Weigner, 1992). Wozniak, Bill Gates, and other computer nerds of the 1970s and early 1980s, who couldn't get a date in high school, were becoming multimillionaires as a result of their association with computers and technology. With that wealth came power, status, respect, and a great deal of press coverage. A 1992 *Forbes* article profiled several successful computer entrepreneurs who were shedding their nerd status mostly as a result of the money they had made and the things they had done with that money. For example Gates was profiled as liking fast cars and tennis, both non-nerd interests (Bell, 1996).

As a result of the press coverage of nerd success stories and the popular media image of underdog to hero, being called a computer nerd in the 1990s was not a condemnation to failure and isolation for life. A person so called possessed skills with technology above and beyond most people. The nerd label was like a merit badge in computers.

Films in the 1990s also began to portray the skilled computer operator in a much different fashion. Instead of a weak background figure, the computer expert became the leading man. Instead of being a social outcast, the computer expert could be the central figure in a team or the main love interest. In *Sneakers* in 1992, Robert Redford played Bishop, the leader of an industrial espionage team that tested banks' security systems. Bishop was a computer expert, but he was far from the computer nerd. His leader status and attractive physical features made him a very masculine figure, far from the image of the 1970s nerd. In *The Net,* a female computer analyst stumbles across a computer conspiracy and ultimately triumphs over a team of bad guys who erased all electronic records of her existence. Bullock, even without makeup and hairdo, is attractive and sought after by men, including Dennis Miller, who loses his life because he is her boyfriend. The 1995 movie *Johnny Mnemonic* starred Keanu Reeves as a super-slick courier with an 80-gigabyte brain implant. Mnemonic triumphs over the corporations and their thugs to release information that helps all humankind.

Hackers, also released in 1995, portrayed a group of high school students who, as underdogs, defeat the adult hacker at his own game. *Hackers* reflected two important aspects of the 1990s computer nerd: the group mentality that binds nerds and provides a sense of belonging and the emerging image of the nerd as evil hacker. In that same era, one cannot forget the superspy Tom Cruise in the 1996 film version of *Mission Impossible.* As Ethan Hunt, Cruise is a clean-cut, all-American man and a driven moral crusader for what is right. Always using his laptop to send cryptic messages or discover some clue, he succeeds even after his entire team has been killed.

1990s TELEVISION: WINNERS AND LOSERS

It would be incorrect to say that the old computer nerd image had completely vanished from the media during the 1990s. Television continued to contribute to the traditional stereotype. For example, a 1995 short-lived primetime television series called *Dweebs* actually borrowed its premise directly from the garage-to-penthouse story of Jobs and Wozniak. In this series, the men of Cyberbyte (a high-tech company) hire a secretary (Carey) to help them develop their social skills and become more at ease with women. Warren, the boss, doesn't know how to complete a sentence. Vic wears sunglasses all the time. And none of the men has much experience talking to women. Carey on the other hand has no computer skills and tries her best to understand and be understood.

Other successful 1990 shows that portrayed the traditional computer nerd stereotype included *Family Matters, Saved by the Bell,* and *The Simp-*

sons. Running for a decade, *Family Matters* focused on the Winslow family and how they dealt with the continued interference of ultranerd Steve Urkle played by Jaleel White. Urkle was the embodiment of the nerd, except that he was black. The white counterpart to Urkle might well be Samuel "Screetch" Powers. One nerd in *The Simpsons* is Bart's best friend, Milhous.

NERD BECOMES HACKER

Somewhere along the line of films and TV series, the computer nerd stereotype mutated and was supplanted in part by the image of a computer hacker. Not a hypermasculine geek, this alternative image of a computer expert is the renegade computer buff of today with the ability to illegally gain entry into any system, whether private, business, or national security. According to "A Portrait of J Random Hacker," this male with sociopathic tendencies is between 13 and 30, his appearance is scruffy, he dresses for comfort and function.[2] He is highly educated and has little time for anyone who is not at the same level. His reading habits are omnivorous and include lots of science and science fiction, but he avoids the cyberpunk magazines such as *Wired.* He is not a drug user, but consumes caffeine in great volume and has a preference for ethnic food, especially take-out. He is sexually open to more counterculture practices and is antiauthoritarian.

The computer hacker's roots can be traced from the basement at MIT, but it is the media and the popular news that keep him in front of the public. He is the creator of the Melissa virus, the young man who broke into the Toys R Us system and the credit card database of Bank of America. The hacker is our worst nightmare brought to us on the news and in film. The power base of this computer nerd gone bad is the antithesis of the original stereotype. Instead of an image of the victim or the hero, the hacker is the villain. Hackers tend toward self-absorption, arrogance, and impatience with other people.

The jury is out on this latest reference to people who possess exceptional skill levels with computers and the Internet. There have been enough real stories about hackers in the press and news to assure that the term and the stereotype will stay on the public agenda. They also have appeared and will continue to appear in the public's entertainment choices. But whether the hacker or nerd image prevails will depend upon the public. These images are, as Lippmann put it, "reflections of our society, not representations of society as it is" (Lippmann, 1961).

CONCLUSION

Throughout this book there are references to the damage stereotypes can do to individuals or a group. In the case of the computer nerd, it is media coverage of the real-life experiences of a few extremely successful men that has helped reshape the stereotype of the computer nerd to something that is not always a negative. In fact, by the mid-1990s the definition of a computer nerd depended largely on the individual's reference point. For outsiders to the world of computers, the term could be used as a derogatory reference to a person wrapped up in computers to the exclusion of everything else. But used within the computer community, *nerd* usually means smarter than or different from the average, and it has a decidedly positive connotation. In this latter view, a nerd likely has the skills needed to get information to help a friend, or to hack into the school computer to change a grade, or to help plan the rescue of a military officer held by an evil enemy.[3]

Females also appear to have made progress in the area of computer comfort. The Internet has a computer nerd Web site for women only. In the South, schools are testing girls only computer clubs with specialized training and programming designed to change the negative stereotyping of the information technology profession. The clubs hope to go nationwide in 2003 ("Girls' Computer Clubs," 2002).

ONE FINAL NOTE

As one traces the creation and re-creation of the computer nerd stereotype from its geek roots to the modern hacker image, there is a clear connection between people who use the technology and the technology itself. As programming advances, so does the role of the character and the meaning associated with use of the term. Where it goes depends on us.

Chapter 27

STEREOTYPING OF MEDIA PERSONNEL

Walter B. Jaehnig

William V. Kennedy is a retired U.S. Army public affairs officer and former journalist. He is also the author of *The Military and the Media: Why the Press Cannot Be Trusted to Cover a War* (1993). In the book's opening chapter, Kennedy provided the U.S. military's justification for restricting news media access to the battlefield, especially during the Persian Gulf War of 1991:

> Why, then, should journalists utterly ignorant and inexperienced in the history, language, organization, methods, and technology of the subject they are covering, when that subject has a bearing on the life or death of thousands (indeed, of an entire nation), be permitted to roam about at will and to report without effective supervision? (p. 11)

This is a view apparently held by many in the U.S. military establishment; indeed, as Kennedy noted, in general, "the people who are attracted to a military career and the people who are attracted to a journalism career don't much like each other" (p. 13). This is because journalists as a group possess characteristics abhorred by those in uniform:

> Skepticism—indeed, often hostility and ridicule—toward religion, patriotism, and authority in general has become the hallmark of the 20th century journalist. At least among American journalists, there is a tendency to avoid mathematics and science in favor of the abstractions and fantasies of litera-

ture, sociology, and political "science." A dislike for any sort of "regimentation" is often expressed by a deliberately cultivated lack of fastidiousness in matters of dress and personal appearance. These characteristics—in particular the ridicule of patriotism—are found frequently enough among journalists to create a stereotype detested by the military. (p. 13)

Apparently Daniel Pearl, the *Wall Street Journal* Bombay bureau chief who was murdered by a radical Islamic group in Pakistan in early 2002, possessed some of these unsoldierly characteristics. According to a *USA Today* story, he was recruited to the *Journal*'s London bureau while wearing a ponytail, and a colleague recalled that when she met him, Pearl was barefoot in the office (Donahue, 2002). More important, the story described him as "(s)keptical about institutions and spin," and not interested in "geopolitical machinations but in explaining to the *Journal*'s affluent readers the day-to-day struggles of ordinary people." Pearl was warm, creative, a lover of music, sympathetic to the Islamic world, and a writer of both whimsical stories as well as stories that questioned "institutional assumptions about government actions."

Clearly, the same personal characteristics can be read or interpreted in totally different ways, depending upon one's view of the world and the journalist's role within it. What has changed since September 11, 2001, is that two overlapping but conflicting stereotypes of professional journalists are developing in the public mind. Whether the journalist's skepticism, humanism, and acts of inquiry contribute value to the wider society increasingly appears to depend upon the eye of the beholder.

STEREOTYPING THE STEREOTYPERS

Journalists, possibly more than any other occupational group, provide the images upon which social stereotypes are based. They are trained and rewarded for describing the world around them; this means they do not often provide insights into their own professional world, even when it might benefit the public to know more about who they are and how they work.

But increasingly, *journalism* as a noun does not play a substantial role in public discourse. We speak more in terms of *the media,* a constituent group thought to have greater and greater influence in American life. *Media* itself is a troublesome word, often loaded with pejorative meanings. It is conventionally used in its plural, collective form, referring to a range of print and broadcast communications organizations (and, accordingly, in the Associated Press stylebook, requiring a plural verb). This is consistent with a pluralistic political philosophy that assigns a limited, informational role to a press institution composed of a diverse range of news organizations, under different ownerships, representing a full range of views in the marketplace of ideas. In a democratic system of checks and balances, the media have no more power and influence than other institutions, and, in a functional sense, the media provide the framework and conduits for public discussion of issues.

In recent years, popular usage of *media* has given it singular connotations (a trend evident to United Press International editors when producing their version of the style manual) that represent more powerful conceptions of informational institutions. Sometimes, *media* seems to refer to television alone, as when the small-market television station reporter shows up at a fish fry, struggling under the weight of camera, light, and battery packs, and someone says, "The media is here!" More often, it is used to refer to a singular, monolithic (and distinctly nonpluralistic) institution with a mind and values of its own in which all news employees are grouped together, no matter who they work for or what they do. Usually this singular usage is antagonistic in character, used by critics on both the left and the right, expressing disapproval of whatever news agencies have done and their perceived power to do it, as if the values displayed by the media differ distinctly from those held by ordinary (nonmedia) people.

If *media* is problematic, *media personnel* is even more so. Clearly, the term refers to much more than newspaper editors, reporters, photographers, and graphic designers, and their occupational equivalents in broadcast organizations. Within the communications industry, we might make significant distinctions among newspaper reporters, soap opera actors, book authors, talk show hosts, television camerapersons, trade magazine publishers, advertising promoters, network commentators, sportswriters, or disc jockeys—to name only a few visible, media-related occupational positions—but it is not at all clear that members of the general public make the same distinctions.

Not only is the term *media* inclusive, but the increasing blurring of lines between traditional media forms and functions complicates it. Televised entertainment programs adopt the newscast format. At the same time the television evening news preoccupies itself with news items of celebrities. Infomercials borrow television talk show formats and purvey product attributes as if they were newsworthy. And with the heavy celebrity orientation of the new media, disc jockeys and sportswriters are as likely to relay newsy bits of information to their audiences as persons conventionally considered to be news reporters.

Finally, even within traditional news media, crucial distinctions might be made between those connected with what has been termed the elite media—usually referring to the Washington/New York/Los Angeles news and entertainment axis—and the rest of the country. The same stereotypes hardly seem to apply to a newspaper photographer in Carbondale, Illinois, and a Washington, DC, political commentator on a Sunday morning television panel discussion, but to members of the audience they both are media. Simply put, is it not difficult to identify nearly a million people working in many occupations, with presumably the similar ideological views, under the same stereotype of media?

JOURNALISTS AS STEREOTYPES

The international conflict since 9/11 has provided an extended look at journalists and the work they do. From this at least two views have grown, related in no small part to the perspective of the viewer. The first is rooted in the story of Daniel Pearl and the other eight journalists who died in Afghanistan and Pakistan since 9/11, as well as many others injured reporting the Israeli/Palestinian conflict in recent months. The Freedom Forum reports that 51 journalists worldwide were killed in the line of duty in 2001, and more than 1,300 have been killed on the job over the past 200 years (Phipps, 2002; Trigoboff, 2002). Their story connects with the romantic image of the trench-coated foreign correspondent, whose work is based in hardship, sacrifice, and courage. The second view is far less flattering to journalists.

In the romantic vision, patriotism means journalists are obligated to ask unpopular questions and provide the sorts of information people in a democratic society need to know. These journalists face many obstacles—from the manipulations of government and military information controls to their own limited language and cultural preparation—but slog on in the public's interest. Their work is expensive, in economic cost and personal privations. These reporters know they are not heroes—that word is reserved for others in the post-9/11 world. When Christiane Amanpour, chief international correspondent for CNN, was asked who were the heroes in her profession, she replied:

> I don't know about heroes, but I think the people who go above and beyond the call of duty are the war correspondents, the war photographers, and all the people who make up a team of journalists who cover wars. In the end, this is the most difficult and the most dangerous. You just

never know; are you going to come back or not. ("Interview: Christiane Amanpour," 2002)

Always lurking behind the work of this new generation of war correspondents is the second view, the sense that a nation at war does not honor and respect their traditional watchdog role. Commenting on U.S. military restrictions on reporting in Afghanistan, Amanpour said, "Let's be very honest. The [Bush] administration has not suffered any public backlash from its restriction of journalists. The public doesn't care how little or how much, apparently, they see of this war. So, that's a problem for us."

Terry Anderson, an Associated Press reporter taken hostage in Lebanon during the 1980s, noted, "[j]ournalism can be a very dangerous profession.... To cover the news, [journalists] have to be in the midst of it. To be neutral and fair means being willing to talk to all sides, to go into the streets and see what is happening, and to do so most of the time without bodyguards or protection" (Anderson, 2002).[1]

As Kennedy suggested, many question journalists' patriotism. They fail to understand Anderson's statement about being "neutral and fair" and talking to all sides. Ultimately, reporters' questions are construed as inappropriate and threatening to the American war effort. Faced with the Bush administration's secrecy policies, coordinated information campaigns, pressure on the television networks, and moral imperatives underlying its war on terrorism, journalists have been branded as opponents—or pressured to climb on board as cheerleaders for the war effort.

This more critical view of journalists has become the basic stereotypical image in recent movies, novels, plays, and television dramatic productions, where reporters are seedy, cynical, and bearers of questionable ethics—especially the foreign correspondents, covering events in the world's seamiest trouble spots. Films such as *Salvador, Under Fire,* or *The Year of Living Dangerously,* and James Woods, Nick Nolte, and Mel Gibson in their sweaty dungarees or military fatigues, anticipated the real-life antics of Geraldo Rivera in Afghanistan, waving his firearm or claiming to have covered battles when he was 50 miles away. Playwright Tom Stoppard, a former journalist himself, cataloged the failings of journalism in *Night and Day,* a play about a rebellion in the fictitious African state of Kambawe. Though supporting the concept of free expression, Stoppard's two key reporters are hardened professionals with warped senses of public responsibility. His third journalist, the idealistic young Jacob Milne, is killed chasing a scoop that fails to be published because of a journalists' union strike.

Michelle Malkin's column in *Human Events* weeks after 9/11 established the tone for this journalistic stereotype:

> The media backlash against public displays of patriotism reveals a lot about modern American journalism's true colors. Many of today's leading purveyors of journalism are simply embarrassed to identify with the average citizen. They view flag waving as a maudlin exercise; gun ownership as fanatical; national pride as politically incorrect arrogance; and the U.S. military as an outdated, hierarchical, racist, sexist, homophobic, and imperialistic institution. (Malkin, 2001)

Malkin declared that the war reporting of Ernie Pyle that earned him a Pulitzer Prize in 1944 "would have gotten him fired today."

Faced with this criticism, especially from conservative groups, what Erik Sorenson, president of MSNBC, referred to as the "patriotism police" (Rutenberg & Carter, 2001), the major issue in the corporate-owned media became not the government's conduct of the war, but how the news organizations could show their patriotic support for it and "get on side" (Knightley, 1975). Television news commentators sprouted red, white, and blue ribbons, as the NBC peacock acquired patriotic feathers, and newspapers promoted the war with jingoistic headlines. Reporters, especially from the broadcast industry, donned battle fatigues and fired home stories of the war-is-fun variety from aircraft carriers and military bases in the Middle East, while their stations and networks ran Pentagon-provided video clips of military equipment and its devastating potential for evil doers in the world at large.

Some journalists who dissented from this view found their opposition unwanted. Tom Gutting, a columnist at the *Texas City Sun,* was fired for writing a column that criticized President Bush. A columnist in Oregon, Dan Guthrie, was fired under similar circumstances (Barton, 2001). Janis Besler Heaphy, publisher and president of the *Sacramento Bee,* was prevented from completing her commencement address at California State University Sacramento for suggesting that the Bush administration had made several attempts "to manipulate the press, encouraging the press to surrender some of its independence and thoroughness in the name of patriotism and security" (Roberts, 2001, p. 2). She also questioned whether the press should agree to censorship measures requested by the government. "Scrutiny by the press of this war on terrorism and publication of dissenting viewpoints are not signs of disloyalty. Rather, they are expressions of confidence in democracy and in the fulfillment of the First Amendment

charge to hold government accountable." The university president apolo-
gized for the heckling Heaphy received and posted her speech on the university's Web site.[2]

PERCEPTIONS AND EXPECTATIONS

It is one of the paradoxes of our time that as public estimation of the
news media seemingly drops lower and lower, people spend more and
more time and money with media products, watching television, going to
movies, buying books, searching electronic information services, and
reading newspapers. The events since 9/11 have accelerated both these
trends. So how do members of the public read these two journalistic stereotypes?

Lewis H. Lapham, editor of *Harper's Magazine,* suggested the American public is being manipulated by both the federal government and the
news media:

> Probably because I'm used to reading the letters to the editor of *Harper's
> Magazine,* I incline to give the American people credit for a higher quotient
> of intelligence and a greater store of idealism than their supervisors in
> Washington think they want or deserve, and I suspect that if given a voice
> in the arrangement of the nation's foreign affairs they would endorse the
> policies (similar to those once put forward by Franklin D. Roosevelt) that
> reflected a concern for human rights, international law, nuclear disarma-
> ment, freedom from both the colonial and neocolonial forms of economic
> monopoly. But the American people don't have a voice at the table, espe-
> cially not now, not during what the media and the government aggressively
> promote as a "time of war." (Lapham, 2002)

Lapham might be only partly right. Results from two major public opinion surveys of media credibility carried out during the summer of 2002
show that the American public accepts *both* journalistic stereotypes: while
they might question journalistic practices and media patriotism, they still
believe news organizations are necessary to hold government agencies
accountable (Paulson, 2002; Princeton Survey Research Associates,
2002). The Freedom Forum's First Amendment Center found in its survey
that nearly half of 1,000 adults surveyed (49 percent) thought the First
Amendment went too far in the rights it guarantees—up from 22 percent
in 2000. The least popular First Amendment right was freedom of the
press, with 42 percent of respondents saying the press has too much freedom, and about half saying the press had been too aggressive in asking

government officials for information about the war on terrorism. Similar results were found in a survey produced by the Pew Research Center for the People & the Press. Only 49 percent of 1,365 respondents thought the news media were highly professional in their work, down from 73 percent in the period following 9/11. And journalists' ratings for patriotism had plummeted by 20 percentage points in that period—to 49 percent.

However, these surveys also support the favorable stereotype of the news media's traditional watchdog role. The Pew survey found the percentage of respondents believing that press criticism prevents political leaders from acting wrongly grew from 54 to 59 percent from November 2001 to July 2002. During the same period, public confidence in government reports on the war on terrorism fell by 20 percentage points—to 60 percent. And according to the First Amendment Center's survey, 57 percent believed the news media should be allowed to freely criticize the U.S. military's strategy and performance. The percentage thinking it was essential that a free press inform the public had grown from 60 to 68 percent between 1997 and the summer of 2002.

These figures seem contradictory in many ways. This might not be surprising in a nation fundamentally divided on many issues and along several fault lines: witness the slim electoral margin in the 2000 presidential election, the narrow majorities in the houses of Congress, and polling results on any number of major public issues. The figures do suggest why two contradictory stereotypical views of journalists and the work they do are evident in the United States today. So far, the evidence suggests that the present crisis in America has accentuated its deep cleavages, not drawn the nation together as some media myth making might suggest.

Part IX

CONCLUSION

Chapter 28

COMMON GROUND AND FUTURE HOPES

Clifford G. Christians

Sticks and stones may break my bones, but words will never hurt me.

This old saw could not be more wrong and destructive. Telling kids to ignore taunting peers is good advice in one sense, of course. But as these chapters document across the board, cruel names and distorted pictures attack our very being. They go for the jugular emotionally. Stereotypes shrivel our humanity. This book's high-level worrying about images that injure is not marginal to media studies but central to them.

In their own way, the authors presume and exemplify a philosophy of symbolic communication. They stake a powerful claim for symbol theory, though their intentions may be elsewhere. Representational forms matter in a symbolic view; these chapters demonstrate how and why. The contributors share a commitment to social justice, but on a deeper level their common ground is epistemological. They each drive a nail in the coffin of mainstream empiricism. Communication ethicists are served with an encyclopedia of material, but the field as a whole benefits also. Stereotypes are a laboratory for examining how symbols function.

MAINSTREAM EMPIRICISM

In the received view, knowledge is built up and communicated brick by brick. The aim is clarity and efficiency in the message. Democratic societies protect it by a sacred First Amendment. We call it the stimulus-response model and go after the in-between, calibrating it empirically, insisting on a feedback loop, and quantifying the noise in the channel. It presumes the Enlightenment's fact-value dichotomy. The statistically sophisticated are assigned the heavy lifting, putting message systems into mathematical form in order to advance scientific prediction and control. In this perspective, ethical questions are left along the fringes for those with divine wisdom or hot-tempered moralists and quasi-academics.

Out of inertia or lethargy, the majority of communication scholars have assumed a priestly role as guardians of the empiricist view; they are busy, in Thomas Kuhn's terms, doing normal science (Kuhn, 1970). Most research money still supports studies that measure observable behavior, finding in such results the precision they desire. Meanwhile, some scholars seek more elaborate and finely tuned procedures, more complex multivariate scales, faster computer banks, and longer-range experiments. It is hoped that improved methods will eliminate the remaining weaknesses.

The accomplishments of the mainstream paradigm are worth noting. We understand more clearly now the significance of audience demographics. Some differences among the media—their varying purposes and potential—have been stipulated. Media messages can be delivered today with greater impact. We speak more informatively about stimulus variables, perception, and attitude change. Sociometric scales have forced explicitness—about the way children read the television text, for instance.

But a paradigm shift is occurring in media studies these days, as in the social sciences, generally. A growing number among us sense deeply that the field of communications needs a fresh theoretical foundation and a more solid set of intellectual questions. A watershed change to interpretativeness is under way. Consequently, many theorists recognize that an outdated model happily marrying political and commercial concerns, although revered by the engineering mentality found in the prestigious sciences, has just about accomplished its potential. A noted insider, Joseph Klapper (1965), himself regretted that after years at the "inexhaustible fount of variables," a systematic description of effects and their predictive applications "becomes the more distant as it is the more vigorously pursued" (p. 316). The received view is breaking up beneath our feet and the protest grows.

Despite good intentions and Herculean effort, communication scholars witness an ever-lengthening agenda of unresolved issues. The received view has produced an elegant handling of details, but today's issues demand a different statement of problems and theoretical inventiveness.

The technically rigid left-to-right transportation model appears congenitally inadequate for the broader problems that trouble us now. The mechanistic definition of communication is unhelpful when the overarching issues of this volume are at stake—multiculturalism, visual thinking, digital technologies, and dehumanization, for example (Alexander & Potter, 2001).

The common view is a friendly companion and has a blue-ribbon pedigree reaching deep into Enlightenment maestros. But it doesn't pound on academic doors with much authority any more. There are bigger fish to fry. Cramped into Enlightenment parameters, the transportation model is little more than the crumbs left over by sociology, psychology, economics, and linguistics. Equipped with a method, we are producing mountains of information, but we lack a conceptual framework that provides connections and perspectives.

We now recognize that mathematical theories of communication are a human invention and not a body of objective truths, as the Enlightenment mistakenly assumed. Though the scientific method made stupendous gains in the natural world, generating empirically testable causal explanations, territorialists correctly insist that the quantitative motif ought not overwhelm the study of society as well. Paul Feyerabend has documented that scientific study is itself conditioned by belief systems and ideological commitments. Indeed, the repudiation of Scientism has been carried forward by a broad range of scholarship, from the Frankfurt School to Karl Popper. The epistemological foundation of social science is being reestablished wholesale over Auguste Comte (1798–1859), who founded the new discipline, sociology, on the natural-scientific model.

SYMBOLIC THEORY

Interpretive research in the Counter-Enlightenment mode seeks insightful pictures rather than lawlike abstractions through fixed procedures. Parsimonious generalizations are still important, as they have been since William of Ockham, but only if they arise from a fully developed introspective capacity—or as Herbert Blumer (1969) calls it, from a "poetic resonance with the data." The interpretive turn recovers the fact of human agency, that is, intentions, purposes, and values. Interpretive research, in Clifford Geertz's (1973) words, "enlarges the universe of human discourse" and expands the horizons of human existence by making publicly available the manner in which "others have guarded their sheep" (pp. 14, 30). Interpretive studies catch hold of the ambulation of history, self-consciously avoiding the assumption that social phenomena are autonomous creations arising by spontaneous combustion (Denzin & Lincoln, 2000).

In communication theory, the Italian philologist Giambattista Vico, who refused to be hoist on the Cartesian petard, established the Counter-Enlightenment option. His philosophy of expressivism was a brilliant achievement, contradicting the dominant doctrine of rational mind. This professor of rhetoric at the University of Naples (1699–1741) placed image over concept, language over mathematics, the mythopoetic over facts, and fantasia over logic. His highly original theory of imaginative universals was a fundamental assault on the raging tide of his age.

The symbolic motif is nurtured in the nineteenth century by Wilhelm Dilthey's *Erlebnis,* Frederick Schleiermacher's *Hermeneutik,* August Schleicher's *Comparative Grammar,* Jacob Burckhart's *Civilization of the Renaissance in Italy* (1860), and George Simmel's *Problems of Philosophy of History* (1892). And it establishes definitive form in an intellectual trajectory from Ferdinand De Saussure's *Course in General Linguistics* (1916) to Ernst Cassirer's mighty four-volume *Philosophy of Symbolic Forms* (1925). For Cassirer, symbolization is not merely the hallmark of human cognition; our representational capacity defines us anthropologically. Cassirer titles his summary monograph *An Essay on Man.* He identifies our unique capacity to generate symbolic structures as a radical alternative to animal rationale that has been established since classical Greece and to the biological being of evolutionary naturalism. Arguing that the issues are fundamentally anthropological rather than epistemological per se, Cassirer's creative being is carved out against a reductionism to intellectus on the one hand, and a naturalistic neurophysiology on the other.

Cassirer collapses the hoary differences among human symbolic systems. Music, art, philosophical essays, mathematics, religious language, and Bacon's scientific method are placed on a level playing field as all symbolic constructs. James Carey (1988, 1997a, 1997b) calls it the ritual view—rituals as ceremonies or sacraments in which we define meaning and purpose, events of celebration (graduation, weddings, birthdays), and not merely exchanges of information. In this book's effort to grapple with ethics while shifting from print to the visual, we finally feel at home theoretically.

Symbol is the critical concept. What atom is to physical science and cell is to biology, symbol is for communication. Cultures are interconnections of symbolic forms, those fundamental units of meaning expressed in words (mention *power* and notice the range of affective responses), gestures (a clenched fist, for example), and graphics (swastikas or a cross burned on the lawn). Realities called *cultures* are inherited and built from symbols that shape our action, identity, thoughts, and sentiment. Communication, therefore, is the creative process of building and reaffirming through symbols. Culture signifies the constructions that result.

Human behavior, in this vision, is symbolic action—action signifying something, as does phonation in speech, pigment in paintings, sonance in music. Our world is an intricate series of piled-up inference and implication. A twitch of the eye is more than a contracting eyelid and may actually be a mischievous wink or indicate a conspiracy. News reading thus becomes a dramatic act. Readers face not pure information but a drama; contending forces are portrayed, nudging one another into patriotism, class antagonisms, resentments, or crusading support. Speak the verbal symbol *death* and listeners will provide their own range of understanding: cessation of brain waves or heartbeat, a disembodied soul meeting God, or separation from a human community.

Our differing definitions reflect diverse values and social purposes. Humans stitch together views of the world to orient themselves and provide social cohesion. We take pieces of cloth and demand that flags be respected as our national emblem. Bread signifies Jesus' body, water purifies from wickedness, and *dogs* become despicable persons. Although not identical to that which they symbolize, symbols participate in their meaning and power; they share the significance of that to which they point. In addition, they illuminate their referents so as to make them transparent; they permit us to express levels of reality that otherwise remain hidden. Symbols open up the human spirit where our worldviews are inscribed.

A symbolic theory of communication recognizes human creativity as this species' distinctive feature. Creative beings do not merely exist in a vast museum, but are curators of their own. Their environments are not coded genetically (as with animal instinct), but organized symbolically without end. *Homo sapiens* is the only species that cooks its food; no balanced diets are built into the genes. Instincts produce perennially identical beaver dams and anthills; cultures are developed and imagined, always transcending biological necessity. Humankind organizes and enlarges its environment; the porpoise cannot. Humans readily displace both time and space; animals act only when stimuli are in fact present. We possess the creative imagination to describe experience, evaluate action, and transmit ideas for public discussion. Animals demonstrate none of these traits.

Consistent with the perspective of this book, I appropriate here a semiotic definition. In contrast to anthropology, where culture refers to entire civilizations as complex wholes, and in contrast to common parlance, where culture is identified as refined manners, symbolic theories of culture concentrate on representational forms. Most definitions of culture (certainly those fostered by anthropology) are expansive, encompassing under the term virtually all social activity. Culture is thus said to involve technologies, customs, arts, sciences, products, habits, and political and social organizations that characterize a people. I find the broad definition inchoate and distinguish culture from political and social structures, from direct efforts to understand nature (such as chemistry, physics, astronomy), and from religious institutions. Culture thus becomes essentially our communicative activities and refers primarily to the products of the arts and language. Images that injure can thus be examined fruitfully, without including all types of harm to the innocent within the research frame. The semiotic focus of this volume follows in the legacy of Jacob Burckhart.

Language is the marrow of community, the public agent through which our identity is realized. H. Richard Niebuhr (1941) recognized that persons are displayed, made accessible, nurtured, and integrated into social units through symbol, myth, and metaphor. Words for him are concrete forms of life. Their meaning derives from an interpretive, historical context humans themselves supply. Symbolic forms are social, not "isolated, separate and therefore meaningless sounds" (p. 96). Our constitutive relations as human beings are linguistic.

Language, from Niebuhr's perspective, is the matrix of humanity; it is not privately nurtured and problematic in the public sphere, as John Locke had argued in the seventeenth century. Niebuhr holds form and content together; concepts are not isolated from their representations. He weaves the social and individual dimensions of language into a unified whole. The symbolic approach to communication ransoms us from Locke's unproductive question, "How can private and isolated minds engage one another?" Through the social nature of language we integrate the message with communal formation. Consistent with this perspective, we document through these chapters that the manner in which race, age, gender, class, physical disabilities, and ethnicity is mediated provides the possibility for a just socioeconomic order. Human bonds are nurtured through language. Our first existential order, in other words, is a symbolic theater.

Symbol theory has been fertile territory—hermeneutics, the semiotics of Roland Barthes, Umberto Eco, and Paul Tillich's extensive work on symbolic language. Narrative discourse gets special treatment in Quentin Schultze's argument that popular culture serves a religious role in constituting our belief systems. Derrida's sliding signifiers, Stuart Hall's ideology, Heidegger's house of language, Baudrillard's simulacrum, and Bahktin's dialogical imagination live out of symbolic theory as well.

However, for all the vast range and depth of this book's symbolic thrust, it reminds me of a persistent problem within symbolism as a whole: its anthropological assumptions need clarification and development. Symbol theory entails a strong claim about *Homo sapiens* that demands further intellectual scrutiny. This first generation of scholarship has invented the wheel, but we are still riding in an oxcart. In the various debates over symbolic theory, I would argue for one that puts the radically human at its epicenter. All symbolic theories are antipositivistic, but they accent the problem of communication in different ways: meaning, political economy, interpretation-text-hermeneutics, history, ideology, power, and so forth. In effect, I believe we should place dialogic theory at the center of a series of increasingly narrow concentric circles—the Counter-Enlightenment, interpretive theory, and human symbolic capacity.

The ancient Greeks first identified—within Western society, at least— the interpretive impulse as a pervasive condition of human existence. They brought the hermeneutical consciousness into focus. The contemporary mind readily recognizes it. Interpretativeness is presumed among symbolic theorists today; however, it took Aristotle's genius to locate this human *ars interpretandi* explicitly within philosophical anthropology as a property of human beings. Aristotle found *hermeneia* (interpretation) worthy of a major treatise by that title, and he outlined a formal theory of communication in his *Rhetoric*. But, as Gadamer reminds us, in the *Nicomachean Ethics,* interpretation is given its richest meaning. Intellection and interpretation are presumed to differ in this Aristotelian classic on ethics. *Hermeneia* belongs to the higher and purer operations of the mind, but it is not just theoretical knowledge (*episteme*). Neither is it practical skill (*techne*), since it concerns more than utility. Making a moral decision, Aristotle argues, entails doing the right thing in a particular circumstance, and to accomplish that successfully demands that we interpret the concrete situation. The moment of discernment requires that we deliberate within ourselves; yet it cannot be confused with logical analysis. In this manner, Aristotle confirmed an orienting process beyond the senses, yet differing from intellection. Discursive penetration (Anthony Giddens' phrase) is born of conscience.

What Aristotle locates in the classical period is primordial, inherent, and fundamental. While he speaks with a Greek cadence, *hermeneia* concerns a universal modality, a constituent feature of our anthropology. The most typical labels are body, mind, and spirit. Others have called it psyche, the moral imagination, and fantasia. One humanly integrated whole of three distinct dimensions is harmonized into a unique species without exception.

Through the hermeneutical modality, we experience epiphanic moments suspended outside our person. These normative manifestations of compelling force are not grounded a priori. We can appropriate everyday reality cognitively, but *hermeneia* enables us simultaneously to engage a world independent of ourselves. As Thomas Nagel (1986) contends in his *View from Nowhere,* through the interpretive impulse, we form an overriding conception of the world with us in it. We are contained within history and do not create ourselves from scratch. Thus humans consider it worthwhile to bring their values and beliefs "under the influence of an impersonal standpoint," even without proof that this more permanent vista is not illusory. An independent reality, experienced phenomenologically, is from nowhere in particular, but we think it "natural to regard life and the world in this way" (pp. 5, 7) Thus in describing our concrete situation, we appeal to the impersonal with such phrases as, "the truth is . . . my dignity has been violated," "justice demands," "innocent victims," and so forth.

Martin Buber's (1958) theory of communication makes the dialogic relation primal in his famous aphorism, "In the beginning is the relation" (p. 69). He intends that ontologically as a category of being. This irreducible anthropological phenomenon cannot be decomposed into simpler elements without destroying it. There are not three components, sender-message-receiver, to be dismembered for scientific analysis. The reciprocal bond is an organic whole forming an interpretive unit centered in human *hermeneia.* All the variables are conjugate relationships, and isolating them is academia's version of Humpty Dumpty. Communications rest in the spirit, in our interpretive capacity—not in the mind, cogito, or intellectus. The commonplace phrase, "We're with you in spirit," is actually a powerful truth; the oneness of our species is born along the stream of consciousness. I resonate through my spirit to the moral imagination of others. Our common humanity is not inscribed, first of all, in politics, economics, transportation, or data. Our human bond is actually an ethical commitment rooted in value-saturated symbols (Cissna & Anderson, 1998).

Buber categorically rejects all dualism between self and culture. And Paulo Freire (1973) maintains the same dialectical unity with this symmetrical summary: "I cannot exist without a not-I; in turn the not-I depends on that existence.... There is no longer an 'I think' but 'we think.' " He writes:

It is the "we think" which establishes the "I think" and not the contrary. This co-participation of Subjects in the act of thinking is communication. . . . Communication implies a reciprocity which cannot be broken. Hence it is not possible to comprehend thought without its double function, as something which learns and something which communicates. . . . Communication is characterized by the fact that it is dialogue. It is not the transference of knowledge but the encounter of subjects in dialogue in search of the significance of the object of knowing and thinking. (pp. 137–139)

In Freire's terms, it is our ontological vocation as creative subjects to live meaningfully within the world while transforming it to suit our purposes. Freire (1970) presumes an explicit anthropology, conceiving of humans as existing not only in everyday reality but also through symbols separating from it in their consciousness (p. 69). Humans are able to adopt postures ranging from nearly undifferentiated spontaneous response to a critical attitude that entails a conscious process of intervention. As with the dialogic tradition generally, Freire sweeps epistemology into his anthropology. He declares that we have understood reality when we have gotten inside the self-in-relation. He presumes a symbolic paradigm with the radically human as the meaningful center (Thomas, Richards, & Nain, 2000).

When symbolic theory revolves around a dialogic axis, the application to stereotyping in mediated images is obvious. Though the world of technological images is our linguistic home and not something alien or frivolous, we can simultaneously nurture personal arenas in dialogic terms. While critiquing mediated structures and transforming them vigorously, human beings can create oppositional symbolic worlds interpersonally within subcultures and neighborhoods. Creating and nurturing symbolic worlds that heal are never automatic anywhere; but in the free spaces, grass roots symbol making is likely to be participatory. Examples of local responsibility for the symbols produced exist all over the globe. Expanding their number is our primary mission for the future.

CONCLUSION

In applying and energizing a symbolic approach, this book helps accomplish for communications what Albion Small earlier attempted for sociology. Albion Small (1903), the president of Colby College in Maine, taught a moral philosophy course to every senior, orienting them to civic responsibility before graduation. Called to the University of Chicago to start what we now know as the Sociology Department, he saw it, in effect, as moral philosophy conscious of its task: "Science is sterile unless it contributes knowledge of what is worth doing" (p. 119).

He wanted to make sociology the organizing center of the social sciences as a whole, but without a discrete subject matter of its own. Small believed that sociology could meet its ultimate test as an index and a measure of what ought to be done.

Extraordinarily influential, he founded the American Sociological Association (ASA) and served as the first editor of the *American Sociological Review*. But subsequent history ruptured his vision. In 1932, William Ogburn assumed the presidency of ASA as Small's successor. And in his presidential address, Ogburn declared: "Sociology as a science is no longer interested in making the world a better place in which to live. In encouraging beliefs. In setting forth impressions of life. In leading the multitudes or guiding the ship of state. Science is interested directly in one thing only, to wit, discovering new knowledge" (Sloan, 1980, p. 18).

Integrating facts and values has been a monumental challenge in academic life since the eighteenth century. Deep inside we agree with Thoreau that there is no sense going to Zanzibar just to count the cats, but objective science is addictive nonetheless (Carey, 1997c). For communications, symbolic theory lays a new foundation on which to work in a visual age, and this book is a prototype of what to build.

NOTES AND REFERENCES

FOREWORD

Notes

1. Lippmann, W. (1922). *Public opinion.* New York: Harcourt Brace & Co.
2. *The American heritage dictionary of the English language* (4th ed.). (2000). New York: Houghton Mifflin Co.

CHAPTER 1: MORAL RESPONSIBILITIES AND THE POWER OF PICTURES

Notes

1. Ethical and moral are used here in a synonymous way.
2. This list of prima facie harms comes from the work of Bernard Gert. See Gert, B. (1998). *Morality, its nature and justification.* New York: Oxford University Press.
3. See Mill, J. S. (1991). *On liberty and other essays.* New York: Oxford University Press.

CHAPTER 2: STEREOTYPING, PREJUDICE, AND DISCRIMINATION

Note

1. The student of journalistic ethics will recognize immediately our indebtedness to Professor Lambeth. In a sense, I am trying to find the philosophic under-

pinnings of his journalistic insights. See, especially, Edmund B. Lambeth, (1986). *Committed journalism: An ethic for the profession.* Bloomington, IN: Indiana University Press.

CHAPTER 3: MEDIA METHODS THAT LEAD TO STEREOTYPES

Note

1. Walsh, T. J. (1994, March 20.) The male daze: Men lost in the vast waste-land. Paper presented at the twenty-ninth annual convention of the Broadcast Education Association, Las Vegas, NV.

CHAPTER 4: UNCONSCIOUS, UBIQUITOUS FRAMES

Note

1. See the American Civil Liberties Union Web site's section on racial profiling.

References

ACLU. (2003). Racial equality: Racial profiling. [Online]. Retrieved July 8, 2003, from www/aclu.org/RacialEquality/RacialEqualitylist.cfm?c=133.

Entman, R. (1993). Framing: Towards clarification of a fractured paradigm. *Journal of Communication, 43*(4), 51–58.

Enteman, W. F. (1996). Stereotyping, prejudice, and discrimination. In P. M. Lester (Ed.), *Images that injure pictorial stereotypes in the media* (pp. 9–14). Westport, CT: Praeger.

Ghanem, S. (1996). *Media coverage of crime and public opinion: An exploration of the second level of agenda setting.* (Unpublished doctoral dissertation, Austin University of Texas. p. 25.

Gitlin, T. (1980). *The whole world is watching: Mass media in the making and unmaking of the New Left.* Berkeley, CA: University of California Press.

Hoffstetter, R. (1976). *Bias in the news.* Columbus, OH: Ohio State University Press.

Liebes, T. (2000). Inside a news item: A dispute over framing, *Political Communication, 17,* 295–305.

Linn, T. (1996). Media methods that lead to stereotypes. In P. M. Lester (Ed.), *Images that injure pictorial stereotypes in the media* (pp. 15–20). Westport, CT: Praeger.

Perkins, D., & Starosta, W. (2001). Representing coculturals: On form and news portrayals of Native Americans, *The Howard Journal of Communication, 12,* 73–84.

Shoemaker, P., & Reese, S. (1996). *Mediating the message*. White Plains, NY: Longman.

Tuchman, G. (1978). *Making news: A study in the construction of reality*. New York: Free Press.

van Dijk, T. (1991). *Racism and the press*. London: Routledge.

Weston, M. (1996). *Native Americans in the news: Images of Indians in the twentieth century press*. Westport, CT: Greenwood.

CHAPTER 5: IMAGES THAT HEAL

Reference

Barthes, R. (1982). *Camera lucida: Reflections on photography*. New York: Vintage/Ebury.

CHAPTER 6: VISUAL SYMBOLISM AND STEREOTYPES IN THE WAKE OF 9/11

Notes

1. See www.onroute.com/guides/keywest/nightlife.html and sloppyjoes.com/history.htm.

2. If for some reason you need to be reminded of the tune and lyrics, head to www.scoutsongs.com/lyrics/godblessamerica.html and sing along with the cheesy electronic accompaniment.

3. Available at: www.loc.gov/exhibits/treasures/trm019.html.

4. Available at: library.brandeis.edu/about/liaison/liaison1298.html.

5. Available at: www.usacitylink.com/flag/history.html.

6. Available at: www.poynter.org/Terrorism/gallery/wedgallery.htm.

7. See the September 24, 2001, issues of *U.S. News & World Report, Newsweek, Time,* and *The New Yorker.*

8. Available at: politicalhumor.about.com/library/images/blterrorpics.htm.

9. Available at: www.topps.com/enduringfreedom.html.

10. Staff and Wire reports. (2001, September 22) Flags invoke feelings. *Albuquerque Journal.* [Online] Retrieved July 8, 2003, from www.abqjournal.com/homes/452284homes09–22–01.htm.

11. Ibid.

References

De Lisser, E. (2002). *Companies flood the market with patriotic-themed wares*. Retrieved November 11, 2002, from www.wsjclassroomedition.com/tj_020502_patr.htm.

Hill, H. (1997, October). *Endangered expressions.* Retrieved July 8, 2003, from www.sabine-mag.com/archive/ar02009.htm.

Lambe, J. L., & Begleiter, R. J. (2002). Wrapping the news in the flag: Use of patriotic symbols by U.S. local TV stations after the terrorism attacks of September 11, 2001. Retrieved July 8, 2003, from www.udel.edu/communication/ COMM418/begleite/patrioticsymbols/symbols.pdf.

Lester, P. M. (2003). *Visual communication images with messages* (3rd ed.). Belmont, CA.: Wadsworth.

Zeller, T. (2002, May/June). Patriotic marketing hits bottom. *Mother Jones, 22.*

CHAPTER 7: TERRORISTS WE LIKE AND TERRORISTS WE DON'T LIKE

Notes

1. Available at: www.pointer.org/Terrorism/kenny6.htm.
2. See Photo of baby suicide bomber called "a joke." (2002). Retrieved July 8, 2003, from www.cnn.com/2002/WORLD/meast/06/28/baby.photo/.
3. Available at: library.nps.navy.mil/home/tgp/tgpmain.htm#definitions.

References

Ahmad, E. (2001). *Terrorism, theirs and ours.* New York: Seven Stories.

Ahmed, A. (2002). Hello, Hollywood: Your images affect Muslims everywhere. Retrieved July 8, 2003, from www.npq.org/archive/2002 spring/ahmed.html.

Sanders, E. (2001, September 27). Understanding turbans: Don't link them to terrorism. *Seattle Times* Retrieved July 8, 2003, from seattletimes.nwsource .com/html/home/.

CHAPTER 8: UNEQUAL COMBATANTS ON AN UNEVEN MEDIA BATTLEFIELD: PALESTINE AND ISRAEL

Note

1. See Bordewich, F. M. (1995, January). A holy war heads our way, *Reader's Digest.* 76–80; Kamm, T. (1995, January 5). Clash of cultures: Rise of Islam in France rattles the populace and stirs a backlash. *Wall Street Journal;* Lewis, B. (1990, September). The roots of Muslim rage. *Atlantic Monthly 226,* 3.

References

Cappella, J. N., & Jamieson, K. H. (1996). News frames, political cynicism, and media cynicism. *Annals of the Academy of Political and Social Sciences, 546,* 71–84.

Esposito, J. L. (1995). *The Islamic threat, myth or reality?* New York: Oxford University Press.

Gamson, W. (1992). *Talking politics.* Cambridge: Cambridge University Press.

Lewis, B. (1990, September). The roots of Muslim rage, *Atlantic Monthly 226*, 3.

Liebes, T. (1992). Our war/their war: Comparing the *Intifadeh* and the Gulf War on U.S. and Israeli television. *Critical Studies in Mass Communication, 9,* 44–55.

The National Conference for Community and Justice reviews "The Siege," a movie about Islamic terrorism, (1998, November 6). *PR Newswire.*

Okwu, M. (2000, April 25). Arab-Americans call for boycott of "Rules of Engagement." [Online]. Retrieved July 8, 2003, from www.cnn.com/2000/showbiz/movies/04/25/rules.of.engagement/.

Ross, S. D. (2003). An American frame: New York Times discourse on Palestine and Israel. *Conflict & Communication.* [Online]. Retrieved on July 9, 2003, from www.cco.Regener_Online.de.

Said, E. (1981). *Covering Islam.* New York: Pantheon.

Schlesinger, P., Elliot, P., & Murdock, G. (1984). *Televising terrorism: Political violence in popular culture.* New York: Scribner.

Shaheen, J. (2002, February 28). Hollywood widens slur targets to Arab and Muslim Americans since Sept. 11. Pacific News Service. Retrieved October 21, 2001 from www.alternet.org.

Shinar, D. (2000). Media Diplomacy and "Peacetalk", the Middle East and Northern Ireland. *Gazette, 62,* 2, 83–97.

Shinar, D. (2002). Peace process in cultural conflict: The role of the Media. In E. Gilboa (Ed.), *Media and conflict: Framing issues, making policy, shaping opinions.* Ardsley, NY: Transnational.

Steuter, E. (1990). Understanding the media/terrorism relationship: An analysis of ideology and the news in *Time* magazine. *Political Communication and Persuasion, 7,* 257–278.

Stossel, S. (2001, October 22). Terror TV. *The American Prospect 12*(18), 35–37.

Tilly, C. (1978). *From mobilization to revolution.* Reading, MA: Addison-Wesley.

Wolfsfeld, G. (1997). *Media and political conflict.* New York: Cambridge University Press.

CHAPTER 9: POST-9/11 DISCRIMINATION AGAINST ARABS AND MUSLIMS

Notes

1. The author gratefully acknowledges the suggestions and research support of Rebecca Brown, Patrick McKeand, Peg Williams, and Deb Perkins. Any errors are the author's.

2. A full description of racial profiling may be found in a U.S. Department of Justice Monograph, A Resource Guide on Racial Profiling Data Collection Systems, by Deborah Ramirez, Jack McDevit, and Amy Farrell. Available at: www.ncjrs.org/pdffiles1/bja/184768.pdf).

3. "Civil Rights in the United States 2001: Accommodating Diversity" by Mohammed Nimmer, published by the Council of American-Islamic Relations, may be downloaded in PDF form at www.cair-net.org/civilrights/ 2001_Civil_ Rights_Report.pdf. This annual report, published since 1996, details harassment complaints by Muslims. The 2001 report indicates a 15 percent increase in complaints over the previous year. The American-Arab Anti-Discrimination Committee also published periodic reports on hate crimes and discrimination against Arab-Americans. The most recent report, "1998–2000 Report on Hate Crimes and Discrimination Against Arab Americans," may be obtained from www.adc.org/index.php?id = 279.

References

Amnesty International. (2001). *September 11 crisis response guide for junior high and high schools.* New York: Amnesty International USA.

Another Kind of War. (2001, September 18). *USA Today,* p. 23A.

Auletta, K. (2002). The Howell doctrine. *The New Yorker.* LXXVIII (15), 48–71.

Burgard, M. (2001, September 21). Unease in Arab community; after terror attacks, some in New York City face blame and bigotry; terror in America: New York City. *Hartford Courant,* p. A3.

Charen, M. (2001, October 28). Expel Arabs, profile truckers. *Baltimore Sun,* p. 3F.

Chavez, S. (2001, September 17). After the attack; the victims; she was Muslim; she was a victim. *Los Angeles Times,* p. 16.

Claffey, M. (2001, November 12). Pakistani groups cite persecution. *Daily News,* p. 33.

Crossroads: Race, rights and national security. (2002, May 10). Washington, DC: Lemelson Center, National Museum of American History, Smithsonian Institution.

Iftikhar, A. T. (2001, October 8). [Letter to the editor]. *Newsweek,* p.14.

Johnston, D. (2001, November 6). Mother survives WTC but son joins Taliban— War on Terror: New York's traitor. *Daily Telegraph,* p. 5.

Marshall, S. (2001, September 20). Dear friends in peace. [Letter to the Islamic Society of North America, Plainfield, IN].

The Muslim wife. (2001, October 14). *Sunday Times.*

Nail, D. E. (2001, October 27). [Letter to the editor]. *Martinsville Daily Reporter.*

Pitts, L., Jr. (2001, October 28).... No, doing so would trash our ideals. *Baltimore Sun,* p. 3F.

Seelye, K.Q. (2002, June 23). War on terror makes for odd twists in justice system: flexible rules raise constitutional issues." *New York Times,* p. 16.

Timeline: Countdown to U.S. air strikes. (2001, October 9). *Courier Mail,* p. 4.

U.S. Catholic Bishops & Muslim Leaders. (2001). The one God calls us to be peoples of peace. In J. Farina, J. (Ed.), *Beauty for ashes: Spiritual reflections on the attack on America* (pp. 2067–2208). New York: Crossroads.

Wertheimer, L. (1993, March 9). William Sessions discusses terrorism on Capitol Hill. *All Things Considered.* Washington, DC: National Public Radio.

CHAPTER 10: ARABS AND ARAB AMERICANS: ANCIENT MIDDLE EAST CONFLICTS HIT HOME

Notes

1. Jones, J. (2001, September 28). Americans felt uneasy toward Arabs even before Sept. 11. Gallup News Service. Retrieved October 20, 2002, from www.alefbeh.com/accordingto/101501/gallup_poll.jsp.

2. American Arab Anti-Discrimination Committee. (2000, April). Statement against "Rules of Engagement." Retrieved October 20, 2002 from www.yementimes.com/00/iss16/report.htm.

3. Available at: www.saja.org.

4. Available at: www.arab-heritage.com.

References

Abraham, S., & Abraham, N. (1983). *Arabs in the New World.* Detroit: Wayne State University Center for Urban Studies.

Behar, R. (1993, October 4). The secret life of Mahmud the Red. *Time.*

Church. G. (1993, July 5). The terror within. *Time.*

Ebert, R. (1998). The Siege review. *Chicago Sun-Times.* Retrieved July 8, 2003, from www.suntimes.com/ebert/ebert_reviews/1998/11/110603.html.

Lamb, D. (1987). *The Arabs.* New York: Vintage Books.

McCarus, E. (1994). *The development of Arab-American identity.* Ann Arbor, MI: The University of Michigan Press.

Merina, V. (2001). Diversity since September 11: Never more important. The Poynter Institute. Retrieved July 8, 2003, from www.poynter.org/content/content_view.asp?id=5063.

Peterson, P. (2002, September/October). Public Diplomacy and the War on Terrorism. *Foreign Affairs.*

Said, E. (1981). *Covering Islam.* New York: Pantheon Books.

Twain, M. (2002). *The Innocents Abroad.* New York: Viking Penguin.

CHAPTER 11: MEDIA STEREOTYPES OF AFRICAN AMERICANS

References

Abraham, L. (1998). *Subtle manifestations of prejudice: implicit visual constructions of black pathology.* Unpublished doctoral dissertation, Annenberg School for Communication, University of Pennsylvania.

Bird, S.E. (1996). CJ's revenge: Media, folklore, and the cultural construction of AIDS. *Critical Studies in Mass Communication, 13,* 53.

Boggle, D. (1991). Toms, coons, mulattoes, mammies, & bucks: An interpretive history of blacks in American films. New York: Continuum.

Boskin, J. (1980). Denials: The media view of dark skins and the city. In B. Rubin (Ed.), *Small voices and great trumpets: Minorities and the media.* New York: Praeger.

Browne, D.R., Firestone, C.M., & Mickiewics, E. (1994). *Television/radio news & minorities.* Queenstown: Aspen Institute.

Campbell, C.P. (1995). *Race, myth and the news.* Thousand Oaks, CA: Sage.

Cowen, P.S. (1991). A socio-cognitive approach to ethnicity in films. In L.D. Friedman (Ed.), *Unspeakable images: Ethnicity and the American cinema.* Urbana and Chicago: University of Illinois Press.

Crowdus, G., & Georgakas, D. (2002). Thinking about the power of images: An interview with Spike Lee. *Cineaste, 26*(2).

Dates, J.L., & Barlow, W. (Eds.). (1990). *Split image: African Americans in the mass media.* Washington, DC: Howard University Press.

Devine, P.G. (1989). Stereotypes and prejudice: Their automatic and controlled components. *Journal of Personality and Social Psychology, 56,* 5–18.

Drummond, W.J. (1990). About face: From alliance to alienation. *The American Enterprise, July/August,* pp. 23–29.

Entman, R.M. (1994a, Summer). African Americans according to TV news. *Media Studies Journal,* 29–38.

Entman, R.M. (1994b). Representation and reality in the portrayal of blacks on network television news. *Journalism & Mass Communication Quarterly, 71,* 509–520.

Entman, R.M., & Rojecki, A. (2000). *The black image in the white mind: Media and race in America.* Chicago & London: The University of Chicago Press.

Gist, M.E. (1990). Minorities in media imagery. *Newspaper Research Journal, 11*(3), 52–63.

Gray, H. (1989). Television, black Americans, and the American dream. *Critical Studies in Mass Communication, 6,* 376–386.

Guerrero, E. (1993). *Framing Blackness. The African American image in film.* Philadelphia: Temple University Press.

Jhally, S., & Lewis, J. (1992). *Enlightened racism: The Cosby Show, audiences, and the myth of the American dream.* Boulder, CO: Westview.

Jones, J. (1998). The Accusatory Space. In Gina Dent (Ed.), *Black popular culture* (p. 96). New York: The New Press.

Lester, P.M., & Smith, R. (1994). African American photo coverage in four US newspapers, 1937–1990. *Journalism Quarterly, 71*(2), 380–394.

MacDonald, J.F. (1992). *Blacks and white TV: African Americans in television since 1948.* Chicago: Nelson-Hall.

Martindale, C. (1996). "Newspaper stereotypes of African Americans," In P.M. Lester (Ed.), *Images that injure: Pictorial stereotypes in the media.* Westport, CT: Greenwood.

Meertens, R.W., & Pettigrew, T.F. (1997). Is subtle prejudice really prejudice? *Public Opinion Quarterly, 61,* 54–71.

Mendleberg, T. (1996, September). *Implicitly racial appeals and the impact of campaigns.* Paper delivered at a seminar for Annenberg Research Fellows, Annenberg School for Communication, University of Pennsylvania.

Messaris, P. (1997). Visual persuasion: The role of images in advertising. Thousand Oaks, CA: Sage.

Messaris, P., & Abraham, L. (2001). The role of images in framing news stories. In S.D. Reese, O.H. Gandy, Jr., & August E. Gant (Eds.), *Framing public life: Perspectives on media and our understanding of the social world.* Mahwah, NJ: Lawrence Erlbaum.

Pease, E.C. (1989). Kerner plus 20: Minority news coverage in the Columbus Dispatch. *Newspaper Research Journal, 10*(3), 17–38.

van Dijk, T.A. (1987). *Communicating racism : Ethnic prejudice in thought and talk.* London: Sage.

van Dijk, T.A. (1988). Introduction. In G. Smitherman-Donaldson & T.A. van Dijk (Eds.), *Discourse and discrimination*, p. 18. Detroit: Wayne State University Press.

CHAPTER 12: ETHNIC STEREOTYPES: HISPANICS AND MEXICAN AMERICANS

References

Ayoso, R. (2002, April 3). Hollywood seeks key to Spanish-language market for films. Retrieved April 11, 2002, from www.HispanicBusiness.com

Del Olmo, F. (1985). Newspaper innovations: Attempts to serve the changing Latino community. *Telecommunications and Latinos,* 41–45.

The Economic Policy Institute. (2001, September 25). *Household income fails to grow in 2000.* Retrieved November 11, 2002, from www.Epinet.org.

Gutierrez, F. (1978, August 13–16). *Through Anglo eyes: Chicanos as portrayed in the news media.* Paper presented at the Association for Education in Journalism 61st annual conference, Seattle, Washington.

A melding of cultures: Latins, the largest new group, are making their presence felt. (1985, July 8). *Time,* 36–41.

Mendosa, R. (1993, July). A love affair with movies. *Hispanic Business,* 12–24.

Obejas, A. (2001, March 21). Census data may get media more interested in Hispanics. *Chicago Tribune.*

Perez-Torres, R. (1988). Chicanos in film; a new portrayal. *Estos Tiempos, 4*(2), 28.

Policy statements on media use of the term "illegal alien." (1993). El Paso (Texas) Association of Hispanic Journalists and Colorado (Denver) Hispanic Media Association.

Rodriguez, R. (1990, April 9). "Daily papers misread Latinos, say leaders. *Hispanic Link Weekly Report,* 1–2.

Torres, J. (2002, April 9). *National Association of Hispanic Journalists statement on ASNE's Newsroom Survey.* Washington, D C: National Association of Hispanic Journalists.

Torres, J. (2000, September 22). *NAHJ releases fifth annual "Network Brownout" report.* Washington, D C: National Association of Hispanic Journalists.

U.S. Bureau of the Census, United States Department of Commerce. (May 2001). *Decennial Report 2000. Profiles of General Demographic Characteristics, 2000; People and families in poverty by selected characteristics: 1999–2000.* Washington, DC: U.S. Department of Commerce.

CHAPTER: 13: EXOTICS, EROTICS, AND COCONUTS: STEREOTYPES OF PACIFIC ISLANDERS

References

Asian American Journalists Association. (1991). *Asian American handbook.* Chicago: National Conference of Christians and Jews.

Barclay, B. (1990). *Our own image.* Auckland: Longman Paul.

Mita, M. (2001, November 10). *Storytelling: A Pacific view.* In *Hawai'i International Film Festival.* Symposium conducted at the University of Hawai'i.

CHAPTER 14: NATIVE AMERICAN STEREOTYPES

Note

1. See American Indian Sports Team Mascots Web site, available at: earnestman.tripod.com/1indexpage.htm.

References

Copeland, D. (1993, August*). "The Skulking Indian Enemy," colonial newspapers; portrayal of Native Americans.* A paper presented at the Association for Education in Journalism and Mass Communication.

Elie, Lolis E. (2002, April 23). Exposing stereotypes of Indians. (New Orleans) *Times Picayune.*

Harjo, S. S. (1990). *Racism in the news* [Video]. Nashville, TN: Spectra Communications, Inc., distributed by Media Action Research Center, Inc.

Rethinking Schools. (1991). *Rethinking Columbus.* [Special edition]. Milwaukee, WI: Rethinking Schools, Ltd. in collaboration with Network Educators of Central America.

Spindel, C. (2000). *Dancing at halftime: Sports and the controversy over American Indian mascots.* New York: New York University Press.

CHAPTER 15: JEWISH IMAGES THAT INJURE

Notes

1. See Jewhoo available at: www.jewhoo.com/ as retrieved on April 21, 2002.

2. See Classical and Christian Anti-Semitism, available at: www.remember.org/guide/History.root.classical.html.

3. Available at: www.jtsa.edu/library/exhib/jewoth/.

4. Available at: motlc.wiesenthal.com/albums/palbum/p03/a0177p3.html.

5. See German Propaganda Archive, available at: www.calvin.edu/academic/cas/gpa/thumb.htm.

6. Available at: www.islam.net.

7. Available at HonestReporting.Com, www.HonestReporting.com/followup/01_tuvia.asp,as retrieved April 21, 2002.

8. See HonestReporting.Com, available at: honestreporting.com/default.asp, as retrieved May 4, 2002.

9. See The Consequences of Right-Wing Extremism on the Internet, available at: www.adl.org/internet/extremism_rw/default.asp, as retrieved April 21, 2002.

10. Available at: www.adl.org/poisoning_web/poisoning_toc.html.

11. Available at: www.adl.org/egyptian_media/media_2001/Intro.html.

12. For a good reference on Jewish images in cinema, available at: www.lib.berkeley.edu/MRC/imagesjews.html.

13. See, Leichter, Harry, Jewish Humor Site, www.haruth.com/jhumorlink.htm.

References

Belasco, D. (1999, October). *After the nanny: Young Jewish women in mainstream culture."* Culture Currents. Retrieved November 11, 2002, from www.jewishculture.org/currents/9910current.htm.

Critics leave Schindler off best directors' list. (1993, December 17). *The Daily Telegraph.*

Dreifus, C. (1993, May). Richard Dreyfuss. *The Progressive,* p. 32.

Glassman, B. (1975). *Anti-Semitic stereotypes without Jews.* Detroit: Wayne State University Press.

Jewish targets in Europe attacked. (2002, April 19). *ABC Today.* Retrieved July 8, 2003, from www.abc.net.au/worldtoday/s535726.htm.

Kaplan, A. (2002). *How Jews revolutionized comedy in America.* Retrieved July 9, 2003, from uahc.org/rjmag/302ak.html.

Keinon, H. (2002). *PR czar: Images beat arguments in media war.* Retrieved November 11, 2002, from www.jpost.com/Editions/2002/01/11/News/News.41518.html.

Raphael, R. (1998, April 17). Jewish kid hitting the big time on TV's outrageous *South Park. Jewish Student Press Service.* Retrieved July 9, 2003, from www.jewishsf.com/6k980417/etsopark.htm.

Singer, J. (2000, April). *Making sense of Jewish stereotypes.* The Future of Freedom Foundation. Retrieved July 9, 2003, from www.fff.org/freedom/0400f.asp.

Wasserman, D. (1994, 19 February). *Visually challenging or visually challenged? A P.C. debate by cartoonists.* [Op-Ed]. *The Boston Globe,* p. 15.

Welles, H.G. (1922). *A short history of the world.* Retrieved July 9, 2003, from www.bartleby.com/86/21.html.

Ziv, A., & Zajdman, A. (1993). *Semites and stereotypes, characteristics of Jewish humor.* Westport, CT: Greenwood.

CHAPTER 16: IMAGES OF IRISH-AMERICANS: INVISIBLE, INEBRIATED, OR IRASCIBLE

Notes

1. An online Lexis-Nexis search of American newspapers found that roughly one-third of the retrieved articles that mentioned Irish Americans were related to St. Patrick's Day.

2. To see representations of this and many of the other illustrations mentioned in this chapter, available at: www.nde.state.ne.us/SS/irish/unit_2.html.

References

Bales, R.F. (1944). *The fixation factor in alcohol addiction: An hypothesis derived from a comparative study of Irish and Jewish social norms.* Unpublished doctoral dissertation, Harvard University.

Breslin, J. (1991, March 19). The cardinal sins of Irish Catholics. *Newsday,* p. 27.

Burton, P., & Cohen, R. (Producers). (1984). The old man and the gun. *Frontline.* Boston: Public Broadcasting Service.

Clayton, J. (2002, March 25). Collection of Ties Bind to Community. *The Union Leader* (Manchester, NH), p. 1A.

Cronin, M., & Adair, D. (2002). *The Wearing of the green, a history of St. Patrick's Day.* New York: Routledge.

Doyle, J. (2002, March 7). Saving the Irish soul. *San Francisco Chronicle,* p. D1.

Fallows, M.R. (1979). *Irish Americans, identity and assimilation.* Englewood Cliffs, NJ: Prentice-Hall.

Feroze, L. (1994, March 17). St. Patrick's Day: Calgary's Irish remember home. *Calgary Herald,* p. A5.

Fitzgerald, M., & King, J. (1990). *The uncounted Irish.* Toronto: P. D. Meany.

Glad, D. D. (1947, December). Attitudes and experience of American-Jewish and American-Irish male youth as related to differences in adult rates of inebriety. *Quarterly Journal of Studies on Alcohol, 8,* 406–72.

Greeley, A.M. (1972). *That most distressful nation.* Chicago: Quadrangle Books.

Ignatiev, N. (1995). *How the Irish became white.* New York: Routledge.

Lebow, R. N. (1976). *White Britain and black Ireland. The influence of stereotypes on colonial policy.* Philadelphia: Institute for the Study of Human Issues.

Louie, E. (1994, March 16). The pub: A center of Ireland in exile. *New York Times,* p. C1.

McGee, J. (2001, November 2). Irish American meat raffle is Nov. 24. *The Patriot Ledger* (Quincy, MA), p. 4.

Nichols, J. (2002, March 15). Irish struggle is example for today. *Capital* (Madison, WI) *Times,* p. 11A.

Nugent, K. (2002, March 11). Naughton named to board of Irish Democrats' group. *Worcester Telegram & Gazette,* p. B4.

Potter, G. (1960). *To the golden door.* Boston: Little, Brown.

Quindlen, A. (1991, March 14). Erin go brawl. *New York Times,* p. A25.

Reel, B. (1993, July 7). When the pot calls another pot Irish. *Newsday,* p. 81.

Richardson, S. A., Goodman, N., Hastorf, A. H., & Dornbusch, S. M. (1961). Cultural uniformity in reaction to physical disabilities, *American Sociological Review, 26,* 244–247.

Rothman, D. (1971). *The discovery of the asylum.* Boston: Little, Brown.

Shannon, W. V. (1963). *The American Irish.* New York: Macmillan.

Solomon, B. (1956). *Ancestors and immigrants.* Cambridge: Harvard University Press.

Steinfeld, P. (1991, March 23). Cardinal says press reports reflect Catholic bashing. *New York Times,* p. 27.

Stivers, R. (1976). *A hair of the dog.* University Park, PA: Pennsylvania State University Press.

Taste–Review & Outlook: Trouble brewing. (2002, March 15). *Wall Street Journal,* p. 15W.

Wittke, C. (1956). *The Irish in America.* Baton Rouge: Louisiana State University Press.

CHAPTER 17: WOMEN AS SEX PARTNERS

References

American Society of Plastic Surgeons (2001). *2001 Cosmetic Surgery Trends.* Retrieved May 15, 2002, from www.plasticsurgery.org/mediactr/costrends 2001.cfm.

Botta, R. (1999). Television images and adolescent girls' body image disturbance. *Journal of Communication, 49*(2), 22–41.

Botta, R. (2000). The mirror of television: A comparison of black and white adolescents' body image. *Journal of Communication, 50*(3), 144–159.

Cosmo Cover Style. (February 2002). *Cosmopolitan*, 184–193.

Dines, G., & Humez, J. M. (1995). *Gender, race and class in media: A text reader.* Thousand Oaks, CA: Sage.

Field, A. E., Camargo, C. A., Jr., Taylor, C. B., Berkey, C. S., Roberts, S. B., & Colditz, G. A. (2001, January). Peer, parent and media influences on the development of weight concerns and frequent dieting among preadolescent and adolescent girls and boys. *Pediatrics, 107*(1), 54–60.

Gross, A. M., Bennett, T., Sloan, L., Marx, B. P., & Juergens, J. (2001). The impact of alcohol and alcohol expectancies on male perception of female sexual arousal in a date rape analog. *Experimental and Clinical Psychopharmacology, 9*(4), 380–8.

Harrison, K. (1997). Does interpersonal attraction to thin media personalities promote eating disorders? *Journal of Broadcasting and Electronic Media, 41,* 478–500.

Harrison, K. (2000). The body electric: Thin-ideal media and eating disorders in adolescents. *Journal of Communication, 50*(3), 119–143.

Hofshire, L. J., & Greenberg, B. S. (2002). Media's impact on adolescents' body dissatisfaction." In J. D. Brown, J. R. Steele, & K. Walsh-Childers (Eds.), *Sexual teens, sexual media.* Mahwah, NJ: Erlbaum.

Howitt, D. (1995). Pornography and the paedophile: Is it criminogenic? *British Journal of Medical Psychology, 68,* 15–27.

Hurst, N. M. (1996). Lactation after augmentation mammoplasty, *Obstetrics & Gynecology, 87*(1), 30–34.

Kalyanaraman, S., Steele, J., & Sundar, S. S. (2000, June). *Communicating objectification: Effects of sexually suggestive advertisements.* Paper presented at the 50th Annual Conference of the International Communication Association, Acapulco, Mexico.

Labre, M. P. (2002). The Brazilian wax: New hairlessness norm for women?" *Journal of Communication Inquiry 26*(2), 113–132.

Marx, B. P., Gross, A. M., & Adams, H. E. (1999). The effect of alcohol on the responses of sexually coercive and noncoercive men to an experimental rape analogue. *Sex Abuse, 1* (2), 131–45.

Neifert, M., DeMarzo, S., Seacat, J., Young, D., Leff, M., & Orleans, M. (1990). The influence of breast surgery, breast appearance, and pregnancy-induced breast changes on lactation sufficiency as measured by infant weight gain. *Birth, 17(1),* 31–38.

Owen, P. R., & Laurel-Seller, E. (2000). Weight and shape ideals: Thin is dangerously in. *Journal of Applied Social Psychology, 30*(5), 979–990.

Stice, E., & Shaw, H. E. (1994). Adverse effects of the media portrayed thin-ideal on women and linkages to bulimic symptomatology. *Journal of Social and Clinical Psychology, 13,* 288–308.

Violence, women, and the media. (2000). *Issue Brief Series.* Studio City, CA: Mediascope. [Online]. Retrieved May 4, 2001, from www.mediascope.org/pubs/ibriefs/vwm.htm.

Ward, C. M. (2001). The breast-implant controversy: A medico-moral critique. *British Journal of Plastic Surgery, 54,* 352–357.

CHAPTER 18: WE'VE COME A LONG WAY MAYBE

Note

1. *The USA Today* Annual Ad Meter Poll was used to identify the national buys.

References

McCarthy, M. (2001, January 25). The changing face of Super Bowl Sunday. *USA Today,* pp. 1B, 2B.

Nielsen Media Research. (2000). *2000 Report on television, January 1961–April 30, 2000.* New York.

Schwartz, J. (2000, January 30). A super day to screen ads. *The Washington Post,* p. H1.

Svetkey, B. (1994, March 18). Here's the beef. *Entertainment,* 26–27.

Welsh, J. (2002, February 5). TiVo Publishes Super Bowl usage report. *DigitalSpy,* 2.

CHAPTER 19: THE CHILD AS IMAGE: MEDIA STEREOTYPES OF CHILDREN

Note

1. Information on both these cartoons, available at: www.cartoonnetwork.com.

References

Barcus, F. E. (1983). *Images of life on children's television.* New York: Praeger.

Signorielli, N. (1991). *A sourcebook on children and television.* New York: Greenwood.

Thompson, T. L., & Zerbinos, E. (1997). Television characters: Do children notice it's a boy's world? *Sex Roles, 37,* 415–432.

Weitzman, L. J., Eifler, D., Hokada, E., & Ross, C. (1972). Sex role socialization in picture books of preschool children. *The American Journal of Sociology, 77,* 1125–1150.

Witt, S. D. (1997). Boys will be boys, and girls will be... hard to find: Gender representation in third grade basal readers. *Education and Society, 15*, 47–53.

CHAPTER 20: GROWING OLD IN COMMERCIALS: NOT ALWAYS A LAUGHING MATTER

Note

1. The ad with this headline appeared in the E-host database found in many university libraries. But when one accesses the *Advertising Age* Web site for Garfield's Ad Review, the headline is different. Why there is a difference is unclear, unless *Advertising Age* responded to criticism of the headline and changed it in the electronic file. The reader can seek out the original copy of *Advertising Age* in a library to see the original headline.

References

Bryant, K. (2001, October 18). They're moving on up. *Los Angeles Times,* Sec. 5, p. 2.

Chura, H. (2002, February 11). Draft codger. *Advertising Age,* 4.

Deets, H. B. (1994, July/August). No more stereotypes, thank you! *Modern Maturity,* 4–5.

Dychtwald, K. (2000). *Age power: How the 21st century will be ruled by the new old.* Boston: J. P. Tarcher.

Ekerdt, D. J., & Clark, E. (2001, March). Selling retirement in financial planning advertisements. [Online]. *Journal of Aging Studies, 15*(1), 55–68. Abstract from AgeLine Database.

Frase-Blunt, M. (2001, April 17). Rejecting life expectancies, Washington [DC] octogenarians and nonogenarians shatter the stereotypes of old age. *Washington Post,* p. T18.

Friedman, S. (2000, August 5). "Geezer jokes" take a toll. *Newsday* [New York], p. B10.

Garfield, B. (2002, April 1). Garfield's Ad Review. Innocence lost: Midas sags to a low with geriatric nudity spot. *Advertising Age,* p. 57.

Hammond, M. (2001, March 4). Baby boomers rewrite aging. *St. Petersburg Times,* p. 7D.

Kaufert, P. A., & Lock, M. (1997). Medicalization of women's third age. [Online]. *Journal of Psychosomatic Obstetrics and Gynaecology, 18*, 81–86. Abstract from AgeLine Database.

Mitchell, S. (1998). *American generations.* Ithaca, NY: New Strategist.

Negative views of aging may harm health of seniors. (2000, August 11). *Parent Care Advisor, 8*(10).

Pensioners in a fizz over negative advertising. (2000, July 20). *Glasgow Herald,* p. 13.

Ylanne-McEwen, V. (2000, Summer). Golden times for golden agers: Selling holidays as lifestyle for the over 50s. [Online]. *Journal of Communication, 50*(3), 83–99. Abstract from AgeLine Database.

CHAPTER 21: THE INVISIBLE CULTURAL GROUP: IMAGES OF DISABILITY

Note

1. Available at: www.kidzworld.com/site/p581.htm.

References

Donaldson, J. (1981, March). The visibility and image of handicapped people on television. *Exceptional Children, 47*(6), 413–416.

Editor wins grant to improve image of the disabled. (1988, October 23). *Louisville Courier Journal,* pp. 1B, 12B.

Johnson, M. (1987, September/October). Where do you get your information about disability issues? *The Disability Rag,* pp. 24–27.

Lester, P. M. (2003). *Visual communication images with messages* (3rd ed.). Belmont, CA: Wadsworth.

Longmore, P. K. (1985a, January/February). A note on language and social identity of disabled people. *American Behavioral Scientist, 28*(3), 419–423.

Longmore, P. K. (1985b, Summer). Screening stereotypes: Images of disabled people. *Social Policy, 32.*

Longmore, P. K. (1990, Fall). The glorious rage of Christy Brown. *Disability Studies Quarterly, 10*(4), 23–25.

Mankiewicz, F., & Swerdlow, J. (1978). *Remote control: television and the manipulation of American life.* New York: Ballantine Books.

People gain roles in ads and on TV. (1991, September 23). *New York Times,* p. 14.

Peyser, M. (2000, February 21). Malcolm lands on top. *Newsweek.*

Wood, D. B. (1989, March 2). Redrawing US portrait of the disabled. *Christian Science Monitor,* p. 14.

Zola, K. I. (1985). Depictions of disability—Metaphor, message and medium in the media: A research and political agenda," *The Social Science Journal, 22*(4), 5–17.

CHAPTER 22: THE BLIND IN THE MEDIA: A VISION OF STEREOTYPES IN ACTION

References

Koestler, F. A. (1976). *The unseen minority: A social history of blindness in America.* New York: David McKay.

The miracle worker. (1963, January). *Esquire.*

Monbeck, M. E. (1973). *The meaning of blindness: Attitudes toward blindness and blind people.* Bloomington, IN: Indiana University Press.

CHAPTER 23: RECAPTURING THE ARCHETYPE: AN INCLUSIVE VISION OF SEXUALITY AND GENDER

References

Boothe, K. (1998, May 11). NLGA deplores unprecedented "bathroom journalism" by TV news. *National Lesbian and Gay Journalists Association news release.*

(GLAAD) Alert. (1996, December 12). The Gay and Lesbian Alliance Against Defamation (GLAAD) Alert.

Goldberg, V. (2002, May 12). When the news in pictures was news. *New York Times,* Arts, p. 25.

Gross, L. (1991). Gays, lesbians and popular culture. In M. Wolf and A. Kielwasser (Eds.). *Gay people, sex, media.* Binghamton, NY: Haworth.

James, C. (2000, October 1). *New York Times.*

Moritz, M. (1996). Reframing gay and lesbian media images: Fundamental problems. In P. M. Lester, (Ed.). *Images that injure pictorial stereotypes in the media* (pp. 143–148). Westport, CT: Praeger.

Moritz, M. (1998). Media. In *Gay and Lesbian Almanac* (p. 399). London: St. James.

CHAPTER 24: THE AVOCADO AND THE ASPARAGUS

References

Barry, A. M. S. (1997). *Visual intelligence: Perception, image, and manipulation in visual communication.* New York: State University of New York Press.

Bechara, A., Damasio, H., Tranel, D., & Damasio, A. (1997). Deciding advantageously before knowing the advantageous strategy. *Science, 275,* 1293–1295.

Graber, D. A. (1990). Seeing is remembering: How visuals contribute to learning from television news. *Journal of Communication, 40*(3), 134–155.

Jung, C. J. (1964). *Man and his symbols.* Garden City, NY: Doubleday.

LeDoux, J. (1986). Sensory systems and emotion. *Integrative Psychiatry 4,* 237–243.

LeDoux, J. (1996). *The emotional brain.* New York: Simon & Schuster.

Lester, P. M. (2003). *Visual communication: Images with messages* (3rd ed.) Belmont, CA: Wadsworth.

Madigan, S. (1983). Picture memory. In Jo C. Willis (Ed.), *Imagery, memory and cognition; Essays in honor of Allan Paivio* (pp. 65–89). Hillsdale, NY: Erlbaum.

McLuhan, H. M. (1967). *The mechanical bride*. New York: Vanguard.

McLuhan, H. M., & Powers, B. R. (1989). *The global village, transformations in world life and media in the 21st century*. New York: Oxford University Press.

Newton, J. (1996). Of the avocado and the asparagus: The dance of the archetypes. In Lester, P. M., (Ed.). (1996). *Images that injure pictorial stereotypes in the media* (pp. 161–164). Westport, CT: Praeger.

Newton, J. (2001). *The burden of visual truth: The role of photojournalism in mediating reality*. Mahwah, NJ: Erlbaum.

Paivio, A., Rogers, T. B., & Smythe, P. C. (1968). Why are pictures easier to recall than words? *Psychonomic Science, 11*(4), 137–138.

Sargent, S. L., & Zillmann, D. (1999, May). *Image effects on selective exposure to news stories*. Paper presented to the annual meeting of the International Communication Association, San Francisco, CA.

Schultz, M. (1993). *The effect of visual presentation, story complexity and story familiarity on recall and comprehension of television news*. Unpublished doctoral dissertation, Indiana University, Bloomington.

Showalter, E. (1990). *Sexual anarchy, gender and culture at the fin de siècle*. New York: Viking.

Sperry, R. W. (1973). Lateral specialization of cerebral function in the surgically separated hemispheres. In F. J. McGuigan & R. A. Schoonover (Eds.), *The psychophysiology of thinking* (pp. 209–229). New York: Academic Press.

Stone, A. R. (1993). The "empire" strikes back: A posttranssexual manifesto (3rd ed.). Retrieved September 26, 2002, from www.sandystone.com/empirestrikes-back. First edition published in 1991 in Kristina Straub and Julia Epstein (Eds.), *Body guards: The cultural politics of gender ambiguity*. New York: Routledge.

Stone, A. R. (1995). *The war of desire and technology at the close of the mechanical age*. Boston: MIT Press.

Williams, R. (1999, Autumn) Beyond visual literacy: omniphasism, a theory of cognitive balance, part I. *Journal of Visual Literacy, 19*(2), 159–178.

Williams, R. (2000, Autumn). Omniphasic visual-media literacy in the classroom part III. *Journal of Visual Literacy, 20*(2) 219–241.

Winson, J. (2002, August). The meaning of dreams. *Scientific American: The hidden mind, 12*(1) 54–61.

CHAPTER 25: DRAWING BLOOD: IMAGES, STEREOTYPES, AND THE POLITICAL CARTOON

Notes

1. In this chapter, the terms *political cartoon* and *editorial cartoon* are used interchangeably; they refer to a drawing that is designed to sway your opinion about a social, political, or contemporary event.

2. This study suggests that there are at least eight different theories that try to explain why something is funny or why it is not: biological, superiority, incongruity, surprise, ambivalence, relief, configurational, and psychoanalytic. "Many of these theories have given special notice to the prevalence or appeal of aggressive humor, and three of them predict in reasonably direct fashion that aggressive humor should tend to be funnier than more harmless kinds of humor" (McCauley, Woods, Coolidge, and Kulick, 1983).

References

Ammons, D.N., King, J. C., & Yeric, J. L. (1988). Unapproved imagemakers: Political cartoonists' topic selection, objectives and perceived restrictions. *Newspaper Research Journal, 9*(3), 79–90.

Can we play through? (1992, May 25). *Newsweek,* 6.

Cartoons. (1993). *Compton's Interactive Encyclopedia.* (Sec. 2, p. 1). London: Compton's NewMedia, Inc.

Dowd, M. (1988, July). The campaign you didn't see. *American Photographer,* 44.

Ethics in editorial cartooning: Cartoonist and editor views. (1988). *Newspaper Research Journal, 9*(3), 91–103.

Freedom Forum. (1997, January). Freedom Forum First Amendment calendar. Arlington, VA: Freedom Forum.

Garland, N. (1989, September). Cartoonist's eye view. *National Review,* pp. 32–33.

Glassman, C. (1994). Why is this man smiling? A cultural analysis of presidential campaign photojournalism. Unpublished master's thesis, Hunter College of the City University of New York.

Grob, G.N., & Beck, R.N. (1970). *Ideas in America.* New York: The Free Press.

Handlin, O. (Ed.). (1960). *American principles and issues.* New York: Holt, Rhinehart & Winston.

Hoff, S. (1976). *Editorial and political cartooning.* New York: Stravon Educational Press.

Love, A.M., & Deckers, L. H. (1989). Humor appreciation as a function of sexual, aggressive, and sexist content. *Sex Roles, 20,* 649–654.

Malcolm, J.P. (1813). *An historical sketch of the art of caricaturing.* London: Longman, Hurst, Rees, Orme, and Browne.

McCauley, C., Woods, K., Coolidge, C., & Kulick, W. (1983). More aggressive cartoons are funnier. *Journal of Personality and Social Psychology, 44,* 817–823.

Nelson, R.P. (1975). *Cartooning.* New York: NTC/Contemporary.

Schlagheck, C. (1992, September). Enough is enough, say columnists," *News Photographer,* 57.

Walker, M. (1994, January 17). Mightier than the sorehead. *The Nation,* pp. 45–54.

CHAPTER 26: TRANSFORMATION OF A STEREOTYPE: GEEKS, NERDS, WHIZ KIDS, AND HACKERS

Notes

1. Available at: www.sci.ameslab.gov/ABC/Biographies.html.

2. See "A Portrait of J. Random Hacker," available at: www.comedia.com/hot/jargon_3.0/APPEND_B/APPENDXB.HTML (10 May, 2002).

3. All of these references are taken from the main plot lines of contemporary popular films.

References

AAUW report says girls shortchanged in computer age. (2000, August). *Reading Today*. Looksmart. Retrieved April 23, 2002, from www.findarticles.com.

American Heritage College Dictionary (3rd ed.). (1997). p. 915. Boston: Houghton Mifflin Co.

Bell, J. (June 1996). Hack the movies: How the Internet fares in Hollywood. *SBA-MUG Newsletter*. Retrieved April 4, 2002, from www.art.net/Studios/Visuals/Jillbell/Movies2.html.

Cultural stereotypes. (2002, April 16). *Crow Magazine*. [Online]. Retrieved from www.crowmagazine.com/culstereo.htm.

Eglash, R. (2000, November 14). *Race sex and nerds: From black geeks to Asian hipsters*. Paper presented at the American Studies Association meeting, Detroit, MI.

Farnall, O., & Smith, K. (1999). Invisible no more: Advertising and people with disabilities. In D. Braithwaite & T. Thompson, T. (Eds.), *Handbook of communication and people with disabilities: Research and application* (pp. 307–318). Hillsdale, NJ: Erlbaum.

First-year female college students found to have less confidence about computer skills than male counterparts. (2001, February 15). *Black Issues in Higher Education*.

Girls' computer clubs fight off "nerd" image. (2002, February 8). TSL Education Limited, *New York Times*. [Online]. Retrieved May 1, 2002, from web.lexis-nexus.com/universe/printdoc.

Jolivette, H. (2002, May 6). ABC replica stopping at Colorado. *Iowa State Daily*, p. A1.

Kendall, L. (1999). Nerd nation: Images of nerds in US popular culture. *International Journal of Cultural Studies, 2*(2), 260–283.

Lippmann, W. (1961). *Public Opinion*. New York: Macmillan.

Schorow, S. (2001, December 8). Net life: Fellowship of fans thrives on the Web. *Boston Herald*. [Online]. Retrieved May 8, 2002, from weblexus-nexus.com/universe/document?_m = 6d8ae,53a840c80367e0f6df24ed08.

Strober, M., & Arnold, C. (1987). *Computer chips and paper clips: Technology and women's employment.* [Online]. Washington, DC: National Research Council. Retrieved July 9, 2003, from www.nap.edu/catalog/951.html/.

Weibel, K. (1977). *Mirror mirror: Images of women reflected in popular culture.* Garden City, NY: Anchor Books.

Weigner, W. (1992, June 12). Revenge of the Nerds. *Forbes.*

CHAPTER 27: STEREOTYPING OF MEDIA PERSONNEL

Notes

1. Many news organizations recently have sought protection for their journalists, paying several British security training companies $400–$600 a day for safety training. The Associated Press estimates that about 400 of its staff have participated in hazard training (Trigoboff, 2002, p. 12).

2. Available at: www.csus.edu.

References

Anderson, T. (2002, February 1). Pearl's kidnappers won't win. *New York Times,* p. A25.

Barton, G. (2001, December). Patriotism and the news. *The Quill,* p.18.

Donahue, D. (2002, June 24). Danny Pearl's words live On. *USA Today,* p. D1.

Interview: Christiane Amanpour. (April 2002). *Proceedings: United States Naval Institute,* 54–56.

Kennedy, W. V. (1993). *The military and the media: Why the press cannot be trusted to cover a war.* Westport, CT: Praeger.

Knightley, P. (1975). *The first casualty.* New York: Harcourt Brace Jovanovich.

Lapham, L. H. (2002, February). Mythography. *Harper's Magazine,* 9.

Malkin, M. (2001, October 8). [Column]. *Human Events.*

Paulson, K. (2002, September). Too Free? Retrieved July 9, 2003, from www.ajr.org/article.asp?id=2621.

Phipps, J. L. (2002, March 11). When journalists become targets. *Electronic Media,* p.14.

Princeton Survey Research Associates. (2002, July). The Pew Research Center for People & the Press survey. [Online]. Retrieved July 9, 2003, from people-press.org/reports.

Roberts, T. (2001, December 28). Inside NCR. *National Catholic Reporter,* p. 2.

Rutenberg, J., & Carter, B. (2001, November 7). Network coverage a target of fire from conservatives. *New York Times,* p.B2.

Trigoboff, D. (2002, May 6). Journalists' survival schools. *Broadcasting & Cable,* p. 20.

CHAPTER 28: COMMON GROUND AND FUTURE HOPES

References

Alexander, A., & Potter, W.J. (Eds.). (2001). *How to publish your communication research: An insider's view.* Thousand Oaks, CA: Sage.

Blumer, H. (1954, February). What is wrong with social theory? *American Sociological Review, 19,* 3–10.

Blumer, H. (1969). *Symbolic interactionism: Perspective and method.* Englewood Cliffs, NJ: Prentice-Hall.

Buber, M. (1958). *I and thou* (2nd ed.). Trans. R.G. Smith. New York: Scribner's.

Carey, J.W. (1997a). The communications revolution and the professional communicator. In E.S. Munson & C.A. Warren (Eds.). *James Carey: A critical reader* (pp. 128–143). Minneapolis, MN: University of Minnesota Press.

Carey, J.W. (1997b). The dark continent of American journalism. In E.S. Munson & C.A. Warren (Eds.). *James Carey: A critical reader* (pp. 144–148). Minneapolis, MN: University of Minnesota Press.

Carey, J.W. (1997c). Ritual. In E.S. Munson & C.A. Warren (Eds.). *James Carey: A critical reader* (pp. 313–316). Minneapolis, MN: University of Minnesota Press.

Carey, J.W. (1988). *Communication as culture.* Boston: Unwin Hyman.

Cissna, K.N., & Anderson, R. (1998, February). Theorizing about dialogic moments: The Buber-Rogers position and postmodern themes. *Communication Theory, 8,* 63–104.

Denzin, N.K., & Lincoln, Y.S. (Eds.). (2000). *Handbook of qualitative research* (2nd ed.). Thousand Oaks, CA: Sage.

Freire, P. (1970). *Pedagogy of the oppressed.* New York: Seabury.

Freire, P. (1973). *Education for critical consciousness.* New York: Seabury.

Geertz, C. (1973). Thick description. In *The interpretation of culture.* New York: Basic Books.

Klapper, J.T. (1965). What we know about the effects of mass communication: The brink of hope. In O. Lerbringer & A.J. Sullivan (Eds.). *Information, influence, and communication.* New York: Basic Books.

Kuhn, T. (1970). *The structure of scientific revolutions.* Chicago: University of Chicago Press.

Nagel, T. (1986). *The view from nowhere.* New York: Oxford University Press.

Niebuhr, H.R. (1941). *The meaning of revelation.* New York: Macmillan.

Sloan, D. (1980). The teaching of ethics in the American undergraduate curriculum, 1876–1976. In D. Callahan & S. Bok (Eds.). *Ethics teaching in higher education.* New York: Plenum.

Small, A. W. (1903). Me significance of sociology for ethics. In *The Dicennial Publication of the University of Chicago* (vol. 4). Chicago: University of Chicago Press.

Thomas, P., Richards, M., & Nain, Z. (Eds.). (2000). *Communication and development: The Freirean connection.* Cresskill, NJ: Hampton.

BIBLIOGRAPHY

AAUW report says girls shortchanged in computer age. (2000, August). *Reading Today.* Looksmart. Retrieved April 23, 2002, from www.findarticles.com.

Abraham, L. (1998). *Subtle manifestations of prejudice: implicit visual constructions of black pathology.* Unpublished doctoral dissertation, Annenberg School for Communication, University of Pennsylvania.

Abraham, S., & Abraham, N. (1983). *Arabs in the New World.* Detroit: Wayne State University Center for Urban Studies.

ACLU. (2003). Racial equality: Racial profiling. [Online]. Retrieved July 8, 2003, from www/aclu.org/RacialEquality/RacialEqualitylist.cfm?c=133.

Ahmad, E. (2001). *Terrorism, theirs and ours.* New York: Seven Stories.

Ahmed, A. (2002). *Hello, Hollywood: Your images affect Muslims everywhere.* Retrieved July 8, 2003, from www.npq.org/archive/2002 spring/ahmed. html.

Alexander, A., & Potter, W. J. (Eds.). (2001). *How to publish your communication research: An insider's view.* Thousand Oaks, CA: Sage.

American heritage college dictionary (3rd ed.). (1997). p. 915. Boston: Houghton Mifflin Co.

The American heritage dictionary of the English language (4th ed.). (2000). New York: Houghton Mifflin Co.

American Society of Plastic Surgeons (2001). *2001 Cosmetic Surgery Trends.* Retrieved May 15, 2002, from www.plasticsurgery.org/mediactr/costrends 2001.cfm.

Ammons, D.N., King, J. C., & Yeric, J. L. (1988). Unapproved imagemakers: Political cartoonists' topic selection, objectives and perceived restrictions. *Newspaper Research Journal, 9*(3), 79–90.

Amnesty International. (2001). *September 11 crisis response guide for junior high and high schools.* New York: Amnesty International USA.

Anderson, T. (2002, February 1). Pearl's kidnappers won't win. *New York Times,* p. A25.

Another kind of war. (2001, September 18). *USA Today,* p. 23A.

Asian American Journalists Association. (1991). *Asian American Handbook.* Chicago: National Conference of Christians and Jews.

Auletta, K. (2002). The Howell doctrine. *The New Yorker,* LXXVIII (15), 48–71.

Ayoso, R. (2002, April 3). Hollywood seeks key to Spanish-language market for films. Retrieved April 11, 2002, from www.HispanicBusiness.com.

Badinter, E. (1989). *Man/woman, the one is the other.* (B. Wright, Trans.) London: Collins Harville.

Badinter, E. (1989). *The unopposite sex, the end of the gender battle.* (B. Wright, Trans.) New York: Harper & Row.

Bales, R. F. (1944). *The fixation factor in alcohol addiction: An hypothesis derived from a comparative study of Irish and Jewish social norms.* Unpublished doctoral dissertation, Harvard University.

Barclay, B. (1990). *Our own image.* Auckland: Longman Paul.

Barclay, B. (2001, November 10). Preserving Pacific media. In *Hawai'i International Film Festival.* Symposium conducted at the University of Hawai'i.

Barcus, F. E. (1983). *Images of life on children's television.* New York: Praeger.

Barry, A. M. S. (1997). *Visual intelligence: Perception, image, and manipulation in visual communication.* New York: State University of New York Press.

Barthes, R. (1982). *Camera lucida: Reflections on photography.* New York: Vintage/Ebury.

Barton, G. (2001, December). Patriotism and the news. *The Quill,* 18.

Bateson, M. (1994). *Peripheral visions: Learning along the way.* New York: HarperCollins.

Bechara, A., Damasio, H., Tranel, D., & Damasio, A. (1997). Deciding advantageously before knowing the advantageous strategy. *Science, 275,* 1293–1295.

Behar, R. (1993, October 4). The secret life of Mahmud the red. *Time.*

Belasco, D. (1999, October) After the nanny: Young Jewish women in mainstream culture. *CultureCurrents.* Retrieved November 11, 2002, from www.jewishculture.org/currents/9910current.htm.

Bell, J. (1996, July). Hack the movies: How the Internet fares in Hollywood," *SBAMUG Newsletter.* Retrieved, April 4, 2002, from http://www.art.net/Studios/Visuals/Jillbell/Movies2.html.

Berelson, B., & Salter, P. J. (1973) Majority and minority Americans: An analysis of magazine fiction. In S. Cohen & J. Young (Eds.), *The manufacture of news* (pp.107–126). Beverly Hills, CA.: Sage.

Billings, D. (Ed.). (2001). *Back talk from Appalachia: Confronting stereotypes.* Lexington, KY: University Press of Kentucky.

Bird, S. E. (1996). CJ's revenge: Media, folklore, and the cultural construction of AIDS. *Critical Studies in Mass Communication, 13,* 53.

Black, J., Steele, B., & Barney, R. (1994). *Doing ethics in journalism: A handbook with case studies.* Boston: Allyn & Bacon.

Blumer, H. (1954). What is wrong with social theory? *American Sociological Review, 19,* 3–10.

Blumer, H. (1969). *Symbolic interactionism: Perspective and method.* Englewood Cliffs, NJ: Prentice-Hall.

Boggle, D. (1991). *Toms, coons, mulattoes, mammies, & bucks: An interpretive history of blacks in American films.* New York: Continuum.

Bolton, R. (1992). *Culture wars, documents from the recent controversies in the arts.* New York: New Press.

Bolton, R. (Ed.). (1992). *The contest of meaning: Critical histories of photography.* Cambridge, MA: The MIT Press.

Boorstin, D. J. (1961). *The image: A guide to pseudo-events in America.* New York: Harper Colophon.

Boothe, K. (1998, May 11). NLGA deplores unprecedented "bathroom journalism" by TV news. *National Lesbian and Gay Journalists Association news release.*

Bornstein, K. (1994). *On men, women and the rest of us.* New York: Routledge.

Boskin, J. (1980). Denials: The media view of dark skins and the city. In B. Rubin (Ed.), *Small voices and great trumpets: Minorities and the media.* New York: Praeger.

Botta, R. (1999). Television images and adolescent girls' body image disturbance. *Journal of Communication, 49*(2), 22–41.

Botta, R. (2000). The mirror of television: A comparison of black and white adolescents' body image. *Journal of Communication, 50*(3), 144–159.

Breslin, J. (1991, March 19). The cardinal sins of Irish Catholics. *Newsday,* p. 27.

Brod, H. (Ed.) (1987). *The making of masculinities, the new men's studies.* Boston: Unwin Hyman.

Brookhiser, R. (1993, March 1). The melting pot is still simmering. *Time,* 72.

Brookhiser, R. (1989, Sept 1). Poison pens. *National Review,* pp. 30–33.

Browne, D. R., Firestone, C. M., & Mickiewics, E. (1994). *Television/radio news & minorities.* Queenstown: Aspen Institute.

Brownmiller, S. (1984). *Femininity.* New York: Fawcett Columbine.

Bryant, K. (2001, October 18). They're moving on up. *Los Angeles Times,* sec. 5, p. 2.

Buber, M. (1958). *I and thou,* (2nd ed.), (R. G. Smith, trans.). New York: Scribner's.

Buck, G. (1992, August 26). And you thought thought-provoking art could only be found in museums. *Chicago Tribune,* p. 16.

Burgard, M. (2001, September 21). Unease in Arab community; after terror attacks, some in New York City face blame and bigotry; terror in America: New York City. *Hartford Courant,* p. 16.

Burton, P., & Cohen, R. (Producers). (1984). The old man and the gun. *Frontline*. Boston: Public Broadcasting Service.

Campbell, C.P. (1995). *Race, myth and the news*. Thousand Oaks, CA: Sage.

Campbell, J. & Moyers, B. (1988). *The Power of Myth*. New York: Doubleday.

Can we play through? (1992, May 25). *Newsweek*, 6.

Cappella, J.N. & Jamieson, K.H. (1996). News frames, political cynicism, and media cynicism. *Annals of the Academy of Political and Social Sciences, 546,* 71–84.

Carey, J.W. (1988). *Communication as Culture*. Boston: Unwin Hyman.

Carey, J.W. (1997a). The communications revolution and the professional communicator. In E.S. Munson & C.A. Warren (Eds.). *James Carey: A critical reader* (pp. 128–143). Minneapolis, MN: University of Minnesota Press.

Carey, J.W. (1997b). The dark continent of American journalism. In E.S. Munson & C.A. Warren (Eds.). *James Carey: A critical reader* (pp. 144–148). Minneapolis, MN: University of Minnesota Press.

Carey, J. W. (1997c). Ritual. In E.S. Munson & C.A. Warren (Eds.), *James Carey: A critical reader* (pp. 313–316). Minneapolis, MN: University of Minnesota Press.

Cartoons. (1993). *Compton's Interactive Encyclopedia*. (sec. 2, p. 1). London: Compton's NewMedia, Inc.

Charen, M. (2001, October 28). Expel Arabs, profile truckers. *Baltimore Sun*, p. 3F.

Chavez, S. (2001, September 17). After the attack; the victims; she was Muslim; she was a victim. *Los Angeles Times*, p. 16.

Christians, C. (1986). Reporting and the oppressed. In D. Elliott (Ed.), *Responsible journalism* (pp. 109–130). Beverly Hills, CA: Sage Publications Inc.

Christians, C., Rotzoll, K., & Fackler, M. (1983). *Media ethics: Cases and moral reasoning*. New York: Longman.

Chura, H. (2002, February 11). Draft codger. *Advertising Age*, p. 4.

Church. G. (1993, July 5). The terror within. *Time*.

Cissna, K.N., & Anderson, R. (1998, February). Theorizing about dialogic moments: The Buber-Rogers position and postmodern themes. *Communication Theory, 8,* 63–104.

Claffey, M. (2001, November 12). Pakistani groups cite persecution. *Daily News*, p. 33.

Clayton, J. (2002, March 25). Collection of ties bind to community. *The Union Leader* [Manchester, NH], p. 1A.

Cobern, C. (1929). *The new archeological discoveries*. New York: Funk & Wagnalls.

Copeland, D. (August, 1993) *"The skulking Indian enemy"; colonial newspapers portrayal of Native Americans*. A paper presented at the Association for Education in Journalism and Mass Communication, Kansas City, MO.

Cosmo Cover Style. (February 2002). *Cosmopolitan*, 184–193.

Cowen, P.S. (1991). A socio-cognitive approach to ethnicity in films. In L.D. Friedman (Ed.), *Unspeakable images: Ethnicity and the American cinema.* Urbana and Chicago: University of Illinois Press.

Critics leave Schindler off best directors' list. (1993, December 17). *The Daily Telegraph.*

Cronin, M., & Adair, D. (2002). *The wearing of the green, a history of St. Patrick's Day.* New York: Routledge.

Crookall, D., & Saunders, D. (Eds.). (1989). *Communication and simulation: From two fields to one theme.* Clevedon, England: Multilingual Matters Ltd.

Crossroads: race, rights and national security. (2002, May 10). Washington, DC: Lemelson Center, National Museum of American History, Smithsonian Institution.

Crowdus, G., & Georgakas, D. (2002). Thinking about the power of images: An interview with Spike Lee. *Cineaste, 26*(2).

Cultural stereotypes. (2002, April 16). *Crow Magazine.* [Online]. Retrieved from www.crowmagazine.com/culstereo.htm.

D'Agostino, P., & Muntadas, A. (Eds.). (1982). *The unnecessary image.* New York: Tanam.

Damasio, A. (1994). *Descartes' error.* New York: Putnam.

Damasio, A. (1999). *The feeling of what happens.* New York: Harcourt Brace.

Dates, J.L., & Barlow, W. (Eds.). (1990), *Split image: African Americans in the mass media.* Washington, DC: Howard University Press.

De Lisser, E. (2002). *Companies flood the market with patriotic-themed wares.* Retrieved November 11, 2002, from www.wsjclassroomedition.com/tj_020502_patr.htm.

Deets, H.B. (1994, July/August). No more stereotypes, thank you! *Modern Maturity, 4–5.*

Del Olmo, F. (1985). Newspaper innovations: Attempts to serve the changing Latino community. *Telecommunications and Latinos, 41–45.*

Dennis, E., & Merrill, J. (1991). *Media debates issues in mass communication.* New York: Longman.

Dennis, E., Ismach, A., & Gillmor, D. (Eds.). (1978). *Enduring issues in mass communication.* St. Paul, MN: West.

Denzin, N.K., & Linclon, Y.S. (Eds.). (2000). *Handbook of qualitative research* (2nd ed.). Thousand Oaks, CA: Sage.

Devine, P.G. (1989). Stereotypes and prejudice: Their automatic and controlled components. *Journal of Personality and Social Psychology, 56, 5–18.*

Dickson, T. (1993, Winter). Sensitizing students to racism in the news. *Journalism Educator, 28–33.*

Dines, G., & Humez, J.M. (1995). *Gender, Race and Class in Media: A Text Reader.* Thousand Oaks, CA: Sage.

Donahue, D. (2002, June 24). Danny Pearl's words live on. *USA Today,* p. D1.

Donaldson, J. (1981, March). The visibility and image of handicapped people on television. *Exceptional Children, 47*(6), 413–416.

Dowd, M. (July 1988). The campaign you didn't see. *American Photographer,* 44.

Doyle, J. (2002, March 7). Saving the Irish soul. *San Francisco Chronicle,* p. D1.

Dreifus, C. (1993, May). Richard Dreyfuss. *The Progressive,* 32.

Drummond, W.J. (1990, July/August). About face: From alliance to alienation. *The American Enterprise,* 23–29.

Dychtwald, K. (2000). *Age power: How the 21st century will be ruled by the new old.* Boston: J.P. Tarcher.

Dyer, R. (1993). *The matter of images, essays on representations.* London: Routledge.

Ebert, R. (1998). The Siege review. *Chicago Sun-Times.* Retrieved July 8, 2003, from www.suntimes.com/ebert/ebert_reviews/1998/11/110603.html.

The Economic Policy Institute. (2001, September 25). *Household income fails to grow in 2000.* Retrieved November 11, 2002, from www.Epinet.org.

Editor wins grant to improve image of the disabled. (1988, October 23). *Louisville Courier Journal,* pp. 1B, 12B.

Eglash, R. (2000, November 14). *Race, sex and nerds: from black geeks to Asian hipsters.* Paper presented at the American Studies Association meeting, Detroit, MI.

Ekerdt, D.J., & Clark, E. (2001, March). Selling retirement in financial planning advertisements. [Online]. *Journal of Aging Studies, 15*(1), 55–68. Abstract from AgeLine Database.

Elie, Lolis E. (2002, April 23). Exposing stereotypes of Indians. (New Orleans) *Times Picayune.*

Emery, M., & Emery, E. (1988). *The press and America.* Englewood Cliffs, NJ: Prentice-Hall.

Entman, R., & Rojecki, A. (2000). *The black image in the white mind: Media and race in America.* Chicago & London: The University of Chicago Press.

Entman, R.M. (1993). Framing: Towards clarification of a fractured paradigm. *Journal of Communication, 43*(4), 51–58.

Entman, R.M. (1994a). Representation and reality in the portrayal of blacks on network television news. *Journalism & Mass Communication Quarterly, 71,* 509–520.

Entman, R.M. (1994b, Summer). African Americans according to TV news. *Media Studies Journal,* 29–38.

Enteman, W.F. (1996). Stereotyping, prejudice, and discrimination. In P.M. Lester (Ed.), *Images that injure: Pictorial stereotypes in the media* (pp. 9–14). Westport, CT: Praeger.

Esposito, J.L. (1995). *The Islamic threat, myth or reality?* New York: Oxford University Press.

Ethics in editorial cartooning: Cartoonist and editor views. (1988). *Newspaper Research Journal,* 9 (3), 91–103.

Fallows, M.R. (1979). *Irish Americans, identity and assimilation.* Englewood Cliffs, NJ: Prentice-Hall.

Farnall, O., & Smith, K. (1999). Invisible no more: Advertising and people with disabilities. In D. Braithwaite & T. Thompson (Eds.). *Handbook of communication and people with disabilities: Research and application* (pp. 307–318). Hillsdale, NJ: Erlbaum.

Feroze, L. (1994, March 17). St. Patrick's Day: Calgary's Irish remember home. *Calgary Herald,* p. A5.

Field, A.E., Camargo, C.A., Jr., Taylor, C.B., Berkey, C. S., Roberts, S.B., & Colditz, G.A. (2001). Peer, parent and media influences on the development of weight concerns and frequent dieting among preadolescent and adolescent girls and boys. *Pediatrics, 107*(1), 54–60.

First-year female college students found to have less confidence about computer skills than male counterparts. (2001, February 15). *Black Issues in Higher Education.*

Fitzgerald, M., & King, J. (1990). *The uncounted Irish.* Toronto: P.D. Meany.

Fox, S. (1984). *The mirror makers.* New York: William Morrow.

Frase-Blunt, M. (2001, April 17). Rejecting life expectancies, Washington [DC] octogenarians and nonogenarians shatter the stereotypes of old age. *Washington Post,* p. T18.

Freedom Forum. (1997, January). Freedom Forum First Amendment calendar. Arlington, VA: Freedom Forum.

Freire, P. (1970). *Pedagogy of the oppressed.* New York: Seabury.

Freire, P. (1973). *Education for critical consciousness.* New York: Seabury.

Freud, S. (1965/1900). *The interpretation of dreams.* (J. Strachey, Trans.), New York: Avon.

Friedman, S. (2000, August 5). "Geezer jokes" take a toll. [New York] *Newsday,* p. B10.

Gamson, W. (1992). *Talking politics.* Cambridge: Cambridge University Press.

Gans, H.J. (1979). *Deciding what's news: A study of CBS Evening News, NBC Nightly News, Newsweek* and *Time.* New York: Random House.

Garfield, B. (2002, April 1). Garfield's Ad Review. Innocence lost: Midas sags to a low with geriatric nudity spot. *Advertising Age,* p. 57.

Garland, N. (1989, September 1). Cartoonist's eye view. *National Review,* pp. 32–33.

Geertz, C. (1973). *The interpretation of culture* (pp. 3–32). New York: Basic Books.

Gert, B. (1998). *Morality, its nature and justification.* New York: Oxford University Press.

Ghanem, S. (1996). *Media coverage of crime and public opinion: an exploration of the second level of agenda setting.* Unpublished doctoral dissertation, Austin University of Texas, p. 25.

Girls' computer clubs fight off "nerd" image. (2002, February 8). TSL Education Limited, *New York Times.* [Online]. Retrieved May 1, 2002, from web .lexis-nexus.com/universe/printdoc.

Gist, M.E. (1990). Minorities in media imagery. *Newspaper Research Journal, 11*(3), 52–63.

Gitlin, T. (1980). *The whole world is watching: Mass media in the making and unmaking of the new left.* Berkeley, CA: University of California Press.

(GLAAD) Alert. (1996, December 12). The Gay and Lesbian Alliance Against Defamation (GLAAD) Alert.

Glad, D.D. (1947, December). Attitudes and experience of American-Jewish and American-Irish male youth as related to differences in adult rates of inebriety. *Quarterly Journal of Studies on Alcohol, 8,* 406–472.

Glassman, B. (1975). *Anti-Semitic stereotypes without Jews.* Detroit, MI: Wayne State University Press.

Glassman, C. (1994). *Why is this man smiling? A cultural analysis of presidential campaign photojournalism.* Unpublished master's thesis, Hunter College of the City University of New York.

Goffman, E. (1974). *Frame analysis: An essay on the organization of experience.* New York: Harper & Row.

Goffman, I. (1979). *Gender advertisements.* New York: Harper & Row.

Goldberg, V. (1991). *The power of photography.* New York: Abbeville.

Goldberg, V. (1993, February 28). Still photos trace the moving image of blacks. *New York Times,* p. H23.

Goldberg, V. (2002, May 12). When the news in pictures was news. *New York Times,* Arts, p. 25.

Graber, D.A. (1990). Seeing is remembering: How visuals contribute to learning from television news. *Journal of Communication, 40*(3), 134–155.

Gray, H. (1989). Television, black Americans, and the American dream. *Critical Studies in Mass Communication, 6,* 376–386.

Greeley, A.M. (1972). *That most distressful nation.* Chicago: Quadrangle.

Grob, G.N., & Beck, R.N. (1970). *Ideas in America.* New York: The Free Press.

Gross, A.M., Bennett, T., Sloan, L., Marx, B.P., & Juergens, J. (2001). The impact of alcohol and alcohol expectancies on male perception of female sexual arousal in date rape analog. *Experimental and Clinical Psychopharmacology, 9*(4), 380–388.

Gross, L. (1988). The ethics of (mis)representation. In L. Gross, J.S. Katz, & J. Ruby (Eds.). *Image Ethics* (pp. 188–202). New York: Oxford University Press.

Gross, L. (1991). Gays, lesbians and popular culture. In M. Wolf & A. Kielwasser (Eds.). *Gay people, sex, media.* Binghamton, NY: Haworth.

Gross, L., Katz, J.S., & Ruby, J. (Eds.). (1988). *Image ethics, the moral rights of subjects in photographs, film, and television.* New York: Oxford University Press.

Guerrero, E. (1993). *Framing blackness. The African American image in film.* Philadelphia: Temple University Press.

Gutierrez, F. (1978, August 13–16). *Through Anglo eyes: Chicanos as portrayed in the news media.* Paper presented at the Association for Education in Journalism 61st annual conference, Seattle, WA.

Hall, J., & Lippmann, J. (1993, February 15). NBC News: A question of standards. *Los Angeles Times,* pp. F1, F15.

Hall, J., & Lippmann, J. (1993, February 26). Logging story leaves NBC redfaced again. *Los Angeles Times,* p. D1–D2.

Hammond, M. (2001, March 4). Baby boomers rewrite aging. *St. Petersburg Times,* p. 7D.

Handlin, O. (Ed.). (1960). *American principles and issues.* New York: Holt, Rhinehart & Winston.

Haraway, D.J. (1991). *Simians, cyborgs, and women, the reinvention of nature.* New York: Routledge.

Harjo, S.S. (1990). *Racism in the news.* [Video]. Nashville, TN: Spectra Communications, Inc., distributed by Media Action Research Center, Inc.

Harrison, K. (1997). Does interpersonal attraction to thin media personalities promote eating disorders? *Journal of Broadcasting and Electronic Media, 41,* 478–500.

Harrison, K. (2000). The body electric: Thin-ideal media and eating disorders in adolescents. *Journal of Communication, 50*(3), 119–143.

Harrison, R. (1981). *The cartoon: Communication to the quick.* Beverly Hills, CA: Sage Publications Inc.

Hartmann, P, & Husband, C. (1987). The mass media and racial conflict. In J. Hawthorn, (Ed.), *Propaganda, persuasion and polemic.* London: Edward Arnold.

Herzog, T.R., & Larwin, D.A. (1988). The appreciation of humor in captioned cartoons. *Journal of Psychology, 122,* 597–607.

Hill, H. (1997, October). *Endangered expressions.* Retrieved July 8, 2003, from www.sabine-mag.com/archive/ar02009.htm.

Hoff, S. (1976). *Editorial and political cartooning.* New York: Stravon Educational Press.

Hoffstetter, R. (1976). *Bias in the news.* Columbus, OH: Ohio State University Press.

Hofshire, L.J., & Greenberg, B.S. (2002). Media's impact on adolescents' body dissatisfaction. In J.D. Brown, J.R. Steele, & K. Walsh-Childers (Eds.), *Sexual teens, sexual media.* Mahwah, NJ: Erlbaum.

hooks, b. (1995). *Art on my mind: Visual politics.* New York: New Press.

Hopcke, R.H. (1989). *Jung, Jungians & homosexuality.* Boston: Shambhala.

Hopcke, R.H., Carrington, K.L., & Wirth, S. (Eds.). (1993). *Same-sex love and the path to wholeness, perspectives on gay and lesbian psychological development.* Boston: Shambhala.

Howitt, D. (1995). Pornography and the paedophile: Is it criminogenic?" *British Journal of Medical Psychology, 68,* 15–27.

Hurst, N. M. (1996). Lactation after augmentation mammoplasty. *Obstetrics & Gynecology, 87*(1), 30–34.

Iftikhar, A. T. (2001, October 8). [Letter to the editor]. *Newsweek,* p. 14.

Ignatiev, N. (1995). *How the Irish became white.* New York: Routledge.

Interview: Christiane Amanpour. (April 2002). *Proceedings: United States Naval Institute,* 54–56.

James, C. (2000, October 1). *New York Times.*

Jewish targets in Europe attacked. (2002, April 19). *ABC Today.* Retrieved July 8, 2003, from www.abc.net.au/worldtoday/s535726.htm.

Jhally, S., & Lewis, J. (1992). *Enlightened racism: The Cosby Show, audiences, and the myth of the American dream.* Boulder, CO: Westview.

Johnson, M. (1987, September/October). Where do you get your information about disability issues? *The Disability Rag,* pp. 24–27.

Johnston, D. (2001, November 6). "Mother survives WTC but son joins Taliban—War on terror: New York's traitor." *Daily Telegraph,* p. 5.

Jolivette, H. (2002, May 6). ABC replica stopping at Colorado. *Iowa State Daily,* p. A1.

Jones, J. (1998). The Accusatory space. In G. Dent (Ed.), *Black popular culture* (p. 96). New York: The New Press.

Judge, L., & West, R. S. (1988, September). Why political cartoonists sell out. *The Washington Monthly,* pp. 38–42.

Jung, C. J. (1961). *Memories, dreams, reflections.* New York: Random House.

Jung, C. J. (1964). *Man and his symbols.* Garden City, NY: Doubleday.

Kalter, J. (1986, May 31). Good news: The disabled get more play on TV, bad news: There is still too much stereotyping. *TV Guide,* 41–42.

Kalyanaraman, S., Steele, J., & Sundar, S. S. (2000, June). *Communicating objectification: Effects of sexually suggestive advertisements.* Paper presented at the 50th Annual Conference of the International Communication Association, Acapulco, Mexico.

Kaplan, A. (2002). *How Jews revolutionized comedy in America.* Retrieved July 9, 2003, from uahc.org/rjmag/302ak.html.

Kaufert, P. A., & Lock, M. (1997). Medicalization of women's third age. [Online]. *Journal of Psychosomatic Obstetrics and Gynaecology, 18,* 81–86. Abstract from AgeLine Database.

Keinon, H. (2002). *PR czar: Images beat arguments in media war.* Retrieved November 11, 2002, from www.jpost.com/Editions/2002/01/11/News/News.41518.html.

Kendall, L. (1999). Nerd nation: Images of nerds in US popular culture. *International Journal of Cultural Studies, 2*(2), 260—283.

Kennedy, W. V. (1993). *The military and the media: Why the press cannot be trusted to cover a war.* Westport, CT: Praeger.

Kitch, C. (2001). *The girl on the magazine cover: The origins of visual stereotypes in American mass media.* Chapel Hill, NC: University of North Carolina Press.

Klapper, J. T. (1965). What we know about the effects of mass communication: The brink of hope. In O. Lerbringer & A. J. Sullivan (Eds.), *Information, influence, and communication.* New York: Basic Books.

Knightley, P. (1975). *The first casualty.* New York: Harcourt Brace Jovanovich.

Koestler, F. A. (1976). *The unseen minority: A social history of blindness in America.* New York: David McKay.

Kovel, J. (1984). *White racism.* New York: Columbia University Press.

Kuhn, T. (1970). *The structure of scientific revolutions.* Chicago: University of Chicago Press.

Labre, M. P. (2002). The Brazilian wax: New hairlessness norm for women? *Journal of Communication Inquiry 26*(2), 113–132.

Lamb, D. (1987). *The Arabs.* New York: Vintage.

Lambe, J. L., & Begleiter, R. J. (2002). *Wrapping the news in the flag: Use of patriotic symbols by U.S. local TV stations after the terrorism attacks of September 11, 2001.* Retrieved July 8, 2003, from www.udel.edu/communication/COMM418/begleite/patrioticsymbols/symbols.pdf.

Lambeth, E. (1992). *Committed journalism: An ethic for the profession.* Bloomington, IN: Indiana University Press.

Lapham, L. H. (2002, February). Mythography. *Harper's Magazine, 9.*

Lebow, R. N. (1976). *White Britain and black Ireland. The influence of stereotypes on colonial policy.* Philadelphia: Institute for the Study of Human Issues.

LeDoux, J. (1986). Sensory systems and emotion. *Integrative Psychiatry 4,* 237–243.

Le Doux, J. (1996). *The emotional brain.* New York: Simon & Schuster.

Lester, P. M. (2003). *Visual communication images with messages* (3rd Ed.). Belmont, CA: Wadsworth.

Lester, P. M., & Smith, R. (1990, Spring). African American photo coverage in *Life, Newsweek* and *Time, 1937–1988. Journalism Quarterly,* 128–136.

Lester, P. M., & Smith, R. (Eds.). (1990). *The ethics of photojournalism.* Durham, NC: NPPA.

Lester, P. M., & Smith, R. (1991). *Photojournalism: An ethical approach.* Hillsdale, NJ: Erlbaum.

Lester, P. M., & Smith, R. (1994). African American photo coverage in four US newspapers, 1937–1990. *Journalism Quarterly, 71*(2), 380–394.

Lester, P. M., & Smith, R. (1995). Photojournalism ethics: Timeless issues. In M. Emery & T. Smythe (Eds.), *Customized readings in mass communication.* Dubuque: Brown and Benchmark.

Lester, P. M., & Smith, R. (1997) Images and stereotypes. In E. Cohen & D. Elliott (Eds.), *Contemporary ethical issues: Journalism.* Santa Barbara: ABC-CLIO, Inc.

Lester, P. M., & Smith, R. (2000). Girls can be doctors and boys can be nurses: Surfing for solutions to gender stereotyping. In M. Carstarphen & S. Zavoina (Eds.), *Sexual rhetoric: Media perspectives on sexuality, gender and identity* (pp. 283–292). Westport, CT: Praeger.

Lewis, B. (1990, September). The roots of Muslim rage. *Atlantic Monthly, 226.*

Liebes, T. (1992). Our war/their war: Comparing the *Intifadeh* and the Gulf War on U.S. and Israeli television. *Critical Studies in Mass Communication, 9,* 44–55.

Liebes, T. (2000). Inside a news item: A dispute over framing. *Political Communication, 17,* 295–305.

Linn, T. (1996). Media methods that lead to stereotypes. In P. M. Lester (Ed.), *Images that injure pictorial stereotypes in the media* (pp. 15–20). Westport, CT: Praeger.

Lippmann, W. (1961). *Public Opinion.* New York: Macmillan.

Longmore, P. K. (1990, Fall). The glorious rage of Christy Brown. *Disability Studies Quarterly, 10*(4), 23–25.

Longmore, P.K. (1985a, January/February). A note on language and social identity of disabled people. *American Behavioral Scientist, 28*(3), 419–23.

Longmore, P. K. (1985b, Summer). Screening stereotypes: Images of disabled people. *Social Policy, 32.*

Louie, E. (1994, March 6). The pub: A center of Ireland in exile. *New York Times,* p. C1.

Love, A. M., & Deckers, L. H. (1989). Humor appreciation as a function of sexual, aggressive, and sexist content. *Sex Roles, 20,* 649–654.

MacDonald, J. F. (1992). *Blacks and white TV: African Americans in television since 1948.* Chicago: Nelson-Hall.

Madigan, S. (1983). Picture memory. In J. C. Willis (Ed.), *Imagery, memory and cognition; Essays in honor of Allan Paivio,* (pp. 65–89). Hillsdale, NY: Erlbaum.

Mahdi, L. C., Foster, S., & Little, M. (Eds.). (1987). *Betwixt & between: Patterns of masculine and feminine initiation.* La Salle, IL: Open Court.

Malcolm, J. P. (1813). *An historical sketch of the art of caricaturing.* London: Longman, Hurst, Rees, Orme, and Browne.

Malkin, M. (2001, October 8). [Column]. *Human Events.*

Mankiewicz, F., & Swerdlow, J. (1978). *Remote control: Television and the manipulation of American life.* New York: Ballantine.

Marchand, R. (1985). *Advertising the American Dream.* Berkeley: University of California Press.

Marshall, S. (2001, September 20). Dear friends in peace.[Letter to the Islamic Society of North America, Plainfield, IN].

Martindale, C. (1996). Newspaper stereotypes of African Americans. In P. Lester (Ed.), *Images that injure: Pictorial stereotypes in the media.* Westport, CT: Greenwood.

Marx, B.P., Gross, A.M., & Adams, H.E. (1999). The effect of alcohol on the responses of sexually coercive and noncoercive men to an experimental rape analogue. *Sex Abuse, 11*(2), 131–45.

McCarthy, M. (2001, January 25). The changing face of Super Bowl Sunday. *USA Today,* pp. 1B, 2B.

McCarus, E. (1994). *The development of Arab-American identity.* Ann Arbor, MI: The University of Michigan Press.

McCauley, C., Woods, K., Coolidge, C., & Kulick, W. (1983). More aggressive cartoons are funnier. *Journal of Personality and Social Psychology, 44,* 817–823.

McGee, J. (2001, November 2). Irish American meat raffle is Nov. 24. *The Patriot Ledger* Quincy, MA, p. 4.

McLuhan, H.M. (1967). *The mechanical bride.* New York: Vanguard.

McLuhan, H. M., & Powers, B.R. (1970). *From cliché to archetype.* New York: Viking.

McLuhan, H.M., & Powers, B.R. (1989). *The global village, transformations in world life and media in the 21st century.* New York: Oxford University Press.

Meertens, R.W., & Pettigrew, T.F. (1997). Is subtle prejudice really prejudice? *Public Opinion Quarterly, 61,* 54–71.

A melding of cultures: Latins, the largest new group, are making their presence felt. (1985, July 8). *Time,* 36–41.

Mendleberg, T. (1996, September). *Implicitly racial appeals and the impact of campaigns.* Paper delivered at a seminar for Annenberg Research Fellows, Annenberg School for Communication, University of Pennsylvania.

Mendosa, R. (1993, July). A love affair with movies. *Hispanic Business,* 12–24.

Merina, V. (2001). Diversity since September 11: Never more important. The Poynter Institute. Retrieved July 8, 2003, from www.poynter.org/content/content_view.asp?id=5063.

Messaris, P. (1997). *Visual persuasion: The role of images in advertising.* Thousand Oaks, CA: Sage.

Messaris, P. & Abraham, L. The role of images in framing news stories. In P. Messaris, (1997). *Visual persuasion: The role of images in advertising.* Beverly Hills, CA: Sage.

Mill, J.S. (1991). *On Liberty and other essays.* New York: Oxford University Press.

The miracle worker. (1963, January). *Esquire.*

Mita, M. (2001, November 10). *Storytelling: A Pacific view.* In *Hawai'i International Film Festival.* Symposium conducted at the University of Hawai'i.

Mitchell, S. (1998). *American Generations.* Ithaca, NY: New Strategist Publications.

Moeller, S. (1989). *Shooting war: Photography and the American experience of combat.* New York: Basic Books.

Monbeck, M. E. (1973). *The meaning of blindness: Attitudes toward blindness and blind people.* Bloomington, IN: Indiana University Press.

Moog, C. (1990). *Are they selling her lips? Advertising and identity.* New York: William Morrow.

Moritz, M. (1996). Reframing gay and lesbian media images: Fundamental problems. In P. M. Lester, (Ed.), *Images that injure pictorial stereotypes in the media* (pp. 143–148). Westport, CT: Praeger.

Moritz, M. (1998). Media. In *Gay and Lesbian Almanac* (p. 399). London: St. James.

The Muslim wife. (2001, October 14). *Sunday Times.*

Nagel, T. (1986). *The view from nowhere.* New York: Oxford University Press.

Nail, D. E. (2001, October 27). [Letter to the editor.] *Martinsville Daily Reporter.*

The National Conference for Community and Justice reviews "The Siege," a movie about Islamic terrorism, (1998, November 6). *PR Newswire.*

Negative views of aging may harm health of seniors. (2000, August 11). *Parent Care Advisor, 8*(10).

Neifert, M., DeMarzo, S., Seacat, J., Young, D., Leff, M., & Orleans, M. (1990). The influence of breast surgery, breast appearance, and pregnancy-induced breast changes on lactation sufficiency as measured by infant weight gain. *Birth, 17*(1), 31–38.

Nelson, R. P. (1975). *Cartooning.* New York: NTC/Contemporary.

Newton, J. (1996). Of the avocado and the asparagus: The dance of the archetypes. In P. M. Lester, (Ed.), *Images that injure pictorial stereotypes in the media* (pp. 161–164). Westport, CT: Praeger.

Newton, J. (2001). *The burden of visual truth: The role of photojournalism in mediating reality.* Mahwah, NJ: Erlbaum.

Nichols, J. (2002, March 15). Irish struggle is example for today. *Capital* (Madison, WI) *Times,* p. 11A.

Niebuhr, H. R. (1941). *The meaning of revelation.* New York: Macmillan.

Niebuhr, H. R. (1963). *The responsible self.* New York: Harper & Row.

Nielsen Media Research. (2000). *2000 Report on television, January 1961–April 30, 2000.* New York.

Nugent, K. (2002, March 11). Naughton named to Board of Irish Democrats' group. *Worcester Telegram & Gazette,* p. B4.

O'Neill, M. (1986). *Terrorist spectaculars: Should TV coverage be curbed?* New York: Priority.

Obejas, A. (2001, March 21). Census data may get media more interested in Hispanics. *Chicago Tribune.*

Okwu, M. (2000, April 25). Arab-Americans call for boycott of "Rules of Engagement." [Online]. Retrieved July 8, 2003, from www.cnn.com/2000/showbiz/movies/04/25/rules.of.engagement/.

Owen, P. R., & Laurel-Seller, E. (2000). Weight and shape ideals: Thin is dangerously in. *Journal of Applied Social Psychology, 30*(5), 979–990.

Paivio, A., Rogers, T. B., & Smythe, P. C. (1968). Why are pictures easier to recall than words? *Psychonomic Science*, *11*(4), 137–138.

Pan, Z., & Kosicki, G. M. (1993). Framing analysis: An approach to news discourse. *Political Communication*, *10*, 59–79.

Parenti, M. (1986). *Inventing reality: The politics of the mass media*. New York: St. Martin's Press.

Paulson, K. (2002, September). Too Free? Retrieved July 9, 2003, from www.ajr.org/article.asp?id=2621.

Pearce, F. (1973). How to be immoral and ill, pathetic and dangerous, all at the same time: Mass media and the homosexual. In S. Cohen & J. Young (Eds.), *The Manufacture of News* (pp. 284–301). Beverly Hills, CA: Sage.

Pease, E. C. (1989). Kerner plus 20: Minority news coverage in the Columbus Dispatch. *Newspaper Research Journal*, *10*(3), 17–38.

Pensioners in a fizz over negative advertising. (2000, July 20). *Glasgow Herald*, p. 13.

People gain roles in ads and on TV. (1991, September 23). *New York Times*, p. 14.

Perez-Torres, R. (1988, Fall). Chicanos in film; a new portrayal. *Estos Tiempos* *4*(2), 28.

Perkins, D., & Starosta, W. (2001). Representing coculturals: On form and news portrayals of Native Americans. *The Howard Journal of Communication*, *12*, 73–74.

Peterson, P. (2002, September/October). Public diplomacy and the war on terrorism. *Foreign Affairs*.

Petty, R., & Cacioppo, J. (1981). *Attitudes and persuasion: Classic and contemporary approaches*. Dubuque, IA: Wm. C. Brown.

Peyser, M. (2000, February 21). Malcolm lands on top. *Newsweek*.

Phipps, J. L. (2002, March 11). When journalists become targets. *Electronic Media*, 14.

Pincus, D., & DeBonis, N. (1994). *Top Dog*. New York: McGraw-Hill.

Pitts, L., Jr. (2001, October 28). . . . No, doing so would trash our ideals. *Baltimore Sun*, p. 3F.

Policy statements on media use of the term "illegal alien." (1993). El Paso (Texas) Association of Hispanic Journalists and Colorado (Denver) Hispanic Media Association.

Potter, G. (1960). *To the golden door*. Boston: Little, Brown.

Potter, R. F., Bolls, P. D., & Dent, D. R. (1997, May). *Something for nothing: Is visual encoding automatic?* Paper presented to the annual meeting of the International Communication Association, Montreal, Canada.

Pratkanis, A., & Aronson, E. (2001). *Age of propaganda: The everyday use and abuse of persuasion*. New York: W. H. Freeman and Co.

Prerost, F. J. (1993). Locus of control as a factor in the appreciation of election year political cartoons. *Psychological Reports*, *72*, 217–218.

Prida, D., & Ribner, S. (1976). A feminist view of the 100 books about Puerto Ricans. In *Racism and Sexism in Children's Books* (pp. 42–48). New York: Council on Interracial Books for Children.

Princeton Survey Research Associates. (2002, July). The Pew Research Center for People & the Press survey. [Online]. Retrieved July 9, 2003, from people-press.org/reports.

Quindlen, A. (1991, March 14). Erin go brawl. *New York Times,* p. A25.

Raphael, R. (1998, April 17). Jewish kid hitting the big time on TV's outrageous *South Park. Jewish Student Press Service.* Retrieved July 9, 2003, from www.jewishsf.com/6k980417/etsopark.htm.

Reel, B. (1993, July 7). When the pot calls another pot Irish. *Newsday,* p. 81.

Reese, S. D., Gandy, O. H., Jr., & Gant, A. E. (Eds.). *Framing public life: Perspectives on media and our understanding of the social world.* Mahwah, NJ: Erlbaum.

Rethinking Schools. (1991). *Rethinking Columbus.* [Special edition]. Milwaukee, WI: Rethinking Schools, Ltd. in collaboration with Network Educators of Central America.

Riccio, B. (1994). *Walter Lippmann-Odyssey of a Liberal.* New York: Transaction Publications.

Richardson, S. A., Goodman, N., Hastorf, A. H., & Dornbusch, S. M. (1961). Cultural uniformity in reaction to physical disabilities. *American Sociological Review, 26,* 244–247.

Rickards, M. (1979). *Posters of protest and revolution.* New York: Walker.

Riffe, D., Sneed, D., & Van Ommeren, R. L. (1985). Behind the editorial page cartoon. *Journalism Quarterly 62,* 378–383, 450.

Ritchin, F. (1990). *In our own image: The coming revolution in photography.* New York: Aperture Foundation.

Roberts, T. (2001, December 28). Inside NCR. *National Catholic Reporter,* p. 2.

Rodriguez, R. (1990, April 9). Daily papers misread Latinos, say leaders. *Hispanic Link Weekly Report,* 1–2.

Ross, S. D. (2003). An American frame: *New York Times* discourse on Palestine and Israel. *Conflict & Communication.* [Online]. Retrieved on July 9, 2003, from www.cco.Regener_Online.de.

Rothman, D. (1971). *The discovery of the asylum.* Boston: Little, Brown.

Rule, J. (1975). *Lesbian images.* Garden City, NJ: Doubleday.

Rutenberg, J., & Carter, B. (2001, November 7). Network coverage a target of fire from conservatives. *New York Times,* p. B2.

Said, E. (1981). *Covering Islam.* New York: Pantheon.

Sanders, E. (2001, September 27). Understanding turbans: Don't link them to terrorism. *Seattle Times.* Retrieved July 8, 2003, from seattletimes.nwsource .com/html/home/.

Sargent, S. L., & Zillmann, D. (1999, May). *Image effects on selective exposure to news stories.* Paper presented to the annual meeting of the International Communication Association, San Francisco, CA.

Schiller, D. (1981). *Objectivity and the News.* Philadelphia: University of Pennsylvania Press.

Schlagheck, C. (1992, September). Enough is enough, say columnists. *News Photographer,* 57.

Schlesinger, P., Elliot, P., & Murdock, G. (1984). *Televising terrorism: Political violence in popular culture.* New York: Scribner.

Schorow, S. (2001, December 18). Net Life: Fellowship of fans thrives on the Web. *Boston Herald.* [Online]. Retrieved May 8, 2002, from weblexusnexus. com/universe/document?_m = 6d8ac,53a840c80367e0f6df24ed08.

Schudson, M. (1978). *Discovering the news: A social history of American newspapers.* New York: Basic Books.

Schultz, M. (1993). *The effect of visual presentation, story complexity and story familiarity on recall and comprehension of television news.* Unpublished doctoral dissertation, Indiana University, Bloomington.

Schwartz, D. (1991). *To tell the truth: Codes of objectivity in photojournalism.* Paper presented at the 74th annual convention of the AEJMC, August 7–10, 1991. Boston, Massachusetts.

Schwartz, J. (2000, January 30). A super day to screen ads. *The Washington Post,* p. H1.

Scott, J. (2000). *Resistance to multiculturalism: Issues and interventions.* New York: Brunner/Mazel.

Scott, J. W. (1988). *Gender and the politics of history.* New York: Columbia University Press.

Seelye, K. Q. (2002, June 23). War on terror makes for odd twists in justice system: flexible rules raise constitutional issues. *The New York Times,* p. 16.

Shaheen, J. (2002, February 28). Hollywood widens slur targets to Arab and Muslim Americans since Sept. 11. Pacific News Service. Retrieved October 21, 2001, from http://www.alternet.org.

Shannon, W. V. (1963). *The American Irish.* New York: Macmillan.

Shinar, D. (2000). Media diplomacy and "peacetalk", the Middle East and Northern Ireland. *Gazette, 62*(2), 83–97.

Shinar, D. (2002). Peace process in cultural conflict: The role of the media. In E. Gilboa (Ed.), *Media and conflict: Framing issues, making policy, shaping opinions.* Ardsley, NY: Transnational.

Shoemaker, P., & Reese, S. (1996). *Mediating the message.* White Plains, NY: Longman.

Showalter, E. (1990). *Sexual anarchy, gender and culture at the fin de siècle.* New York: Viking.

Signorielli, N. (1991). *A Sourcebook on children and television.* Westport: Greenwood.

Singer, J. (2000, April). Making sense of Jewish stereotypes. The Future of Freedom Foundation. Retrieved July 9, 2003, from www.fff.org/freedom/ 0400f.asp.

Sloan, D. (1980). The teaching of ethics in the American undergraduate curriculum, 1876–1976. In D. Callahan, & S. Bok (Eds.), *Ethics teaching in higher education.* New York: Plenum.

Small, A. W. (1903). Me significance of sociology for ethics. In *The Dicennial Publication of the University of Chicago* (vol. 4). Chicago: University of Chicago Press.

Smith, R. F., & Goodwin, H. E. (1999). *Groping for ethics in journalism* (4th ed.). Ames, IA: Iowa State University Press.

Snitow, A., Stansell, C., & Thompson, S. (Eds.). (1983). *Powers of desire, the politics of sexuality.* New York: Monthly Review Press.

Solomon, B. (1956). *Ancestors and immigrants.* Cambridge: Harvard University Press.

Sperry, R. W. (1973). Lateral specialization of cerebral function in the surgically separated hemispheres. In F. J. McGuigan & R.A. Schoonover (Eds.), *The psychophysiology of thinking,* (pp. 209–229). New York: Academic Press.

Spindel, C. (2000). *Dancing at halftime: Sports and the controversy over American Indian mascots.* New York: New York University Press.

Spivak, G. C. (1988). *In other worlds, essays in cultural politics.* New York: Routledge.

Spivak, G. C. (1990). *The post-colonial critic, interviews, strategies, dialogues.* New York: Routledge.

Staff and Wire reports. (2001, September 22) Flags invoke feelings. *Albuquerque Journal.* [Online] Retrieved July 8, 2003, from www.abqjournal.com/homes/452284homes09–22–01.htm.

Stangor, C. (Ed.). (2000). *Stereotypes and prejudice: Essential readings.* New York: Psychology Press.

Steinfeld, P. (1991, March 23). Cardinal says press reports reflect Catholic bashing. *New York Times,* 27.

Steuter, E. (1990). Understanding the media/terrorism relationship: An analysis of ideology and the news in *Time* magazine. *Political Communication and Persuasion, 7,* 257–278.

Stice, E., & Shaw, H. E. (1994). Adverse effects of the media portrayed thin-ideal on women and linkages to bulimic symptomatology. *Journal of Social and Clinical Psychology, 13,* 288–308.

Stivers, R. (1976). *A hair of the dog.* University Park, PA: Pennsylvania State University Press.

Stone, A. R. (1993). The "empire" strikes back: A posttranssexual manifesto (3rd ed.). Retrieved September 26, 2002, from www.sandystone.com/empire-strikes-back. First edition published in 1991 in K. Straub & J. Epstein (Eds.), *Body guards: The cultural politics of gender ambiguity.* New York: Routledge.

Stone, A. R. (1995). *The war of desire and technology at the close of the mechanical age.* Boston: MIT Press.

Stossel, S. (2001, October 22). Terror TV. *The American Prospect 12*(18), 35–37.

Strober, M., & Arnold, C. (1987). *Computer chips and paper clips: Technology and women's employment*. [Online]. Washington, DC: National Research Council. Retrieved July 9, 2003, from www.nap.edu/catalog/951.html.

Svetkey, B. (1994, March 18). Here's the beef. *Entertainment,* 26–27.

Taste–Review & Outlook: Trouble brewing. (2002, March 15). *Wall Street Journal,* p. 15W.

Thomas, P., Richards, M., & Nain, Z. (Eds.). (2000). *Communication and development: The Freirean connection.* Cresskill, NJ: Hampton.

Thompson, T. L., & Zerbinos, E. (1997). Television characters: Do children notice it's a boy's world? *Sex Roles, 37,* 415–432.

Tilly, C. (1978). *From mobilization to revolution.* Reading, MA: Addison-Wesley.

Timeline: Countdown to U.S. air strikes. (2001, October 9). *Courier Mail,* p. 4.

Torres, J. (2002, April 9). National Association of Hispanic Journalists Statement on ASNE's newsroom survey. Washington, DC: National Association of Hispanic Journalists.

Torres, J. (2000, September 22). NAHJ releases fifth annual "network brownout" report. Washington, DC: National Association of Hispanic Journalists.

Trigoboff, D. (2002, May 6). Journalists' survival schools. *Broadcasting & Cable,* 20.

Tuchman, G. (1978). *Making news: A study in the construction of reality.* New York: Free Press.

Twain, M. (2002). *The Innocents Abroad.* New York: Viking Penguin.

U.S. Bureau of the Census, United States Department of Commerce. (May 2001). *Decennial Report 2000. Profiles of General Demographic Characteristics, 2000; People and families in poverty by selected characteristics: 1999–2000.* Washington, DC: U.S. Department of Commerce.

U.S. Catholic Bishops & Muslim Leaders. (2001). The one God calls us to be peoples of peace. In J. Farina (Ed.), *Beauty for ashes: Spiritual reflections on the attack on America* (pp. 2067–2208). New York: Crossroads.

van Dijk, T. A. (1987). *Communicating racism: Ethnic prejudice in thought and talk.* London: Sage.

van Dijk, T. A. (1988). Introduction. In G. Smitherman-Donaldson & T. A. van Dijk (Eds.), *Discourse and discrimination* (p. 18). Detroit, MI: Wayne State University Press.

van Dijk, T. A. (1988). *News as discourse.* Hillsdale, NJ: Erlbaum.

van Dijk, T. A. (1991). *Racism and the press.* London: Routledge.

Vestergaard, T., & Schrøder, K. (1985). *The Language of Advertising.* Oxford: Basil.

Violence, women, and the media. (2000). *Issue Brief Series.* Studio City, CA: Mediascope. [Online]. Retrieved May 4, 2001, from www.mediascope.org/pubs/ibriefs/vwm.htm.

Walker, M. (1994, January 17). Mightier than the sorehead. *The Nation,* 45–54.

Walsh, T.J. (1994, March 20.) The male daze: Men lost in the vast wasteland. Paper presented at the twenty-ninth annual convention of the Broadcast Education Association, Las Vegas, NV.

Ward, C.M. (2001). The breast-implant controversy: A medico-moral critique. *British Journal of Plastic Surgery, 54,* 352–357.

Wasserman, D. (1994, February 19). Visually challenging or visually challenged?/A P.C. debate by cartoonists. [Op-Ed]. *The Boston Globe,* p. 15.

Weibel, K. (1977). *Mirror mirror: Images of women reflected in popular culture.* Garden City, NY: Anchor.

Weigner, W. (1992, June 12). Revenge of the nerds. *Forbes.*

Weitzman, L.J., Eifler, D., Hokada, E., & Ross, C. (1972). Sex role socialization in picture books of preschool children. *The American Journal of Sociology, 77,* 1125–1150.

Welles, H.G. (1922). A short history of the world. Retrieved July 9, 2003, from www.bartleby.com/86/21.html.

Welsh, J. (2002, February 5). TiVo publishes Super Bowl usage report. *Digital-Spy,* 2.

Wertheimer, L. (1993, March 9). William Sessions discusses terrorism on Capitol Hill. *All Things Considered.* Washington, DC: National Public Radio.

Weston, M. (1996). *Native Americans in the news: Images of Indians in the twentieth century press.* Westport, CT: Greenwood.

Wilcox, D., Ault, P., & Agee, W. (1992). *Public relations: Strategies and tactics.* New York: HarperCollins.

Williams, R. (1999, Autumn). Beyond visual literacy: omniphasism, a theory of cognitive balance, part I. *Journal of Visual Literacy, 19*(2), 159–178.

Williams, R. (2000a, Spring). Visual illiteracy and intuitive visual persuasion, part II. *Journal of Visual Literacy, 20*(1), 111–124.

Williams, R. (2000b, Autumn). Omniphasic visual-media literacy in the classroom, part II. *Journal of Visual Literacy, 20*(2), 219–241.

Willis, J. (1991). *The shadow world: Life between the news media and reality.* New York: Praeger.

Winson, J. (2002, August). The meaning of dreams. *Scientific American: The Hidden Mind, 12*(1), 54–61.

Wisan, J. (1965). *The Cuban crisis as reflected in the New York press (1895–1898).* New York: Octagon.

Witt, S.D. (1997). Boys will be boys, and girls will be...hard to find: Gender representation in third grade basal readers. *Education and Society, 15,* 47–53.

Wittig, M. (1992). *The straight mind and other essays.* Boston: Beacon.

Wittke, C. (1956). *The Irish in America.* Baton Rouge, LA: Louisiana State University Press.

Wolf, M.A., & Kielwasser, A.P. (Eds.). (1991). *Gay people, sex, and the media.* New York: Harrington Park.

Wolf, M. A., & Kielwasser, A. P. (2001). The news media and peace processes, the Middle East and Northern Ireland. *Peaceworks, 37,* 2.

Wolfsfeld, G. (1997). *Media and political conflict.* New York: Cambridge University Press.

Wood, D. B. (1989, March 2). Redrawing US portrait of the disabled. *Christian Science Monitor,* p. 14.

Wood, R. (Ed.). (1990). *Film and propaganda in America.* New York: Greenwood.

Ylanne-McEwen, V. (2000, Summer). Golden times for golden agers: Selling holidays as lifestyle for the over 50s. [Online]. *Journal of Communication, 50*(3), 83–99. Abstract from AgeLine Database.

Yntema, S. (Ed.). (1997). *Americans 55 & older: A changing market.* Ithaca, NY: New Strategist Publications.

Young, D. (1997, April). Crusader cartoonists. *Southern Living,* 150–154.

Zeller, T. (2002, May/June). Patriotic marketing hits bottom. *Mother Jones,* 22.

Ziv, A., & Zajdman, A. (1993). *Semites and stereotypes, characteristics of Jewish humor.* Westport, CT: Greenwood.

Zola, K. I. (1985). Depictions of disability—metaphor, message and medium in the media: A research and political agenda. *The Social Science Journal 22*(4), 5–17.

INDEX

ABOUT THE CONTRIBUTORS

Linus Abraham is an assistant professor of visual communication, cultural studies, multimedia production, and new media studies at the School of Journalism and Mass Communication, University of Minnesota. His research interests include visual persuasion, the structure, interpretation, and social functions of visual media, cultural determination of ethnicity/ race in the media, and the role of visual imagery in contemporary forms of racism.

Tom Brislin is a professor of journalism and the founding chair of the School of Communications at the University of Hawai'i-Manoa. His teaching and research interests include journalism ethics, international and intercultural mass communication, and visual media and popular culture. He directs the Parvin/Freedom Forum Fellowship Program in Journalism Studies for Journalists from the People's Republic of China and the Carol Burnett Fund for Responsible Journalism.

James W. Brown is professor of journalism and associate dean for the Indiana University and Purdue University at Indianapolis program of the Indiana University School of Journalism. He teaches visual communication and new media courses and is working on a book about Delaware Indians. Brown is usually seen wearing black leather while he guides his K1200LT motorcycle under police radar.

Ramón Chávez is chair of the Department of Contemporary Media and Journalism and curriculum coordinator for the American Indian Journalism Institute at the University of South Dakota. He has taught at Denver's Five Points Media Center, San Jose State University, and The University of Texas-El Paso. He has worked for the El Paso *Herald-Post,* Albuquerque *Tribune,* and the Yakima *Herald-Republic,* and graduated from Texas Tech University and the University of Washington.

Clifford G. Christians is a research professor of communications and professor of media studies and journalism in the Institute of Communications Research at the University of Illinois-Urbana. He is author or coauthor of such books as *Media Ethics: Cases and Moral Reasoning* (6th ed.); *Jacques Ellul: Interpretive Essays*; *Good News: Social Ethics and the Press; Communication Ethics and Universal Values;* and *Moral Engagement in Public Life: Theorists for Contemporary Ethics.* His teaching and research interests include the philosophy of technology, media ethics, and communication theory.

Michael Colgan is currently completing his Ph.D. at the University of South Carolina after a two-decade career in radio broadcasting and management. His research centers on journalism ethics and political communication. In addition to his broadcast experience, Colgan is also a published cartoonist, illustrator, and documentary filmmaker.

J.B. Colson has been teaching the practice, history, and criticism of photography at the University of Texas at Austin since 1968. Before teaching fulltime, he was a nontheatrical filmmaker. In the 1980s his documentary photography of Mexican village life was widely exhibited in that country.

Everette E. Dennis is the Felix E. Larkin Distinguished Professor at Fordham's Graduate School of Business in New York City. He is author of various books on media, an educator, and an institution builder.

Bonnie Drewniany is an associate professor and director of the advertising and public relations sequence at the College of Mass Communications and Information Studies at the University of South Carolina. After watching 14 years of Super Bowl games, she still doesn't know the first thing about football.

Deni Elliott is the Poynter-Jamison Chair in Media Ethics and Press Policy at the University of South Florida, St. Petersburg. She is faculty affiliate in the Department of Philosophy at the University of Montana. Her most recent book is *Teaching Ethics in the First Person;* she also coauthors a monthly column with Paul Martin Lester, "Ethics Matters," for *News Photographer* magazine.

Willard F. Enteman has spent much of his professional life with oxymorons. For one example, he once became president of Bowdoin College in Maine to demonstrate the possibility of rational college administration. Failing at that, he turned to other examples by writing about business ethics and media ethics. Still not having learned his lesson, recently he has been preparing a book providing a philosophical examination of higher education. Thus far, the pages are blank.

Olan Farnall is an associate professor in the advertising sequence at California State University, Fullerton. He holds a doctorate in communication from the University of Alabama and an M.S. from the University of Illinois. His primary research interests include Web-based communication and ability-integrated advertising.

Lucy A. Ganje is the originator of applied research with a focus on cross-cultural visual literacy and interpretation. She is the founder of the Native Media Center at the University of North Dakota. Ganje writes and creates visual communication pieces about the use and appropriation of cultural symbols. She is currently studying the effects of reservation newspapers on race relations. Her coursework includes classes in visual communication, graphic design, media diversity, and semiotics.

Nancy Beth Jackson is an adjunct associate professor at the School of International and Public Affairs at Columbia University. She holds a doctorate in international studies from the University of Miami, Coral Gables, and has worked as a journalist in Africa, Asia, Europe, and Latin America, as well as in the United States.

Walter B. Jaehnig is director of the School of Journalism at Southern Illinois University at Carbondale. He is a former reporter for the Louisville *Courier Journal* and graduated from the Medill School of Journalism at

Northwestern University. He has a doctorate from Essex University in England and formerly taught at Indiana University and the University of Wyoming.

Keith Kenney is an associate professor at the University of South Carolina. His professional interests are documentary photography and film. His research interests are visual communication and theory.

Paul Martin Lester enjoys hikes in the woods that end with a natural hot springs, sunsets after a volcanic eruption, barbequed free-range shrimp, and working on his Web site at commfaculty.fullerton.edu/lester.

Travis Linn was a professor at the Reynolds School of Journalism, University of Nevada, Reno. His professional background included work as a television news director and network news bureau chief. To our great sadness, Travis died before this edition was completed.

Kathy Brittain McKee is associate provost and professor of communication at Berry College in Rome, Georgia. She has a B.A. in communication and religion/philosophy from Shorter College and an M.A. in journalism and Ph.D. in mass communication from the University of Georgia. She is one of the coauthors of *Media Ethics Cases in Moral Reasoning* and has published journal articles and book chapters in media ethics, visual imagery, communication pedagogy, and student-press regulation.

Marguerite Moritz is professor and associate dean at the School of Journalism and Mass Communication, University of Colorado at Boulder. She has written about gay representation for the last 15 years and most recently worked on the documentary, *Scout's Honor,* about the Boy Scouts of America's anti-gay policies. She has served on the Gay & Lesbian Alliance Against Defamation's board of directors and is currently on their National Research Advisory Board. Her documentary, *Covering Columbine* explores issues of media ethics and trauma. Dr. Moritz has lectured in more than 17 countries and was named a Fulbright Senior Specialist in Media in 2002.

Jack A. Nelson taught communications at Brigham Young University for 25 years, specializing in the media and the disabled. He is the author of a

1994 book, The Media, the Disabled, and the Information Age. He retired in 2000 and now writes novels from his Provo, Utah, home.

Julianne H. Newton, University of Oregon associate professor of visual communication, is editor of *Visual Communication Quarterly,* a juried research journal that reaches 12,000 professionals and scholars. For 15 years she taught at The University of Texas at Austin, where she also was head of the Photojournalism Program. Newton has worked as a reporter, designer, editor, broadcast journalist, and photographer. Newton is author of *The Burden of Visual Truth: The Role of Photojournalism in Mediating Reality* (2001).

Susan Dente Ross is an associate professor at the Edward R. Murrow School of Communication at Washington State University where she directs the undergraduate program in media and the law. In addition to conducting research on media portrayals of minorities, she is a First Amendment scholar who specializes in speech at the margins and the former head of the Law Division of the Association for Education in Journalism and Mass Communication.

Ted Curtis Smythe, Ph.D., is professor of communication emeritus in the School of Communications, California State University, Fullerton. Recent research and publications include *The Gilded Age Press, 1865–1900* in the Journalism History series edited by Wm. David Sloan and James D. Startt, in press with Greenwood Press, and "The Diffusion of the Urban Daily, 1850–1900," in the journal *Journalism History* (2002). He was Distinguished Scholar in Residence at Sterling College, Sterling, Kansas for four years after early retirement from California State University, Fullerton.

Kim Walsh-Childers is a Professor in the Department of Journalism at the University of Florida. Her teaching areas include journalism ethics, newswriting, a graduate seminar in mass media and health and magazine feature writing. Her research focuses on print media news coverage of health issues, mass media effects on individual health and health policy, and the relationship between mass media content and adolescent sexual beliefs and behavior.

Lee Wilkins is a professor on the broadcast news faculty at the Missouri School of Journalism. She is a coauthor of a media ethics text, and her current research interest includes how journalists make ethical decisions. She is a member of the founding editorial board of the *Journal of Mass Media Ethics*.

Rick Williams has been a commercial and documentary photographer for more than 30 years. Since 1990 he has taught photography and visual and media communication at the University of Texas at Austin and currently at the University of Oregon. Mr. Williams' theories on visual communication have been published in journals and books and have brought him note as an author, lecturer, and teacher. His award-winning photographs have been widely displayed and published and are in the permanent collections of major museums.

Marsha Woodbury is a lecturer in the Department of Computer Science, University of Illinois, Urbana-Champaign. She is the former national chair of Computer Professionals for Social Responsibility and author of *Computer and Information Ethics* (2002).

Library
St. Louis Community College
Forest Park
St. Louis, Missouri